Coming Out to Parents

Coming Out to Parents

A Two-way Survival Guide for Lesbians and Gay Men and Their Parents

Revised and Updated

Mary V. Borhek

THE PILGRIM PRESS
CLEVELAND, OHIO

The Pilgrim Press, Cleveland, Ohio 44115

Biblical quotations, unless otherwise indicated, are from the Revised Standard Version of the Bible, © 1946, 1952, 1971, 1973 by the Division of Christian Education of the National Council of the Churches of Christ in the United States of America, and are used by permission

Some names have been changed to protect individuals' privacy

Printed in the United States of America
The paper used in this publication is acid free and meets the minimum requirements of American National Standard for Information Sciences-Permanence of Paper for Printed Library Materials, ANSI Z39.48–1984

98 97 96 95 94 93   5 4 3 2 1

Library of Congress Cataloging-in-Publication Data

Borhek, Mary V., 1922-
    Coming out to parents : a two-way survival guide for lesbians and gay men and their parents / Mary V. Borhek.
        p.   cm.
    "Revised and updated."
    Includes bibliographical references and index.
    ISBN 0-8298-0957-0
    1. Lesbians—Family relationships.   2. Gay men—Family relation-ships.   3. Parents of gays.   4. Adult children.   5. Coming out (Sex-ual orientation)   I. Title.
HQ75.5.B68   1993
306.874—dc20   93-23919
                                                    CIP

To my children—
Emily, Barbara, and Eric—
and to Hans and Brian,
who have become part of
the family circle

Contents

Introduction: A Two-way Mirror

When the first edition of *Coming Out to Parents* was published in 1983, a major continuing anxiety for lesbians and gay men was whether they should come out to their parents and how they should do it. AIDS, acquired immune deficiency syndrome, was not a term in general circulation. Although the gay communities of New York and San Francisco had known for some time about this new disease, as had the Centers for Disease Control, AIDS had not yet taken on the consuming focus it would hold later in the 1980s.

The time has now come to revise the earlier book, with the major change being the addition of a chapter about AIDS. Because the subject is so vast, I have chosen to address only the emotional impact of AIDS on the gay or lesbian person and his or her family and to offer help in dealing with this aspect of the disease. I have also made considerable changes in the chapter on religion because of changes in Jewish thinking in particular, and also because a number of Christian books cited in the original version have gone out of print.

The first thing that should be said about AIDS is this—and it must be said in capital letters:

BEING GAY DOES NOT MEAN YOU HAVE TO GET AIDS.

During a conversation with Kate Royston, who is in charge of AIDS education for the Berks AIDS Network in Reading, Pennsylvania, she said to me: "You tell them that *being gay does not mean you have to get AIDS."* The emphasis was in her voice. Several times more in our conversation she repeated these words. They are particularly important for young people to remember, and it's important for them to know the ways in which they can avoid contracting the virus.

If you are HIV positive, meaning you have acquired the human immunodeficiency virus, or if your child is HIV positive, this can be the main fact of your life now. However, all of the other difficulties that a lesbian or gay person encounters in a mainly heterosexual world are still there. Young people continue to discover their sexual orientation and to need ways of communicating this to their parents. So this book is still necessary, and it is still a two-way mirror that can help parents understand their children and children to understand their parents.

It would be impossible to deal in one book with all the situations in which lesbians and gay men come out to their parents. For example, certain ethnic and racial backgrounds pose particular problems; other cultural circumstances also make coming out more difficult. I have written mainly out of my own experience and the experiences of those with whom I have come in contact.

In writing this book I have had difficulties with terminology. At present there are no terms related to sexual orientation that please everybody. Homosexuality is a clinical term many gay men find offensive; many lesbians feel the word applies only to men, not to women. Gay, which used to apply to men and women, now applies, in most geographical areas, only to men and should be used as an adjective, not as a noun. Some want it to be capitalized and others are satisfied to let it be spelled with a lowercase *g*. Women usually prefer to be referred to as lesbians.

To avoid using the words homosexuality and homosexual in most of the book, I have used same-sex orientation and same-sex-oriented. Again, these are not satisfactory choices to some people, because they sound too clinical and seem to ignore the affectional aspect of the orientation. Since the publication of the first edition, the terms same-gender orientation and same-gender-oriented have come into use. Despite being even clumsier than the same-sex terms, they take the focus away from only the sexual, that is, genital, aspect of the orientation and give it a more inclusive character. Not everyone will like this new designation; in fact, I have chosen to continue to use the same-sex terms.

The word orientation itself also is not wholly satisfactory, because it implies that a person can be oriented or adjusted in a particular sexual direction. It is an improvement, however, over the words sexual preference, which indicate to some people that a man or woman has made a conscious choice to relate lovingly and sexually to persons of the same gender rather than to persons of the opposite gender.

The authors of the book *Sexual Preference* deal with the erroneous meaning of this term.

> Although we have entitled our present work *Sexual Preference*, we do not mean to imply that a given sexual orientation is the result of a conscious decision or is as changeable as the many moment-by-moment decisions we make in our lives. Neither homosexuals nor heterosexuals are what they are by design. . . . There is no reason to think it would be any easier for homosexual men or women to reverse their sexual orientation than it would be for heterosexual readers to become predominantly or exclusively homosexual.[1]

A paper prepared for study and discussion at a 1979 conference in Milwaukee for Lutheran campus ministers states: "We are using 'sexual orientation' here in its broadest reference to our sensations and perceptions of our-

3

selves in relation to others, in terms of not only interpersonal attraction but also such 'non-sexual' enterprises as achieving success, child-rearing, etc."

I have written this book as a two-way mirror for both the same-sex-oriented person and her or his parents. I hope daughter or son and mother and father will want to read all the chapters. (Chapter 9, "Religious Issues and a Same-Sex Orientation," has been included for parents for whom religion is an issue in their difficulties with their child's orientation.) This way the adult child can gain some understanding of the parents' perspectives and of her or his own adjustment to life. The parent who reads the book will gain a perspective of his or her own life situation as well as that of the same-sex-oriented daughter or son. Both sides can come to understand why the child's sexual orientation may seem so shocking, can come to understand the changes and upheavals going on within the parents, and thus can begin to cope constructively with the situation.

Generally, the chapters are best read in sequence, but chapter 9 may be read at any point. Parents who are having particular problems with the religious aspect of a same-sex orientation may want to turn to this chapter first.

I am sad that such elaborate preparation is necessary in order for a gay or lesbian child to be open with his or her parents about the person the child really is. Society through the centuries—largely because of a lack of genuine information—has laid a cruel burden on the same-sex-oriented person. Only now is the world at large beginning to deal more realistically and less hurtfully with this orientation.

I dream of a time when parents can realize without anguish that their son is gay or their daughter lesbian, because society will have learned that a same-sex orientation is not sick, dangerous, or evil. What a person, whether heterosexual or homosexual, does with his or her sexuality may indeed be evil, sick, or dangerous, but in either case the orientation itself is not.

What if there were no persecution of lesbian and gay persons, no fear in being one's total self, and no agonized coming out to oneself, to one's parents, to others? Obviously, society has not yet incorporated this vision. Many battles are still to be fought before there can be mutual understanding, respect, and acceptance between heterosexual and same-sex-oriented persons.

As a gay or lesbian child, in coming out to your parents and in helping them deal with your sexual orientation you are taking a step in the direction of mutuality. If you as parents make an effort to come to terms with your child's sexuality, you also are moving in a constructive direction.

Some people do not consider this movement constructive. To them, these ideas are destructive of all the values they hold dearest. If you are one of these people, please do not throw this book aside in fear, anger, and disgust. Its real purpose is not to present a theory of sexual and social evolution that may or may not come to pass. Rather, it is designed to help you deal with a difficult fact in your life.

Whatever your ideas about a same-sex orientation, you are being forced to cope with the information that your child is lesbian or gay. You can cut off contact or communication with your child, but this will not change her or his sexual orientation, *because she or he cannot and should not change in the way that you want—should not* because this would violate the person your child really is. How much better to maintain contact with him or her and give yourself time to learn more about yourself, your child, and the situation in which you find yourself.

Although my name appears as author, this book, including the new material, could not have come into being without the assistance—sometimes substantial—of many people. Some can be named; others prefer to remain anonymous or be referred to by fictitious names.

Douglas Elwood, John Grace, Jennifer Feigal, Sylvia Rudolph, and Rabbi Moshe Adler gave me much help in writing the first edition. My children by birth or by relationship with a family member, as well as many lesbians and gay men, and in some cases their families, also provided a great deal of assistance.

A number of people provided help and information for the chapter on AIDS. John Grace in particular was unfailingly helpful. Alan Peura, director of the Berks (County) AIDS Network, Reading, Pennsylvania, and Deborah McCone, Kate Royston, and Norman N. Jeffrey, Jr., of the network, gave valuable help, as did Stephan Peura, director of Rainbow House, Wernersville, Pennsylvania. Ann Huey of the Lehigh Valley Hospice and Linda Lobach of AIDS Outreach, both of Allentown, Pennsylvania, as well as Ron Ostrosky and Robert Roush, both of AIDS Service Center, Bethlehem, Pennsylvania, provided information. Others who assisted include Rev. Nancy Adams, Dr. Keith Battin, Ted Bowman, Lee Cappiello, Dr. Eli Coleman, Mary Ann Dwyer, Phyllis Edwall, Jennifer Feigal, Susan Fraser, Linda Hessey, Allen H. Kostenbader, Sue Marx, Charlotte and Gus Sindt, Rev. Peter Skelly, Rev. Charles Staples, Rev. Leo J. Tibesar, Jr., and Norma Wilson.

The book would not have come into being had it not been for Pearl P. Rosenberg, Ph.D., who at the time of its writing was assistant dean of admissions and student affairs of the University of Minnesota Medical School. In 1978 she addressed the second annual workshop sponsored in Minneapolis by Families of Gays and Lesbians (later to become a Parents and Friends of Lesbians and Gays—P-FLAG—group) in cooperation with the Neighborhood Counseling Center. She was the first person to point out to me that parents go through a grieving process when a lesbian or gay child comes out to them. From this beginning I put together a talk I used for a number of lesbian/gay groups, which ultimately developed into this book.

Those who find this book helpful do so because of the persons I have mentioned. The pain a family experiences when it learns one of its members is same-sex-oriented or has AIDS may be lessened a bit because of the willingness of these people to share their stories or serve as advisers.

For any parent reading this book the journey ahead may not be easy, but life was not designed to be easy—exciting, difficult, depressing, monotonous, at times heartbreaking, at times joyous, but never easy.

Chapter 1

So You Want to Come Out
to Your Parents

So you want to come out to your parents. You want to tell them an important fact about yourself of which, in all probability, they are unaware: If you are a woman, you want to tell them you are a lesbian; if you are a man, you want to tell them you are gay.

Or you have already come out to them, and the ensuing explosion has left you angry, alienated, wounded, and bitter.

Or you have told your parents, and they have not referred to the matter since. It is as if you had not said anything.

Or they want you to talk with their minister, priest, or rabbi. Or they want you to seek counseling. (Obviously, they hope you can change.)

Or they keep handing you literature published by ex-gay organizations—groups (usually with a strong religious orientation) that promise help in changing from a same-sex orientation to a heterosexual orientation or support in living a celibate lifestyle.

Or they let you know, not too subtly, that *you* are welcome at home, but your friend is not.

Or possibly they have let you know, quickly and definitely, that you are no longer their daughter or son.

Your parents' reactions to the news that their child is same-sex-oriented are likely to be emotional and, unfortunately, negative. Why must it be like this, you wonder. Why can they not be loving and accepting of this aspect of yourself? It may have been hard for you yourself to accept your sexual orientation. If they could receive your information with at least a measure of equanimity, it would be much easier for you. When they seem greatly disturbed, you are forced to retrace all the agonizing steps you have taken, as you wait for them to work through their difficulties with your gayness or lesbianism.

If you want to help them deal with what you are going to tell them—or have already told them—you need some understanding of the social and sexual climate in which your parents matured. Until the late 1960s your parents never saw the word homosexuality in magazines or newspapers—at least not the ones most people read. The word appeared in dictionaries, in some encyclopedias, in scholarly publications, and in books that wanted to be slightly daring. Homosexuality was not a topic of general social conversation, although there were plenty of crude jokes about fairies, homos, queers, dykes, amazons, and lezzies. As for the church, homosexuality was not mentioned from the pulpit or discussed at church meetings. It was hardly even breathed at counseling sessions in the privacy of the pastor's study, and almost never did it find its way into the confessional.

Until I was seventeen I had never heard the word homosexual. I came across it as I was reading a rather unorthodox book that had been recommended to me by a self-consciously iconoclastic young friend. When I looked up the word in the dictionary I was shocked. The definition was restrained, as definitions in dictionaries are apt to be, and was taken care of in one brief phrase: "n., eroticism for one of the same sex."

I was confused. I had been led to believe that such feelings could happen only between men and women, not between persons of the same sex. How was it possible for a man to have sexual feelings for another man or a woman for another woman?

For some time I mulled over this information. Apparently, persons of the same sex could become sexually excited about each other. I did not understand how this was possible. Nor did I realize that feelings of genuine love could accompany the sexual feelings.

During my first year of college I was confronted with what appeared to be too intimate a relationship between two young women in my circle of friends. The rest of the group frequently discussed the situation when the two women were not present. I cannot remember anyone ever saying the word lesbian—if indeed we even knew the word. No one ever verbalized why we were concerned about the situation or what we thought was actually going on when the two women were together in one or the other's room, with the door closed. We just knew this kind of thing was not done.

We never learned whether our suspicions were correct. Neither woman returned the following year. One transferred to a college near her family's new home; the other married her steady boyfriend during the summer.

As I moved into adulthood I discovered that there might be unpleasant consequences to being homosexual. Because at that time homosexuality was considered a crime and a sin rather than an orientation toward life, it was not surprising that persons who were homosexual were subject to blackmail, that they could face professional and social ruin if their homosexuality were discovered, or that they could even be jailed. No one questioned *why* homosexuality was a crime. The law said it was, and no one was motivated to argue with the law. If people chose to be perverse, they had to suffer the penalty.

This is the climate in which most parents grew up. People did not know much about homosexuality and saw no reason to learn more. If you, a lesbian or gay person, were born in the 1950s, 1960s, or 1970s you probably cannot entirely understand the feelings with which your parents may have to struggle, because the social climate has changed significantly in the past twenty to twenty-five years. Your parents are laboring under a whole body of unconscious assumptions, most likely never even specifically formulated, gathered from a word here, an innuendo there, a significant silence, a whispered remark. Most parents do not know why they think about homosexuality in the way they do or from what sources they have inherited their ideas.

This kind of unconscious "information" is the hardest to deal with or change. Straight people never thought to question their ideas about homosexuality. They "knew" certain things about it and none of these things was good.

In addition to your understanding something of the climate in which your parents grew up, it will be helpful for you to see your parents as persons rather than as father and mother. Now that you are an adult, your parents are no longer responsible for raising, disciplining, and training you. For you to relate to them in the former parent/child ways is no longer helpful or desirable. You need to see them and relate to them as adult to adult. (If you have not yet attained legal majority, the situation is different.)

Separating the real personhood of a parent from her or his parental role is not always easy. Attitudes and habits formed over the first fifteen to twenty years of one's life are hard to change. An adult child often slips back unconsciously into former patterns of relationship with his or her parents, and the parents often deal with their grown-up child in parental rather than adult ways. Outwardly, parents and child are adults, but inwardly, the adult daughter or son may retain a vague sense of being the little girl or boy relating to the grown-up persons who for many years held the reins of power and who seemed to be so much wiser and more competent than the child. The parents also find it hard to remember that this person, their child, who for years needed guidance and discipline, no longer requires this type of care. Not to slip back at least slightly into old habits of relating to each other is difficult for parents and grown child.

In addition, try to gain a perspective on the problems your parents are facing at this particular time in their lives. What are the pressures they may be feeling? Are they dealing with thwarted dreams of career or status? Are they coming face to face with the inevitability of aging and consequent mortality? Are they having problems with *their* parents? Are they also being confronted by difficulties with other children in your family? The more you can see your parents as two individuals struggling with their own issues of personhood as well as with the demands of the older and younger generations of the family, the better you will understand their reactions to your coming out to them.

Although you may have some trouble visualizing it, once upon a time—perhaps not so long ago—your parents were young. Life stretched before them with wonderful and seemingly endless possibilities. In those days their chins were firmer and single, their hips narrower, their stomachs flatter, their hair one color, and their muscles did not feel like tired rubber bands. Now, even though they may look youthful, with each passing day they realize that life is not the same as it used to be.

Twenty to thirty years ago they had hopes and dreams and goals. They could be whatever they wanted to be, accomplish whatever they set themselves to accomplish. Opportunity beckoned; the future was bright, the horizon almost limitless.

Your parents may be realizing gradually that many of these marvelous dreams will never be fulfilled. Somehow they have slipped into certain patterns, and the difficulty and pain of altering these patterns may be more than they care to undertake. All of us live with a psychological as well as a physical law of inertia that makes it easier to remain in a known routine—even though it may be uncomfortable—than to change course and take a new direction. Leaving the safety of the known for the risk of the unknown can be frightening.

With each passing year your parents may be increasingly aware of their unfulfilled dreams, their mistaken decisions and choices in the past, the things they have not done that now may never be accomplished. They begin to realize that while they used to be able to keep going strong until 1 A.M., now they begin to wilt at 10 or 11 P.M. They find their eyes at half-mast over the evening paper. They fall asleep watching television. The french fried onion rings they used to be able to eat by the basketful now cause indigestion, and feet that never hurt before start aching. The signs are there: *I am getting old.*

They do not *say* that to themselves. They joke about the little aches and pains, about going to sleep over the newspaper or while watching television. But underneath, well concealed from others and perhaps partially hidden from themselves, uneasiness and frustration due to these creeping limitations may be building. At times they may experience a touch of panic: "What will become of me?"

They may not be conscious of these thoughts. All they know is they feel vaguely unhappy or slightly depressed, as if the sun that had shone so brightly had retreated behind a cloud.

Other pressures are also common to most parents in the middle or later years. They want life to be better for their children than it was for them. This in itself is natural and commendable. The problem arises when the parents discover that their idea of better may not coincide with the adult son's or daughter's idea of better. It may be difficult—or even impossible—for the parents to understand how a particular course of action or a philosophy of life can be satisfying to their child when it is so unpalatable to them.

Whether they are aware of it or not, most parents have an instinctive sense that their children are their—the parents'—second chance at life. Usually, such parents are sophisticated enough to realize they cannot push their children into a particular profession or vocation in order to satisfy their own unfulfilled dreams. Still, they want their children to be richer and smarter and better and wiser—and possibly happier—than they have been.

This wish is not a totally unselfish one. Although your parents want you to do well in life for your own sake, they also need you to do well so they can prove to themselves that they are not failures as parents.

In addition, children provide continuity into the future for the parents, who may not be conscious of this feeling. Those who believe in life after death feel they do not need grandchildren and great-grandchildren to achieve immortality. And yet . . . and yet . . . despite all one's rational knowledge and belief, a visceral kind of yearning wants one's genes, one's name, one's bloodline carried on into the future.

Then comes the child's announcement, "I am lesbian" or "I am gay." One brief sentence strikes at the heart of all the unconscious hopes and dreams and wishes with which the parents have surrounded their child. Can you understand why such an announcement arouses deep feelings within parents?

Another aspect of your parents' lives may be affected by your announcement of your sexual orientation. Although they may never have talked about this with you (in all likelihood they have not), there was probably a time when their sex life was fairly intense. And now? Like many other things at this time in their lives, their sexual energy may be scaling down also.

Your announcement that you are lesbian or gay, relating as it does to your sexual nature, could be upsetting, because it touches the area that may be most sensitive to your parents. Because sexual drives are connected with some of the deepest instincts of the human race, sex is never impersonal. No one can approach the subject neutrally. The fact that we are male or female, the unspoken sexual messages as well as the spoken ones (if any) when we were children, the accumulation of our sexual experience or lack of it—all these influence each of us so that it is impossible to deal with sexual matters from a wholly neutral standpoint.

In addition, it is often difficult for parents to face the fact that their children are sexual beings. Generally, parents expect their children, as they grow up, to begin dating and eventually become engaged, to marry and in time have children. Parents know their children are sexual persons, but the sexual development parents visualize takes place within the forms prescribed by society. Sexuality that manifests itself in the standard heterosexual mode—dating, marriage, children—is not nearly as threatening or upsetting as sexuality that departs from this pattern.

In telling your parents you are lesbian or gay you are telling them you are indeed a sexual being, but that your sexuality is not channeled into the ordered patterns that are safe and familiar. Suddenly, you are a stranger. The sexual fears, prohibitions, and taboos that have been bred into your parents throughout their lives are activated by your information. If your parents go into a tailspin, this is hardly surprising. You are bringing the sexual revolution home to them in a personal, unmistakable, upsetting way.

You, their child, belong to the forces that seem to be trying to undermine the traditional values of home and family life.

Such a perception does not take into account several factors. The overwhelming majority of lesbian and gay people want to remain part of their family of origin. This hardly qualifies as a wish to damage the family structure. In addition, lesbian and gay people without children often look after infirm parents, whereas siblings who have families to raise are not as apt to become the caretakers. Many gay men and lesbians who have been married and have children are eager to maintain their relationship with their children after the divorce. Increasingly, also, a number of lesbian couples are becoming parents through artificial insemination. While such families may not fit what has been considered the traditional model—father, mother, and children—still they embody concern for the physical, mental, and emotional health of past and coming generations. Thus in a time when more than half of all family units do not conform to the traditional pattern, we can be grateful for every person who wants to maintain relationships with those connected to him or her by blood or by adoption.

As One Parent to Another

So far in this chapter I have addressed same-sex-oriented children. I am shifting now and speaking as one parent to other parents.

Earlier in this chapter you may have read much with which you could identify. Or you may have felt that what was stated did not touch you, that nothing bore much relation to your life. You may even have felt some resistance: "This isn't how it was or is for me." Perhaps you are right.

But sometimes it is difficult for us to see what is closest

at hand, *because we do not choose to.* I am not speaking of a conscious, rational choice that lines up the facts, pro and con, and from this information makes a decision. I am speaking of choices made because our unconscious psychic antennae warn us that these facts will make us uncomfortable. And so we do not allow ourselves to be aware of such facts or situations. We never admit them to our conscious minds.

To face the facts of our middle and later years, especially in today's youth-oriented culture, is not easy. We do not want to deal with the human ambivalence that wants "the best" for our children both because we want our children to be happy and because we want them to bring credit to us. Often we do the right thing, not for the wrong reasons, but for both the right *and* the wrong reasons. Mostly, *we do not want to probe into the matter of sexuality—ours or our children's.* We were raised in a simpler age, when we knew which kind of sexual behavior was accepted and which was taboo. Now our children are asking us to make major revisions in our thinking, feeling, perceiving—our understanding of being. More than this, our children are asking us to go against inherited information accepted for centuries as truth.

I have found it illuminating to discover the roots in antiquity of many of the erroneous beliefs about homosexuality that are still generally accepted as fact. A hundred years' worth of emerging scientific information about homosexuality has made only a dent in the popular understanding of a same-sex orientation.

Although you may not believe it now, your child's coming out to you can be a vehicle for greater self-understanding and deeper relationships with others. "The experience of change, . . . of being on unfamiliar ground, of doing things differently is frightening. It always was and always will be," M. Scott Peck has written in *The Road Less Traveled.* And yet, he says, "it is in this whole process of meeting and solving problems that life has its meaning."[1]

Unquestionably, as the parents of a lesbian or gay child, you have been presented with a real challenge—but also with a real opportunity for growth in your life. You may not welcome this opportunity, but often we do not welcome those situations that strip us of our comfortable insulation, that force us to leave our secure cocoon and venture forth into new and unchosen territory.

Chapter 2

The Big Decision

If you are a gay man or a lesbian who has not yet come out to your parents, you may be apprehensive or downright scared. You do not know how to tell your parents so the pain—for them and for you—will be minimal. Is it best to tell them in person? If a continent lies between where you live and where they live, should you write them a letter or call them on the phone? Or should you wait until you and your parents are together?

You have constructed a hundred different scenarios about your telling them and every one is bad. Avoiding such things as tears, anger, and pain seems impossible. Or you visualize the worst: "You are no longer our daughter (son)."

You wish the scenario could go something like this: "We're glad you've told us. This information doesn't change our feelings for you, except perhaps to make us love you even more because we realize you went through some tough times by yourself when you discovered you are lesbian (gay)." It is unlikely your coming out will be received in quite this manner. You are hoping for an immediate reaction that, realistically, may take months or years to achieve.

How can you tell your parents so they will not react negatively? Unfortunately, the answer to this question is that there is no way you can be sure how your parents will react. They may seem to hold liberal beliefs. Yet when they are confronted with your alternative sexual orientation, they may react with surprising intolerance. Anyone who has seen the Katharine Hepburn/Spencer Tracy movie *Guess Who's Coming to Dinner* has had a glimpse of the discrepancy between what people say they believe and how they feel and react when the reality confronts them.

Other parents, when they learn of their children's same-sex orientation, may draw on reserves of strength and love they were not aware they had. I remember the scene in the television movie *Sergeant Matlovich vs. the U.S. Air Force* in which Matlovich and his father face each other for the first time after the father has learned that his son is gay. He is angry with his son, not because Leonard is gay, but because he has not allowed his father to share the pain through which he had gone in learning to face and deal with his sexual orientation. This is not the reaction Sergeant Matlovich had expected from his father.

In my own case, when I was confronted with the fact that my son, Eric, is gay, I reacted in a way no one could have foreseen. Because I had already lost one member of the family—my husband, through divorce—I dared not let the family shrink further. Even though Eric was gay, which I (at that point) totally condemned, I needed him as a continuing member of the family. Eventually, I moved far beyond this simplistic attitude of condemnation to understanding and acceptance of a same-sex orientation, as I have described in *My Son Eric*.[1]

As you can see, parental reactions are not predictable. Your parents may react in ways you cannot foresee. Perhaps, however, when you tell your parents of your sexual orientation, your worst fears will be realized. As you decide whether or not to come out to them, you need to face up to this possibility but not let it lead you to conclude that you should not tell them about your sexual orientation. It could help you assess more realistically what you are asking of your parents and realize that changing attitudes on this scale takes time, that you will need love and patience as they struggle to replace their former ideas with new information and comprehension.

There are a lot of good reasons why you may want to come out to your parents. Pretending to them, year after year, that you are someone you are not is hard. If your parents do not know the totality that is you, including your lesbianism or gayness, an invisible barrier exists between you and them.

You have to watch carefully everything you say so you do not let slip some piece of information that might give away your secret. "After we've talked about the weather and my job, I have nothing more to say to my parents, because all my leisure activities take place in the gay community and they don't know I'm gay," one young man said, in a discussion about coming out to parents. His problem is not unusual in the gay or lesbian community. If your parents do not know of your sexual orientation, a growing sense of estrangement is apt to develop between your family and you because you are not being yourself with them. You are always playing a role.

Sometimes specific events provide good reasons for coming out to your parents. For instance, self-disclosure becomes rather urgent if you are a visible lesbian or gay activist. If there is a chance that your picture or a statement you make may be printed in a newspaper—any newspaper—it would be better for you to tell your parents about yourself, rather than having them learn the truth from a clipping sent to them by a friend or acquaintance. Do not assume this could not happen, even though you may be living in California and your parents are in Maine. The world is shrinking, news can travel in the most unexpected ways.

A visit by your parents to the town or city where you

live might also cause you to give serious thought to coming out to them. More than one lesbian or gay couple has had to set up elaborate subterfuges when parents come to visit if the parents have no idea of the true state of affairs. Either the couple has to pretend they are friends sharing living quarters (and you better have two bedrooms, each with a bed in it) or the partner has to move everything out of the house or apartment for the length of the visit. During the parents' stay there is continual fear that some telltale evidence has been overlooked and not removed. ("Have I hidden my gay/lesbian books and magazines well enough so my parents will not stumble on them? Is there something that might reveal the truth, some sign to which I have become so accustomed that I am no longer aware of it?")

Often the psychic cost of concealing from your parents the information that you are same-sex-oriented is high. You are implicitly denying the worth of your true self and the worth of your relationship with your lover. You are living out the idea that a same-sex-oriented person *is* a second-class citizen and family member and that the relationship with a partner really *is* inferior to the relationship between married persons. This kind of self-disparagement is so subtle you may not realize that it *is* disparaging.

But the most difficult task you face may be coming out to your parents. A thousand unconscious ties, beginning at the moment of birth and perhaps before, bind us compulsively to our parents. In the case of adoptive parents, the ties may be slightly different but possibly even more compulsive because of the lack of a biologic bond.

Augustus Y. Napier, a psychologist specializing in family therapy, has caught the essence of the adult child's dilemma in *The Family Crucible*, when he writes about "the power of the primordial parent, the source of all oppression and of final deliverance."[2] This is what our parents represented to us when we were helpless babies. At that age we had no words with which to frame our conclusions. Nevertheless, the idea is indelibly entered in our internal mental and emotional "computers." It is one of the unconscious components of our lives—and I am referring to every human being, not only lesbian and gay persons. We can deal with these compulsive bonds only by bringing them into consciousness, at the cost of greater or lesser emotional pain, after which we can begin to deal with them on a maturer level.

Coming out to your parents is usually a highly emotional issue. It cannot be resolved on a purely rational level because of the deep, unconscious emotional bonds as well as the unconscious awareness of your family's rules, those unstated guidelines to the way your particular family deals with life in all its varied aspects, guidelines you absorb seemingly by osmosis.

If you have a partner, the issue is complicated by your need to give the relationship importance and your need for your partner to be part of the family. Any decision—whether to tell or not to tell—carries risk to the familial relationship and to the partner relationship.

The reasons you choose not to tell your parents may be overriding. If one or both of them are old or have serious health problems that might be aggravated by your information or if you feel there is a strong possibility they may disown you, you may choose to say nothing. A more likely result you may envision is that your parents will never be able to come to terms with your information, and you therefore do not want to subject them or yourself to a never-ending tug-of-war.

Perhaps you feel no need to tell your parents. This may be a psychologically sound decision for you, based on realistic wrestling with the issue. But Don Clark, a gay therapist and author of *Loving Someone Gay*, warns that if in your imagination you find yourself again and again telling a particular person you are lesbian/gay, you had better tell that person about your sexual orientation. You are using too much precious emotional energy to maintain your secret. Similarly, he says, if you have to go to some effort to hide your same-sex orientation from a specific person, "you must, for your own survival, tell him or her sooner or later."[3]

If you do decide to come out, are you going to tell only one parent or both? If your parents are divorced, telling only one parent presents no particular problem. Be sure, however, that the parent who has been told knows that the other parent has not. Otherwise you may be setting up a sticky situation for yourself.

If your parents are not divorced but you feel inclined to confide in one and not the other, there may be some family dynamics in action to which you have not heretofore given much thought. You have not analyzed *why* it is always easier to talk with Mom than with Dad or vice versa. It is a fact of life that she (he) seems to understand you better or is not as likely to get upset as the other parent.

Much more is involved in this situation than is apparent at first. Some elements may have to do with whether one parent treats you more as an adult whereas the other still sees you, at least to some extent, as a child. More likely these reflect the pattern of interaction between your parents, and your decision to tell one parent and not the other follows lines of communication and action that your parents have established unconsciously as the family's way of living together.

As an adult, you need not follow the prevailing family pattern. If you do choose to follow it, it might help your own self-understanding to be aware of why you are choosing to tell one parent only. Obviously, you are choosing not to tell one of your parents because you envision an uncomfortable conflict over your sexual orientation. You may have to balance your desire to avoid such discomfort against the fact that you may be putting a strain on the parent you tell by asking that parent to keep the information secret from her or his partner. You are forming an alliance with one parent against the other. Almost certainly this is not a new alliance, but further evidence of a rift that has existed between your parents—as well as between yourself and one parent—for a considerable period. If there is such an emotional split between your parents, telling both of them may mean they are polarized even more as one feels the need to defend you to the other.

There are no easy answers to such a dilemma, but I think you, as a son or daughter of such parents, need to recognize *you are not and never have been* the cause of the division between your parents. The relationship probably has a flaw that can be traced back to its beginning.

The issue is too complex to discuss in detail here, but some exploration of your family relationships might help you make your decision. Reading one or more books dealing with family dynamics (several are listed at the end of this book) will give you some insight into the unconscious rules in your family as well as into your own feelings and your relationships within your family. *The Family Crucible* in particular clearly shows the actual dynamics of family "triangulation" (chapters 12, 13 14).[4] If counseling is available and you feel the need to examine your family system with someone who can help you gain insights, it might be wise to seek this outside help.

Before you decide whether to tell or not to tell your parents you are lesbian or gay, the matter is worthy of your best research and effort, even though this may require a considerable investment of time and energy and perhaps money.

Whether the outcome of your revelation—should you decide to make it—is good (your parents accept and continue to love you) or bad (they never do come to terms with your information), the experience will not have been wasted. Your action may have been painful and, from your point of view, may seem to have been unsuccessful (your parents did not provide the approval/understanding/acceptance you desired). Yet if you emerge from the process with a greater understanding of yourself and of the dynamics of person-to-person and family interaction, you will have been rewarded for whatever time, work, emotion, and money you put into the effort. Self-knowledge and self-understanding usually do not come easy.

Possibly, by being honest with your parents about your real self you are giving them an opportunity to grow. The results may be far better than you can imagine. In time—and I want to emphasize this—*in time* you may be closer to your parents and family because you risked entrusting them with the knowledge of who you really are. You may have a clearer sense of your own identity and a new sense of freedom and self-respect because now you are not hiding your real self. You may have a new sense of yourself as a responsible adult because you have dealt straightforwardly with a difficult issue. You may have a clearer understanding of yourself in your intimate relationships—those with family, partner, and close friends. You may now be able to share joyfully and with a sense of well-being with the significant persons in your life because you have taken the positive step of being real with them.

In other words, by risking coming out to your parents you have given yourself and them an opportunity to grow.

Chapter 3

Grief Often Does Not Look Like Grief

"How could you do this to us?"

This question is one of the commoner reactions of parents to the news that they have a lesbian daughter or a gay son. Sometimes it is asked in anguish, sometimes in anger.

Some parents ask themselves a companion question: "Where did we go wrong?"

Neither query is asked in order to receive objective information. Both are reflexive, knee-jerk reactions to sudden shock and pain.

Undoubtedly, many thoughts and feelings are going through your parents' heads. If it were possible to get a slow-motion reading of these thoughts and feelings, it would probably include shock, confusion, pain, anger, guilt, and a desire to get rid of some of the guilt by shifting the blame.

You have challenged some sensitive traditional beliefs your parents hold. Any challenge to convention is likely at first to provoke bewildered resentment.[1] In addition, your parents are apt to feel tremendous guilt. Anything that happens to their child is *their fault*. They have failed. They must have been bad parents. Their child is gay or lesbian because of what they have done or left undone. Instinctively, they voice a question in order to shift some of the heavy guilt that has descended on them: *"How could you do this to us?"* If your parents have not been afraid to be angry with you, they may ask the question in anger. If they feel that *good* parents do not get angry, they may ask the question with anguished tears in their eyes. Either way the question can be devastating to you. (But then your information has been devastating to your parents.)

The disclosure that you are lesbian or gay has set in motion grief reactions within your parents. And chances are they have not the slightest idea they are experiencing grief. In fact, this may surprise you and your parents. After all, you are alive and in good health. Why should your parents grieve?

Ira J. Tanner, in his book *Healing the Pain of Everyday Loss*, lists different types of losses.[2] The death of a loved one, divorce, and loss of one's job are not the only causes of grief. Moving to a new house; the death of a favorite pet, plant, or tree; job promotion (surprisingly); loss of family heirlooms; seasonal loss, such as the passing of summer, fall, Christmas—all these can cause grief reactions of varying intensity.

But you are alive and healthy, so what have your parents lost?

They have lost an image of you, an idea about you, the identification of you as a heterosexual person. From the moment of your birth they have been creating and adding to a mental picture of who you are. As you have grown and developed they have added details. One assumption about you they probably have never questioned. Most likely they assumed you were heterosexually oriented and that you would someday marry, settle down, and raise a family, like they did.

Now this fundamental assumption about you has been

demolished. Your parents discover that they do not know as much about you as they thought. They have been deceived!

They *have* been deceived but not with malicious intent. In large measure they have deceived themselves by making an assumption they never thought to verify. In addition, you *have* deceived them by letting them continue to assume you are straight. You may have actively encouraged them to think this by various means. Often lesbian and gay young people lie and make omissions about who they are seeing, when, how. Dating is generally the alibi used to conceal lesbian or gay relationships. Such young persons invent names, places, and what happened on these dates in order to hide the truth they are not ready to disclose to their parents, because disclosure could blow the young persons' precarious world to pieces. Probably, these young persons who are becoming aware of their different sexual orientation are struggling with at least some self-loathing; after all, society has graphically told lesbians and gay men how sick, sinful, despised, and repulsive they are. Whatever deception you have engaged in has been undertaken as a means of self-preservation, not consciously to defraud or wound your parents.

Besides other losses your parents are experiencing, they are experiencing a loss of faith in one of their fundamental beliefs, that *of course everyone is born heterosexual unless he or she is sick, neurotic, rebellious, or perverse.* Your parents are therefore grappling with a double grief: the loss of the *you* they thought they knew in every aspect of your being and the loss of a basic tenet, that everyone is born heterosexual and deviates from this only because of calamity or willful perversity. Of course your parents are experiencing loss. Of course they will need to grieve.

Related to their primary loss are allied sources of pain. For instance, they may feel you have forsaken their value system. Almost certainly your parents had hoped you would help perpetuate the things they have valued in their lives: the establishment of a home and family, the value of monogamy (even if they are divorced, they may still believe in one-at-a-time monogamous commitments), and if they are religiously inclined, the upholding of their beliefs about sin and righteousness. Your new and unfamiliar sexual attitudes may threaten to cast them adrift from familiar moorings.

Although they may not realize it at first, perhaps they see this conflict between value systems as a personal defeat. Is it not up to the parents to shape their child's values, to pass on to the coming generation the beliefs and attitudes they deem important and necessary for a full and moral life? Somewhere along the way, they believe, they have failed to transmit to you the ideas they value. Suddenly, insidiously, their own child is the enemy. They are suffering defeat and loss at the hands of their child.

They may also see your apparent forsaking of their values as a loss of power over their child's life. Or they may interpret this supposed loss of power as a rejection of themselves. Unconsciously, most parents mistakenly believe that if their children really honor and love them, the children will adhere closely to their parents' values.

Another grief your parents may be experiencing concerns their loss of expectation of a son- or daughter-in-law. There will be no beautiful wedding to which they can invite relatives and friends, none of the excitement that surrounds such an event, no showers and gifts. Before you dismiss this loss as shallow and trivial, remember that these are deeply ingrained cultural patterns that have their roots in the establishment of a protective environment where children may be created and nurtured.

A new development, the service for the Blessing of Relationships within a religious setting, can provide a ceremony that corresponds to the heterosexual "beautiful wedding." I have witnessed services that in every way fit that description and radiated a depth of meaning and commitment that would do credit to any heterosexual marriage ceremony. Unfortunately such a service may not qualify in the parents' eyes as one to which they want to invite relatives and friends. This is regrettable, because the desire to take another person as a life partner, whether of the same or opposite sex, and to "witness this before God and these witnesses" is a step of the utmost solemnity and commitment and should be greeted with gratitude and support. Such commitment indicates a maturity, a seriousness of purpose, that is a welcome antithesis to the stereotypical assumption that gay men in particular are by definition promiscuous.

In addition to feeling sorrow over the lost expectation of your marriage, your parents may be grieving the loss of potential grandchildren you might have given them. If you have already been married and have had children, in all likelihood you and your mate are getting or have gotten a divorce, and this, too, grieves your parents.

Clearly, both you and your parents need to be aware that they will experience some psychic losses when you tell them of your lesbian or gay orientation. Because these losses are real, it is important that your parents grieve—and that you should be willing for them to do so.

Many gay or lesbian persons I talk with tell me the same thing: "I have told my parents, but they aren't dealing with it at all. I've given them books to read, but they won't read them. We never talk about it." I can hear the hurt in their voices, because their parents seem to be denying the very personhood of their daughter or son.

Denial is a common way of expressing one's grief. What the parents are denying, however, is not the personhood of their child; they are denying to themselves this one fact about their child because they are unwilling or unable to face it and deal with it. And, of course, this is the one fact their child wants them to face—and accept.

The odd thing about grief is that often what people do in its throes does not appear as grief, but rather resembles anger, guilt, blaming, bargaining, denial, and depression. Eventually, the result of all this will be—one hopes—acceptance.

These aspects of grief may not be exhibited as well-defined stages. In fact, they probably will not. They are likely to be more or less scrambled together. Anger may be expressed in a relatively straightforward way, or it may be leaked out in blaming. If anger is repressed and given no outlet, it can lead to depression—anger turned inward. Similarly, guilt may be experienced as guilt, or it may be channeled into other aspects, such as blaming, bargaining, or anger. In addition, all these ungrieflike feelings may be experienced again and again, in no discernible sequence.

Anger in the face of grief may seem to be an odd, sometimes even irrational reaction. When we probe beneath the surface, however, we discover the reasons for it. They are connected to the fight side of the physiological fight-or-flight mechanisms by which the body deals with crises. In addition, grieving persons experience discomfort and confusion because their lives have been disrupted, because they have suffered loss of control over the circumstances of their lives. And so they become angry at themselves for losing control, at others who caused the loss of control, and perhaps ultimately at God or fate or whatever caused this disruption of their lives.

Anger may be expressed in a number of ways. It may rush out explosively, for example, as in the classic "How could you *do* this to us?" or it may be expressed by total silence on the subject. How often have you heard someone say, "I was so angry I couldn't even talk about it"? Your parents' silence may indicate denial, or it may stem from a consuming anger at the blow life has dealt them. Unfortunately, they may be localizing this anger on you rather than on the more abstract designation of "life." They may even be angry that life has dealt such a blow to you, their child. Yet they may be unable to recognize that they are angry or know why. One way or the other, they may be denying feelings.

Many times you have probably greeted the announcement of bad news with the words "Oh no!" or "You're kidding!" This is a manifestation of the wish to deny that a calamity has occurred. Denial serves as an anesthetic in the first flush of grief. It can separate us for a time from pain that is too intense to bear, and by doing this it can help preserve our emotional equilibrium until the time when we can begin to deal with the crisis. Denial functions as a circuit breaker when the emotional circuits become overloaded.

To survive emotionally and continue to function, a person may deny certain information—in this case that his or her child is lesbian or gay. I remember the parents of a gay man saying at a Families of Gays and Lesbians meeting,[3] "Between meetings we kind of forget that Jack is gay, and we get along fine. Then we see the meeting date on our calendar, and it forces us to remember that Jack is gay. Every month we struggle with the decision of whether to come to the meeting and think about his being gay, which makes us feel bad, or not to go to the meeting and forget about his gayness."

When denial becomes a way of life it is damaging to the one who denies and to those around him or her. The results of denial have been graphically portrayed in the book and film *Ordinary People*.[4] Unable to deal with the death of her older son, Beth Jarrett eventually finds it necessary to flee from her husband and younger son, disrupting their lives as well as her own.

The real problem with prolonged denial is that it is a prison in which one locks oneself, and only the imprisoned person holds the key to the door. Storming the fortress from without is rarely successful. Patient love may eventually bring results, but it is an exceedingly difficult gift to give.

Guilt is another strong, universal component of grief. Even when no cause and effect relationship exists between a person's actions and the cause of grief, the human reaction usually is, "If only I had done this" or "If I hadn't done that, it wouldn't have happened."

In the case of a child's same-sex orientation, most parents are inundated with guilt. In my own case I knew immediately *why* Eric is gay: *It was because of the home in which he had grown up.* A number of years and a good bit of information later I know it was not my husband's or my fault, that the causes of a same-sex orientation are complex. Thousands of factors, many of which are not yet understood, may contribute to a child's sexual orientation, whether hetero- or homosexual. Nevertheless, most parents of gay or lesbian persons ask themselves sometime or another, "Where did we go wrong?"

Where there is guilt, there has to be blame. And so parents blame themselves or you or outside circumstances.

"How could *you* do this to us?"

"If only we hadn't let him play with dolls (let her play football with the boys) this wouldn't have happened."

"Some evil person must have seduced my child."

"It there wasn't so much publicity in the newspapers and on TV about homosexuality, this wouldn't have happened." And so on and on.

Guilt can be lessened by bargaining. "Well, it's all right if"—if you seek counseling, if you will try to change, if you will live a celibate life. Bargaining is an attempt by your parents to reduce the anxiety level produced by guilt.

A variation of bargaining can be redefinition. Although the thought may not even be verbalized, it can take many forms: "He (she) will change"; "She will meet the right man (He will meet the right woman)"; "This is just a phase." Wishful thinking and false hope can encourage such redefinition. Hope can keep people alive, and without hope they would at times die. But hope can also be a tormentor, particularly if it is founded on unsubstantiated claims. Thus, every assertion that someone has changed will torment your parents—and possibly you, if they keep reminding you of these claims and assertions. Such shreds of hope can torture your parents and you for years.

Depression can also be a means of shifting guilt to others. "Look how bad you have made me feel" may be the unconscious message being conveyed. Because the other person does not want to accept the guilt, the temptation is to tell the depressed one to cheer up or snap out of it. Unfortunately, this does no good. It is more helpful to *validate* or confirm the reality of the depression by telling the person he or she is experiencing a natural reaction and that it is probably only temporary. If depression continues or deepens, the depressed person may need professional help.

Acceptance is the goal toward which all the foregoing grief reactions are moving. But when it begins to appear, it often vanishes again quickly. One week your parents may seem to be feeling pretty good about you and life, and the next week, unaccountably, they are back to all the old struggles. You may breathe a sigh of relief the first time your parents *finally* seem to have accepted you only to find the next time you see them or talk with them on the phone or get a letter from them they have fallen back into denial, guilt, depression, and so on. "Won't they *ever* accept me?" you wonder.

You may be able to deal with these shifts more calmly if you realize that grief reactions do not progress in a neat and orderly fashion. Your parents are likely to ricochet around among the various aspects of grief, living through each of them not only once, but many times and in no predictable order. Yet if they have touched on acceptance once, they will probably touch on it again and perhaps hold on to it longer the next time. One hopes the time will come when their grief work is completed and acceptance becomes their permanent possession.

Your awareness of the process in which your parents are involved can help you to be patient as they work through their feelings. If parents realize they are in the throes of grief and have some idea of what to expect, they are not as likely to panic but will understand that their feelings of guilt, anger, and depression are normal. These are not comfortable feelings, but at least they are normal. In time their intensity will subside, and what was once the sharpest pain will either be gone or remain only as a dull, residual ache.

Time by itself is not a complete healer, but often the passage of time does lessen the original pain. Time should not be reckoned in weeks or even months, but rather in half years and years. Do not expect today what is appropriate six months or a year from now.

Does any person ever learn the lesson of patience completely? Probably not. But if you allow your parents time to work through their flood of feelings and if they give themselves time to do this, several years from now you may all be surprised and pleased with the results.

Chapter 4

Getting Ready to Make the Big Announcement

Now that you, as a lesbian or a gay man, have some idea of what reactions to expect from your parents when you tell them of your same-sex orientation, let us look at your preparations for telling them and some methods you can use to convey your information.

Do Not Hint

One way *not* to come out to your parents is by dropping hints in your conversation. Many same-sex-oriented persons use this indirect method, thinking that in time their parents will put all the hints together and draw the obvious conclusion. In most cases this technique does not work. Your parents may have been putting bits and pieces of casual information together—or they may not. It is amazing how parents can overlook and ignore those things in their children that they do not care to deal with. Unless your parents really seem to be picking up on the clues you drop, do not expect much from this type of advance preparation.

Some same-sex-oriented persons unconsciously carry on a variation of this form of coming out. Without knowing it, they drop broad hints and clues in their conversation. One young friend of mine was unwisely scattering inferences about her sexual orientation to her colleagues in a career situation that would end abruptly if her coworkers began paying close attention to her repeated hints. Another friend and I pointed out to her the seriousness of what she was doing. In time she came out to her mother (her father is dead) and to her supervisor. Because this greatly eased the pressure she had been feeling, she no longer had an unconscious need to hint about her lesbianism.

Role Reversal

Generally, the advice regarding coming out to parents has been relatively simple: Wait until you yourself feel comfortable about your sexuality, present the information in as kind a way as possible, supply some helpful reading material about homosexuality, and then hope for the best. These are all good ideas, but you can do a lot more to help them and yourself.

As you prepare to come out to your parents, it is important for you to recognize a fact so basic and so obvious that you may have overlooked it. You have had time—perhaps a long time—in which to prepare to make the announcement to your parents about your sexual orientation. You can choose the occasion, the place, and the method of telling. Your parents cannot.

Between one minute and the next their world changes. Suddenly, your parents' role and your role are reversed. All through the years of your growing up your parents cared for you because they had more information about the world than you did. Now the positions are reversed. Now *you* are the one who has more information about same-sex orientation, and you will have to care for your parents as they move into this area that is new to them. Of course, you will not be a "parent" to them in the same way they were to you when you were growing up. You do need to be the guide, however, in the unfamiliar territory to which you are introducing them.

As discussed in chapter 3, your parents will probably experience grief reactions; perhaps these reactions will be intense. Almost certainly they will have no idea that their words and feelings in response to your information *are* grief reactions. You must be prepared to help them understand their feelings, because at first you may be the only person available to do this.

Many parents, when they learn of their children's same-sex orientation, feel isolated, cut off from their usual world. They have no way of knowing that millions of other parents also have same-sex-oriented children and that therefore they are not alone. All they know is that they have been thrust into a world where everything is new and strange. Worst of all, it seems impossible for them to talk to anyone about what has happened.

Among your parents' friends and acquaintances there may be no one who can help them at this point. The usual people you might suggest may not be equipped to handle the situation. For instance, many pastors, priests, and rabbis have not dealt with their own feelings concerning homosexuality and could not therefore help others. The only thing your parents might be told is that you are a sinner and that they should pray for you and encourage you to seek help in order to change. They might not fare much better if they seek help from their doctor. Even if the doctor has the inclination to attend to emotional as well as physical problems, she or he may not have up-to-date information about homosexuality. Or the doctor may be uncomfortable with this subject. As for your parents' talking with a close friend, this may not be practicable. Most of their friends are not any better equipped to deal with the subject than they are. In addition, there are the questions of whether the friend would keep the information confidential and whether the friend might reject your parents. As you can see, even though you are the one who has precipitated the crisis, you have great potential for serving, at least in part, as a healer.

One way you can prepare is to learn about grief. Check the library and the bookstore for books on the subject, and read one or two. Several books dealing with grief that you might find helpful are listed in "For Further Reading."

If a counselor, your pastor, or an older friend is available, talk with him or her about grief. If you cannot explain to the person what you are planning to do and why you want to talk about grief, find someone else with whom you can be honest.

Another direction your preparation might take was indicated in chapter 2: Learn why families behave as they do. Read one or more books on the subject, and possibly consult a counselor if the relationships in your family seem particularly difficult.

Preparing Through Imagination

An important aspect of your preparation involves acting out what you think is going to take place when you tell your parents. What words are you going to say? Try them out in your mind or, better yet, on paper. You may want to write down what you would like to say so you can work with it from several angles.

What do you want to accomplish in this encounter with your parents? All you can hope to do in this initial session is to share yourself straightforwardly, lovingly, and confidently, and then be available to help your parents begin to deal with the information. Therefore, consider the impression your words will create. You can readily understand that if you say, "Dad and Mom, I have something I want to tell you that may upset you," you are setting the stage for one kind of reaction. But you are setting the stage for a different kind of reaction if you say, "Dad and Mom, I've been wanting to share something with you for some time because it's pretty important to me and because you two are pretty important to me." This approach does not guarantee they will receive your news gladly, but you *have* conveyed two positive messages: You have told your parents that the information means a lot to you and that you care about them.

Do not string out your introduction with an overabundance of words or talk around what you want to say. This will give the impression that what you have to say is so awful you are trying to postpone the telling. A short lead, in which you use a past experience as a point of contact, may be helpful, such as, "You know you've asked me from time to time about girl (boy) friends, and I've always kind of put you off." Move on at once to, "The time didn't seem right then to say what I want to tell you now, that I'm gay (lesbian)." Or: "Remember when we had the big discussion about homosexuality? Were you aware that I was the one who brought it up?" Continue with something like, "The reason I wanted to talk about homosexuality is that I'm very much interested in the subject. You see, I'm lesbian (gay)."

Having decided what you want to say to break the news to your parents, you now want to imagine a range of possible reactions they may have to your news. Perhaps they will react quite differently from the scenarios you create. Imagining a number of possible responses, however, should make you more surefooted in dealing with whatever situation arises.

Imagine one way your parents might respond. How would you feel if they reacted this way? Would you be angry? Tearful? Panicky? Even though none of these reactions would be helpful in the actual situation, just realizing that you might have these feelings can be useful; they are clues to the unconscious interaction between you and your parents. Why do you feel angry or tearful? What are you afraid of?

On the contrary, in response to your parents' reactions, you may wish you had a short, punchy retort that would put them in their place. Such a response could not possibly bring any of the results you are aiming for in this encounter. Why do you want to retaliate with a sarcastic or wounding reply? Sarcasm is a hostile reaction that can inflict pain or cause angry feelings to escalate.

This type of imaginative work can be upsetting and emotionally draining, but in the long run it could make a significant difference in your family's final accommodation to the news. In your imagination try out as many possible reactions from your family as you can think of and your responses to these reactions. You may do this in your head, on paper, or with a wise, patient, and understanding friend. (Be sure not to choose friends who have axes of their own to grind!)

The point of this exercise is to weed out all the unthinking responses that can undermine what you are trying to do. An angry response from you is not apt to cause your parents to change their minds. More likely it will generate a response that is angrier and shriller than yours, which in turn will probably generate a one-up response from you, and you and your parents are off to a needless, first-class family row.

As you try out various imagined scenarios, do you find yourself feeling like a naughty child, cowering before disapproving parents? You may discover that you are still trying to earn their approval, that you still feel the need to be the best little boy or girl in the world. This, as well as all your other possible reactions, is important information for you as you think about coming out to your parents.

Time, Place, Cast of Characters

Now that you have considered the *content* of your initial coming-out encounter with your parents, let us look at some of the actual methods you can use to convey your information, such basic considerations as time, place, and cast of characters.

There is probably no gay man or lesbian who is not familiar with the horror stories about how some parents have reacted when they found out their children were same-sex-oriented. Not quite so well known are the parental horror stories about hurtful ways in which children have come out to their parents.

For instance, I have a friend whose gay son chose to come out to her late one night in a busy restaurant. Allison, her son, and a friend of hers had gone to the theater that evening. Afterward, in a noisy, crowded restaurant, her son said to her, in front of her friend, "Mother, I want to tell you I'm gay."

Her immediate reaction to his words was an overwhelming desire to stand up in the middle of the restaurant and scream. Instead, she made her way to the ladies' room, where she vomited and wept. For several weeks she was in a state of shock. Her son made no effort to contact her during this time. After three weeks she pulled herself together enough to contact him and begin bridging the gaping hole he had made in their relationship, not by his being gay, but by the painful way in which he had thrust this information on her.

If he had chosen a quiet time and place to tell her, with opportunity for her to feel emotion in private, to talk with him about it, she would probably not have been thrown into such an acute state of shock. The terrible need to scream, the involuntary reaction of her stomach, the deep feeling of shock that disoriented her for a number of weeks—the intensity of all these reactions might have been substantially lessened if his method of telling her had been more humane.

He was young at the time. Obviously, he was panicked by the task he had set himself or he would not have chosen such an inept way of doing it. This woman is capable of great understanding and compassion, and today, some years later, the breach between her and her son has been mended. They have a good relationship, and she is proud of him.

This incident underscores an important prerequisite for coming out to parents: The more at ease you are with your sexuality, the more healthy your self-esteem will be and the better able you will be to help your parents as you come out to them.

This incident also underscores the importance of choosing a suitable time—a quiet, private, unhurried time with as little chance of interruption as possible. Which location is best? Your parents' home? Yours? Neutral territory? What neutral territory might be available to you that also provides privacy? If there are younger children in your family who do not know you are lesbian or gay, make sure they will not interrupt this time with your parents.

Must you take full responsibility for making all the decisions connected with this first encounter, or is there some way to include your parents in the decision-making process? You might say something like, "I want to talk with you privately about a personal matter—none of the other kids present. When would be a good time and where can we talk?" If one of your siblings already knows and is going to be present as support for both you and your parents, you should, of course, let your parents know that this family member will be included.

Do not invite your parents for a festive event—a lovely gourmet dinner, for example—and then drop your bombshell. You will not soften the blow by doing this. Instead, almost certainly they will be left with the unpleasant feeling of having been cheated and betrayed. You promised something pleasant but delivered something quite different. It is much better to live up to whatever you have implicitly promised.

Consideration of what else is going on in your parents'

lives can also be important. If one of your parents has just lost his or her job, if they have just found that your sister is pregnant although single or that one of your siblings is on drugs, or if they are on the verge of divorce, your coming out to them will work out better, in all likelihood, if you can wait until the acute stage of their crisis has passed. Similarly, the day after Christmas is better than the day before. Your parents can deal with your information in a more pressure-free atmosphere after the festivities are over. And do not plan to break the news to them at ten o'clock at night—any night.

These last few cautions about the timing of your announcement to your parents depend more on common sense and courtesy than on deep psychological insight. *Your* readiness to make your announcement in no way guarantees your parents' readiness to receive it. They may never be really ready, but they should not be struggling with six other serious problems; the immediate timing and setting should be chosen with as much consideration as possible.

Another way of coming out to your parents involves having a counselor or psychotherapist present when you do the telling. As with any method, there are pros and cons. Your parents should know ahead of time that a counselor will be present. Perhaps the simplest and most truthful explanation would include the information that you have talked with a counselor and that it would be helpful if he or she could sit down with you and your parents to discuss a few matters. Mentioning the counselor as a "friend," or inviting your parents without mentioning the counselor, has the drawback of leaving your parents unprepared for the presence of this person who is a stranger to them and, again, could leave them feeling duped. This is a consideration you must weigh as you decide how to get them together with the counselor.

The counselor or therapist should be one in whom your

parents could reasonably be expected to have confidence. If your parents are conservative, for instance, a male counselor who wears an earring could conceivably fail to inspire them with confidence in the validity of his judgment, because they would immediately peg him as "the enemy," recruited to brainwash them. A sensitive, low-key person, however, who *hears* them nonjudgmentally and gives them an opportunity to express their real feelings may be effective in defusing a potentially explosive situation. Some parents might feel comfortable with the additional, trained person present. Other parents might feel that any psychological-type person is suspect, and his or her presence would make a touchy situation even worse. Again, you have to weigh the possible reactions of both parents and make your choice. And if you guess wrong, do not berate yourself. You need have no regrets, no "if onlys," no feeling that "I should have *known* it wouldn't work." You are not a fortune-teller or a mind reader. You are trying to help your parents in a situation you think might be difficult for them, and if it does not turn out as you hope, you are not to blame and neither are they. You have no guarantee that the results would be any better if you told them without the counselor present.

Dealing with Your Parents' Responses

Up to this point the emphasis has been on the feelings and reactions you become aware of within yourself as you imagine the encounter with your parents. Now let us look at various reactions you imagine they may have. For instance, what will you do if they respond with anger? Or tears, guilt, blame, shock? Suppose they respond *too* well: "We've suspected it, dear, and we're glad you told us." And then they change the subject. Possibly—just possibly—real acceptance? If this is the case, they probably figured out your sexual orientation long ago and have been waiting for you to tell them.

Try to listen to the underlying message their words convey. For instance, anger that lashes out at you may really be anger at themselves, at their supposed failure as parents, displaced onto you. Denial may be their way of saying, "Give us time." Whatever your parents' reactions, they should not be taken as a definitive statement of how your parents are going to feel about you for the rest of their lives. Different people react to shock and pain in different ways.

All that is necessary in this encounter, after you have given your information, is for you to listen sympathetically and let your parents ventilate their feelings. Are they angry? All you need to say is, "You seem to be feeling a lot of anger, and that's understandable to me." Tears? A more appropriate response than "Don't cry" might be, "I think I can understand your sadness." Expressions of guilt? "I can understand why you feel guilty, but there's no need to blame yourselves because being gay (lesbian) isn't anybody's 'fault.' It's something that just happens." And so on.

"Wait a minute," you may be thinking. "Shouldn't I try to stop their feelings of anger or their tears?"

No. At this stage your parents need acceptance of their feelings, not attempts to deny them. They need to hear you say that the feelings they are experiencing are normal. Ira Tanner says, "If another values our feelings, we 'own' them within ourselves and do not deny the grieving process."[1]

As I mentioned earlier, because you may be the only person available, you may have to serve, at least for a time, as the validator of their feelings. It is important for you to realize that by doing so you are not assuming blame for their *anger, tears,* or *guilt.* You are saying only that these are real and normal *feelings* for this period of their grief process.

But suppose your parents say practically nothing or

change the subject. Try to draw them out: "How do you feel now that you know I'm lesbian (gay)?" If they do not respond, do not force them. Talking may come later.

If they respond with misinformation and stereotypes about homosexuality, brief and unemotional statements will do far more good than heated denials: "Statistics show that there are many more heterosexual than homosexual child-molesters." "A lesbian (gay) life-style isn't always promiscuous." "A gay (lesbian) person doesn't have to have a lonely old age." Even though your parents may seem to brush your statements aside, later they are more likely to remember and think about what you have said than if you get into head-to-head combat over their ideas or give them a lengthy and involved lecture.

What your parents may be trying to express, in addition to their grief and shock, is that they care about you and want the best for you. Your parents are not your adversaries. Rather, they are persons you love who are in pain, and you want to help them deal with their pain.

Wrapping It Up

How are you going to conclude this meeting with your parents?

Try to sum up the tone of the encounter *briefly*. "This seems to have been pretty upsetting to you, and I think that's understandable. I was pretty upset six years ago when I realized I was gay (lesbian). Maybe we can talk more about this later, when you've had time to think about it." Or: "You seem to have taken my news pretty calmly, but you may have some other feelings later. Lots of parents do. It's sort of a delayed reaction. If you do feel bad later, let's talk about it."

Let them know it is OK for them to have negative feelings and that it is not going to throw you if they do. Also, leave the door open for further dialogue. You may want to point out to them that parents almost universally suffer grief reactions on learning of their children's homosexuality. If they are in an acute stage of reaction, maybe all you will want to do is convey to them that it is all right for them to have these feelings, that many parents *are* upset, confused, in pain, when they are told such news.

Be sure to relate—again—that you have told them you are gay (lesbian) because you love them and do not want barriers between you and them. A hug, a kiss, an arm around their shoulders, a warm touch may be reassuring to them. But perhaps they may not want you to touch them, as if you were suddenly a carrier of the plague. This may hurt you deeply, but if you have mentally prepared yourself for this possibility, you need not be thrown by it. If they shy away from physical contact, respect their wishes without comment. Confine yourself to an expression of verbal caring. You can give way to tears if you want after you have left them.

Time may take care of this problem of being treated like a leper. If it does not, let them know later that their hands-off policy hurts you. This could open up discussion of the notion of same-sex-oriented persons as untouchables and could provide an opportunity for an exchange of feelings.

If you want to let them know immediately that their not wanting any physical contact with you hurts you, remember this standard advice: Do not say, "*You* did thus and so." Talk of *your* feelings: "I feel rejected when you . . ." They may be so involved in their own pain that they give no thought to your pain at their physical rejection of you.

Possibly, you may have no problems in this area because your family members have never expressed their feelings of love by physical contact or by words. You will have to decide whether or not you want to go against your family's unspoken rules and indicate your feelings. By thinking and planning ahead you will be able to go into the encounter with more confidence than if you do not prepare.

Practice various possible dialogues over a period of a few days, a week, a month—whatever timetable you feel you need. The words you actually say when the encounter does take place will probably be very different from those you planned, because you are becoming comfortable in your new role of helper, validator, and comforter in this situation.

Additional Considerations

Words, tones of voice, facial expressions, and actions are powerful tools in conveying one's real meaning to others. The right words may be ruined by voice, expression, or action. You might find it interesting to say, "I love you very much" while standing in front of a mirror. Try saying these words with a loving feeling; then say them in anger, with boredom, jokingly, and in a businesslike way. Match your facial expressions and actions to your tone of voice. Now try mixing, for example, the facial expression of anger with actions suggesting boredom, but still using words about love, and you will see that you are sending contradictory messages. Which are to be believed—your words, your tone of voice, or your actions?

You can have everything else right but wound deeply or arouse anger—or calm inflamed feelings—by your choice of words and the way you state what you want to say. A soft answer still turns away wrath. Listen to yourself, how you phrase ideas, which words you choose. Listen to the words others use, and analyze why some persons automatically arouse your ire, while others make you glad to have encountered them.

Words *can* wound. Words can also heal. They will be important in your continued dealings with your parents.

But suppose you do lose your cool in this or any other

encounter with your parents. All need not be lost. An apology is not a sign of weakness. It can be a sign of inner strength and can sometimes open doors that otherwise might have remained closed. Your expression of regret should be for losing your temper or for making a sarcastic or cutting remark. Apologizing is not synonymous with groveling, and you should ask to be pardoned for your actions only, *not* for a deeply held opinion—and certainly not for being gay or lesbian in the first place.

What do you do if your parents start asking you difficult questions, such as, "How do you have sex?" or "Tell me about your first sexual encounter," or "How many women (men) have you had sex with?" There is no good reason to describe your first sexual encounter to your parents or to tell them the number of different persons with whom you have had sexual experiences. A brief statement of your feelings is all that is necessary, such as "Sex is kind of a private matter. I wouldn't feel comfortable discussing the details of your sex life or mine."

Later perhaps one of your parents may sincerely want to know how same-sex persons "do it." One gay man I know has discussed the mechanics of homosexual sex with his father because his father genuinely wanted to know. Conversely, the mother of a lesbian asked her daughter, in anger, to describe a sexual encounter. The daughter, to punish the mother, did as she was asked. Obviously, much anger existed between this mother and daughter, and both question and answer were expressions of a larger problem between the two.

If your parents ask you if you have a partner and you do, you can say, "Yes, it's Jim (Julia), and someday I'd like you to meet him (her)." In this initial encounter a long, drawn-out discussion of partners can only be a distraction from the main purpose of your meeting, and if your parents do not bring up the issue, there is no need for you to introduce it now. Later will be time enough.

Phone, Letter, or Proxy?

So far only a face-to-face encounter with your parents has been discussed. What if you want to come out to them, but you cannot be with them? Should you write a letter? Would it be better to tell them on the phone? Or should you have someone else—for instance, a brother or sister—break the news to your parents?

Any of these methods might make good sense, depending on your particular situation. Any of these methods could also be used as a way of avoiding a face-to-face encounter, a means of distancing yourself from your parents and from the full impact of their possible anger and pain. You may not yet be secure enough in your sexual orientation to deal with their reactions in person, in which case perhaps you should postpone the telling, if your situation permits.

If you tell your parents on the phone, you have to depend on their words (and perhaps their silences or tears) to provide you with information about their feelings. Visual information is lacking. If you tell them in a letter, you cannot offer them immediate help and support. If someone else tells them, you lost the personal interaction between you and your parents at an important time in both your lives. This method may also give them the nonverbal message that a same-sex orientation is so unacceptable you cannot bear to confront them with this flaw in yourself.

If you feel, after considering the various options, that delegating the telling to someone else is the best way in your particular situation, make sure your parents understand why you feel this way. You might consider writing a letter the intermediary could read to your parents, as one young man did with positive results.

As for coming out in a letter, there may be good reasons this makes sense in your particular circumstances. For instance, you may be on the opposite side of the continent from your parents, and it may be imperative that you get this information to them. You may prefer writing to them instead of phoning because yours is a family in which expressing oneself in writing is easier and more natural than emotional verbal encounters. By writing a letter you have the advantage of selecting just the right words, without the risk of losing them in the nervous excitement of the meeting.

Write the letter and put it away for a week or longer, then get it out and reread it. How does it sound? Timid? Angry? Brusque? Protesting too much? Maybe there are some good sentences and some at which you cringe. Cut out all words or sentences that sound angry, sarcastic, or joking. This is no time for venting negative feelings or attempting humor. Include one or two expressions of caring. Let your parents know that you are telling them of your sexual orientation because you love them and want to share your true self with them. Let them know that you are happy being who you are. (If you are not happy with who you are, perhaps you need to do more soul-searching before you write.) Invite them to call you with their reactions and questions. Or set an approximate time when you will call them: "I'll call next weekend so we can talk."

In discussing coming out in a letter with two parents whose daughter used this method, I found it interesting that the father's and mother's reactions were different. The young woman was away at college but came home frequently on weekends, so it would have been easy for her to tell her parents in person. She chose, however, to write a letter. To the mother, it was a natural thing for her daughter to do this, because the young woman was interested in writing and often used this means of expressing herself. To the father, however, using a letter indicated that his daughter was not comfortable with her sexuality. Because of his questions about her self-acceptance, the parents immediately drove to her college, a four-hour trip, in order to talk with her and assure her of their love and acceptance of her.

Earlier I referred to a young man—Rick—who used the combination of a letter and an intermediary. Rick had come to the point of wanting to come out to his family. He knew the family members would be together for Christmas Day in the midwestern city where they lived, but he could not be with them. Previously, he had come out to one of his brothers, who proved to be supportive. Accordingly, Rick arranged with this brother that, on Christmas evening, he would read a letter from Rick to the assembled family (see Appendix 1). Rick would be waiting by his phone in New York in case any family members wanted to call and talk with him after the letter had been read.

In this family's case the plan worked well. The family *did* call Rick, and each member—mother, brothers, and sisters-in-law—talked with him. Looking back, after several years, his mother felt that Rick's way of telling them "was well thought out, and the proper groundwork was laid. . . . [The letter] answered so many questions and explained so many things that had occurred—especially in the preceding year. He [had] seemed distant and often noncommittal about his activities." She summed up her feelings by saying, "For us, Rick used a good method of communication."

Worst-case Scenario

Inevitably, one comes to the worst possibility, that which every gay and lesbian person has probably had nightmares about at some time: "Suppose my parents throw me out, disown me." This reaction occurs in fewer cases than the prevalence of this fear suggests. Yet it does occur frequently enough that the possibility cannot be discounted.

Usually, when one thinks of parents disowning a child, the reference is to a material and legal disinheriting. It is also possible for parents to disown a child emotionally, even though they may not cut off the child's formal inheritance. Just as emotional divorce can exist between persons who remain legally married to each other, so can emotional divorce exist between parents and a gay or lesbian child.

If, as time goes by, you become aware of an estrangement between you and your parents that grows more and more unbridgeable, you will need to grieve over the withdrawal of your parents' love. If it seems to you that I mention grief incessantly, you are right. You are dealing with change and with many different types of loss, and each change or loss needs to be felt, dealt with, and given due attention if you are to maintain good mental health.

Suppose your parents disown you. What would you do? If this reaction is at all likely, you need to deal with it in two ways. One is a practical approach. How would this action change your life? Would it affect your place of residence, your ability to support yourself? If so, what contingent plans could you make? If you are young and still living at home and this reaction is a possibility, you may want to rethink your decision to come out to your parents. If you still feel you must come out at this time, you had better do some serious, realistic thinking and planning. Crashing with the first person who offers you space may turn out to be disillusioning, and hustling is a hard and dangerous way to make a living.

The other type of preparation you need to make is emotional. Although no one can be totally prepared for possible emotional trauma, recognize ahead of time that rejection by your family cannot help but be extremely painful. Be aware that you will experience grief reactions over a prolonged period—at least a year, if not longer. If you try to avoid grief, if you do not allow yourself to experience it, if you pretend it is not there, if you do not spend time grieving, you simply postpone the day of reckoning. Initially, you may think you can bypass the normal cycle of grief. You may deceive your conscious mind, but you never deceive your body or your inner, unconscious self. Grief undealt with can cause many different kinds of future problems—physical or psychic or both. It is better for you to do your grief work—and it *is* emotional *work*—at the appropriate time. In so doing you can pick up the threads of your life and encounter less ultimate disruption than if you attempt to ignore your grief.

In chapter 3, I mentioned briefly Beth Jarrett's reaction to the loss of her older son in *Ordinary People*.[2] Her younger son, Con, also reacted strongly and much more immediately. As the story unfolds it becomes apparent that Con did not allow himself to acknowledge and experience the grief of losing his brother and the guilt and shame he felt for surviving while his older brother did not. Because the guilt and shame were false—in the sense of not being realistically deserved—does not mean the feelings were less violent or devastating. They were so intense in fact that he attempted suicide. An experienced gay male counselor told me that many of his clients identified with the younger son's reactions because his inner life closely paralleled their own.

If your parents do disown you, whether legally and emotionally or only emotionally, you are likely to feel a great deal of guilt and shame in addition to your sadness at your loss. Again, the guilt and shame are false, undeserved. A same-sex orientation is not in itself a cause for such feelings, even though society tries to tell you it is.

How can you deal realistically with the devastating grief of parental rejection? On the one hand, you do not want to react with such complete abandonment to grief that you cannot function. On the other hand, to stifle your feelings and deny them so completely that you experience no grief at all is not healthy. Somehow you have to find a way that includes allowing yourself to face your real feelings of pain, anger, depression, and so on, while still managing to cope with the problem life has handed you.

When I was in therapy my counselor gave me some tips on how to feel and cope. "You don't have to allow yourself to be inundated with grief all the time," she told me. She suggested I set aside some time—once a day, twice a day, several times a week, whatever seemed necessary—and give myself up to my feelings for this period. It might be five minutes or a half hour. During the rest of the time, if grief feelings assailed me, I could assure them that if they waited until evening or whenever the next grief period came, I would let them express themselves fully. It may seem odd to you to address your feelings as separate from you, but it *does* work. During the period of your grief, if you find the feelings taking over in an unhealthy way— for instance, with self-destructive thoughts or a need to inflict physical pain on yourself—you can tell your feelings, "That's enough now. I'll come back and grieve tomorrow." You *do* need to acknowledge your feelings and give them a place in your life. You do not, however, need to allow them to take over your life. If self-harming thoughts continue to come, make every effort to seek responsible counseling. If you are still incapacitated by grief after a considerable period, you may also want to consider therapy. This is not weakness. Such a decision can demonstrate strength and wisdom.

Rejection by those whom we rightly expect to love us is an extremely painful experience. As far as you are able, remember that the rejection says more about your parents' problems than it does about you. They have rejected you, not because you are inherently unlovable, but because of their own insecurities, their own fragile hold on their self-esteem. If they did not disown you before they knew you are lesbian or gay, it is not *you* they are disowning, but what they see as a threat to themselves. This rationale may not appreciably diminish the pain for you, but it may help you keep a needed perspective.

If you have the courage and the inner resources, keep the door open to your parents. After some time has passed—three months, six months, a year—if you can and want to do it, make contact with them and ask how they are feeling. A cataclysmic decision, reached in the first shock of finding out about your sexual orientation, may not be the decision they want to live with the rest of their lives. Can you forgive enough to try a tentative overture to them? Do you want to? Feel your way carefully. Do they want you back so they can vent their feelings on you? Do you want to return to the fold because you have a need to receive their condemnation? Or have they grown in the interim? Have you grown? Proceed with caution, and examine your reactions and theirs as objectively as possible. There has to be a balance between your need for self-preservation and your parents' needs, whatever they may be. Move warily but not bitterly or cynically.

Limited Relationship

You may have to settle for a limited relationship. I was much older than I should have been before I realized that my mother was too involved in my life, and that I could not confide all my actions to her unless I was prepared to accept endless streams of advice about the way I conducted my life. She did not hesitate to let me know if she thought I was too involved in church work or that my garden was too big for me to take care of or that I ought to feed my family more or less of certain foods. Obviously, what she worried about had nothing to do with the deeper issues of life. She simply wanted to continue to control me.

Her reasons, if she could have formulated them, would have been complex indeed. To retain a sense of self-worth, she needed to control every situation. She had to have the final word. Because of circumstances beyond her control very early in life, she had been gravely wounded psychologically, and because she grew up in a time when psychiatric help was not a possibility for most people, all her life she remained an emotional cripple.

For me to survive emotionally and maintain my own mental health, I had to determine how I could relate to her without damaging my own ability to cope with life. I discovered that if I wanted to survive as a (healthily) independent person, I could not confide all my day-to-day activities to her. I would have to communicate only those things that were noncontroversial.

I think the reason I continued to confide everything to her long after I should have quit lay in my unconscious programming. As a child, I had absorbed the idea that good little girls told their mothers everything. I did not question this idea for a long time, because I was not aware that this was what I thought. You cannot change what you think until you become aware that you are thinking it.

The necessity for a limited relationship with parents may stem from causes that have nothing to do with sexual orientation. Parents bring their own problems to the task of raising their children. Be aware of this so you do not assume guilt for everything that goes wrong in your relationship with your parents. Every relationship is a joint enterprise. One party alone is not responsible for the interaction and the success of a relationship. Both must work at it.

Hidden Anger

One aspect of coming out does necessitate a considerable amount of soul-searching on your part if you are to avoid wounding your parents and perhaps alienating them permanently. Most of this chapter has been concerned with telling your parents of your sexual orientation because you love them and want to share your complete, real self with them. You should also realize that sometimes motives for coming out are not entirely loving and kind. They may in fact spring from deeply buried anger and pain.

Let us go back to the time when the lesbian or gay person is beginning to realize "I *am* different. I *am* lesbian (gay)." A dismaying host of feelings begins to confront the same-sex-oriented person: fear of his or her emerging sexuality, which seems so different from that of his or her peers; the painful realization that he or she is part of a despised and outcast minority; anger at having to deal with this immense, unasked-for problem; guilt at being the awful person society says he or she is. In this maelstrom of pain the young person thrashes about, looking for reasons why this has happened, looking for someone to help carry the crushing load of shame and guilt.

Just as society has provided your heavy burden through its lesbian and gay stereotypes, so it also provides the scapegoat: your parents. This has happened to you because of your father, your mother, the family system, the home in which you grew up. You are suffering because of *them*. If only you could somehow get back at them for what they have done to you.

And, of course, you can by letting them know what kind of person you really are. You can vent your anger by shattering the image they have of you and letting them know how different your values are from theirs.

Naturally, you do not reason this out in logical sequence, as I have done here. The ideas are mostly hidden from yourself in a murky cloud that whirls and seethes below the surface of your mind. What you do and say is not consciously planned. It simply seems to happen. All of us tend to siphon off unconscious anger in many ways—a sarcastic remark, picking a fight, quiet stubbornness, choosing to do the opposite of what someone wants us to do. In *The Angry Book* Theodore Isaac Rubin has detailed the many ways in which hidden anger leaks out.[3]

There are other sources of pain for the same-sex-oriented person who is becoming aware of his or her sexuality. Because the parents automatically deal with their same-sex-oriented child as a heterosexual person, the child has a vague, undefined sense of not having his or her needs met, as if he or she were forever holding out a hand to the parents and the parents were forever reaching for the child's hand in a different place. Parents and child never seem to connect. Eventually, a feeling—probably not even articulated—builds up in the same-sex-oriented person that "they have never been the parents to me that I really needed. They haven't given me what I longed for."

Gradually, the parents become the adversary. If they sense something different about their child, if they unconsciously sense pain or questioning or asking, they may—equally unconsciously—try to reduce their and their child's anxiety by suggesting remedies that are not remedies. To sons: "Why don't you go out for the baseball team?" "Gym class can't be that bad." "Why don't you ask Sally for a date to the prom?" Or, to daughters: "Wouldn't you rather have some dancing lessons instead of so many team sports?" "But you look so nice in that ruffled blouse." "Maybe you shouldn't have broken up with Bob."

Even though the parents are just trying to help, every time they attempt to move the child in the direction of male or female heterosexual stereotypes, the same-sex-oriented child may perceive the parents as insensitive and authoritarian. It is hardly their fault that they are doing it all wrong.

In a sense no parents give—or even *can* give—their children everything they want in an emotional way, no matter what the sexual orientation of the children. But often gay and lesbian children have a special feeling of being cheated by their parents because the homosexual part of them was not loved and accepted. How could this be? The parents had no way of knowing this part of their child. Even the child may not have understood at that point how she or he was different, only that something seemed vaguely to be missing or out of kilter in life. Because of these feelings of frustration, of anger, of loss that build up in the same-sex-oriented person as she or he grows up, the adult child may come out to the parents in a way that creates distance and vents unconscious anger.

How are you going to know whether you are angry at your parents? It may not be easy, because often such anger is largely unconscious and therefore hidden. For a time, monitor your thoughts about your parents, the ways in which you speak of them to other people, the general tenor of your dealings with them. Is there a persistent undercurrent of irritation, rebellion, hostility, sarcasm, opposition, devaluation? Does it seem impossible for them to do *anything* right?

If you detect some hidden feelings of anger, do whatever is necessary to work through these feelings *before* coming out to your parents. Only as you bring such feelings to light, acknowledge your anger, feel again the pain of their abandonment of a certain part of you—only as you grieve for what you missed can you get beyond the anger and begin to build a better relationship with your parents. Your anger is real and, under the circumstances of your growing up, it was valid. Now it is time to move beyond your anger, to realize that your parents *could not have known* what was troubling you. They were not intentionally "bad" parents. Most likely they may have been faintly bewildered ones.

Many parental horror stories about the hurtful ways in which a son or daughter has come out to his or her parents have originated in the anger of the child who wanted to get back at the parents. The parents do not know this, and the child may not know it. The trauma of such a coming out can be prevented if you take the time to search your soul diligently to uncover your real feelings. Again, you may need or want to seek professional help as you do this.

Not Too Late

What if you have already come out to your parents in a hurtful fashion? It is not too late to deal with your anger, and then go to them and let them know why you were angry. Tell them you understand now that they could not have known your needs. Also ask forgiveness for your harsh words. Such an action could heal the rift between you. Even if it does not, you have done what you could.

In any coming out there needs to be a time when you talk with your parents about your past feelings, thoughts, fears, and struggles as you first became aware of who you really are and then began to deal with the information. The initial encounter may not be the time for this, but it should be soon afterward. All too often we want our loved ones to react in a certain way, and we expect them to read our minds, to know what we want from them. If they really loved us, we think, they would intuit our desires and respond accordingly. Of course, it doesn't work this way. (If it did, they might be able to read our minds when we did not want our minds read!). You need to express your feelings, to share with them something of your struggle over the years if there is going to be a basis for their understanding of what you have experienced. How can you expect them to understand your feelings if they have no idea what you went through?

To those parents who have been deeply wounded by their lesbian or gay child, I say this: Perhaps the last few pages have given you some insights into why your child behaved toward you in angry, hostile ways. If he or she has not come to you to talk about the pain of his or her growing-up years, perhaps you can introduce the subject.

It was not your fault, any more than it was your child's fault. The real culprit is society's continuing cruelty to same-sex-oriented persons, and its misunderstandings, ostracism, and condemnation of a group of people with only one difference from the rest of society. If you and your child can begin to understand that each of you has been at the mercy of society's wrongheaded ideas, you can begin to build a bridge between you instead of a wall.

Every coming out is a risk, a gamble. You have no fool-proof means of predicting your parents' reactions. Embarking on this venture with loving, adequate preparation can help. Although success cannot be guaranteed, the chance of failure can be minimized. Your parents' reactions in the initial encounter are immaterial. What happens in the succeeding months is what counts.

Chapter 5

Working Through
Grief—Together

The initial step has been taken. The first encounter with your parents has been accomplished. Whatever the results, neither they nor you will have to go through that particular event again. At times I have been thankful that there is no way of inadvertently getting caught in a time warp and having to live a particular day over.

Where do you go from here? What are the next steps?

Usually, the next step has been for the gay man or lesbian to supply his or her parents with information, lending or giving them whatever books might help them to understand a same-sex orientation. In so doing the gay man or lesbian may be omitting a few important intermediary steps. The parents may not yet be ready to read about homosexuality.

A Peculiar Situation

Remember that your parents are in a peculiar situation. They have entered a grief process for a person—you—who is definitely very much alive, whom they can see, and with whom they can communicate, and that is what creates the problem. This point was touched on in chapter

3, but let us look at it now in more detail. The *you* they thought they knew is gone, and yet the *you* they see and deal with now seems hardly any different. This is why it may be hard for them not to hope that somehow this trauma will vanish and everything will return to the way it used to be. They need to grieve, but it is difficult for them to do this when you are obviously alive and well.

For you, there are unpleasant undertones to their mourning. Even talking about sadness in connection with your sexual orientation indicates that the person you really are is so unacceptable that they need to grieve. Unfortunately, this is the message your parents have gathered from society's attitudes toward a same-sex orientation. It is not their fault they are reacting this way, and your getting impatient with them will not do much to hurry them along or improve your mutual relationship.

Is there anything you can do other than wait for them to work through their grief? Considering that it usually takes two years or longer for parents to accept fully a child's same-sex orientation, you certainly hope so!

Actually, you can do a number of things for your parents.

Several days after the initial revelation of your sexual orientation drop in to find out how they are doing or phone them. Even if it means paying for a 3,000-mile long-distance call, spend the money. There are times when it is better not to economize.

Let them know you are making this contact because you are concerned about *their* welfare, not because you are trying to find out how they are feeling about your sexual orientation. Are they having difficulty sleeping? Eating? If they are, this is not at all surprising, and you can reassure them that their reaction is not unexpected.

If you have not told them that they are most likely experiencing grief reactions, you could tell them now. Perhaps they realize this, but if not, you are the logical person to tell them. Unless they have been able to talk with their minister, priest, or rabbi or their doctor, a counselor, a friend, or other family member—which they probably have not—you are the primary source of help and information.

If they want to talk, be available to them. If not, do not force them.

Helpful Books for Parents

During this period you might suggest they read one or more of the books written especially for parents. *Now That You Know,* by Betty Fairchild and Nancy Hayward, has been updated and is a classic in this field. An excellent all-around book dealing with both religious and general aspects of a same-sex orientation is Letha Scanzoni and Virginia Mollenkott's *Is the Homosexual My Neighbor?* You could offer to lend or give your parents a copy of this book, pointing out in particular the chapters written for parents. Several other books for parents are listed in "For Further Reading."

During this period, if you see that your parents are experiencing aspects of grief reactions you could suggest they read the material in chapter 3 of this book that might be helpful to them in understanding their feelings. Several other books on grief are listed in "For Further Reading." One of them, *Good Grief* by Granger E. Westberg, is short and has chapters of only a few pages each, so it is easy to pick up and read a bit now and then. If your parents are not interested in reading about grief, accept their decision. There is no particular time schedule according to which they must accept your sexual orientation. Try not to crowd them because of your impatience.

If as time goes on your parents keep returning in conversation to such statements as, "I don't know where we went wrong" or "I just wish we knew why you are lesbian (gay)," you might point out that such guilt is very likely an expression of their grief at finding you are different from the person they thought you were. Keep your eyes and ears open, and if your parents' remarks seem to indicate one of the stages of grief, suggest to them that these are normal phases they are going through.

You might think the books that helped you come to terms with your sexual orientation would also help your parents. Experience has often proved different. What met your needs will probably not meet your parents' needs, and the books you found particularly helpful may be all wrong for them. At this point in trying to deal with the information about your sexual orientation, they are more likely to trust heterosexual authors, especially other parents.

Important Source of Information

It is good that you should offer to lend or give books to your parents if they indicate an interest or that you should recommend they obtain such books from a library or bookstore. This should not be a substitute, however, for your willingness to sit down with them and discuss your lesbianism or gayness. You are an important source of information for your parents.

One of the most helpful things you can do for your parents is give them an opportunity to ventilate their feelings and fears. This may be uncomfortable for you and difficult to deal with. When people direct any sort of negative feelings toward us, our instinctive reaction is to defend ourselves by flinging the negative feelings back at them. When they attack, we deny or counterattack, and before we know it we are on a collision course.

If your parents attack, it is because they are experiencing uncomfortable feelings and are trying to deal with them. If you can realize this and try to interpret their feelings to them—"You're feeling pretty bad about this, aren't you?"—you do not run as much risk of getting into a verbal free-for-all as if you undertake to show them how wrong they are or to change their ideas about you conclusively.

The reverse of this is that you also have a right to express your feelings—"I feel as if you disapprove of me, and that hurts." Trying to change someone or tell him or her what he or she is doing wrong invites trouble. If I can say how *I* am feeling instead of attacking the other person, the way is opened for constructive dialogue. An honest ventilation of feelings rather than accusations can lead to a more understanding relationship on both sides.

After a while your parents may want to discuss with you their fears concerning a same-sex orientation. Many of these fears may be the old stereotypical ideas, and you may be impatient at having to deal anew with this misinformation. If you can see each erroneous statement they make as an opening for you to present the facts *calmly and objectively,* without hostility or condescension, you may begin to look on their statements and questions as opportunities and welcome the chance to provide more accurate information. Sometimes it may seem that you are not getting through, but if you keep giving them sound information, without a display of anger or annoyance, in time the information—and your attitude—may significantly change their thinking.

Sometimes your anger or annoyance at one or both parents may have less to do with your sexual orientation than with other facets of your relationship with them. I encountered a gay friend at a time when he was distressed with his parents. Both parties had been battling about his orientation for some time without making any progress toward resolution. When I saw him a month later the stalemate had finally been broken. He and his family were in business together, and he had been feeling a great deal of resentment toward his parents, because they had not clearly defined his duties and authority. He was expected to function in whatever ways he was needed, but he had not been told what those ways were. After he explained to his parents the problems he was experiencing in the business, the three of them were able to work out a satisfactory arrangement, and his sexual orientation no longer served as a focus of the problems that had existed between them.

It is easy for parents who have a lesbian or gay child to think that all problems concerning this daughter or son result from the different sexual orientation. This became especially apparent to me in the Families of Gays and Lesbians group. Many times I spoke with distraught parents out of my experiences with my straight daughters rather than with my gay son. This indicates to me that the problem bothering the parents is connected more with the normal friction between parents and child than with difficulties specifically caused by a different sexual orientation. It may be easier to wrangle endlessly about gayness or lesbianism than focus on the real issues, such as freedom and control, which may be more threatening to the parent-child relationship than sexual orientation.

Just Like Anybody Else

What facts about a same-sex orientation might be reassuring to your parents? One of the things that quieted my fears, although I did not realize it until later, was the ordinariness of the life my son and his partner were leading. They went to work in the morning and came home to their apartment at night to cook meals, wash clothes, shop, clean. They began to redecorate the apartment, doing all the work themselves. They went to church on Sundays and to movies, plays, and concerts. Now and then they entertained friends. In spring and fall they would go in with others and have a garage sale. Their life together was so typical of any young couple that it was impossible for me to regard them as strange or alien beings. The Eric I was seeing was no different from the person he had been before I "found out."

You also might reassure your parents and help them understand you by letting them know you have the same needs, feelings, and desires as a straight person. You need food and shelter, work and play, companionship and love. The same things create pain for you that create pain for everyone: loss of a loved one, loss of friends, loss of a job, quarrels with a partner, loneliness, rejection. You may think it is obvious to your parents that homosexual persons do not have one kind of feelings and heterosexual persons another. Yet quite possibly they do not understand that gay and straight persons share the same *kinds* of human feelings. Only the sex of the loved one may differ.

Do not assume that your parents know these basic facts about you, and do not be angry that you may have to tell them you are just like other people. For several thousand years society has been giving heterosexuals the opposite impression, that same-sex-oriented people belong to some strange and peculiar breed that has no normal human needs or feelings and that is obsessed with thoughts of sex.

It may be reassuring to your parents to know that they are not the *only* ones with a same-sex-oriented child; there are literally millions of parents like them. If you consider that an estimated 5 to 10 percent of the population is same-sex-oriented and that each gay man or lesbian has two parents, you can easily get a rough idea of how many parents are facing or have faced the same questions as your parents. Of course, many parents do not know they have a lesbian or gay child. Many more are not telling other people. Those who are not afraid or ashamed to let others know they have a same-sex-oriented child are comparatively few, which is why your parents may think their situation is unique.

Although your parents may not think so at first, it does

help to talk with other people who are going through similar experiences. If a Parents and Friends of Lesbians and
Gays group is available nearby, your parents could be
comforted, helped, and informed by attending meetings.
If no group is organized where your parents live, possibly
another set of parents would be willing to correspond with
your parents. Although I know of no organized effort to
put parents of same-sex-oriented children in touch with
one another by mail, this should not stop you. All you
need is a gay or lesbian friend whose parents have made
some measure of peace with their child's orientation and
who would agree to exchange letters with your parents
now and them, if they are interested.

It might be helpful to your parents to know that many
fine people are lesbian or gay. If one day every same-sex-
oriented person turned green, we would soon discover
the truth of the placards carried in gay rights parades: "We
are everywhere." One would see green doctors, nurses,
teachers, priests, pastors, bus drivers, politicians, researchers, secretaries, service station attendants, accoun-
tants, athletes, assembly line workers, artists, actors, mu-
sicians, broadcasters, airplane pilots, flight attendants,
computer operators and technicians, police officers, law-
yers, judges, and on and on. By far the greatest proportion
of lesbians and gay men are leading quietly constructive
lives. They are like the great mass of heterosexual people
who also live quietly constructive lives. Neither group
makes many headlines.

Throughout history same-sex-oriented persons have
contributed greatly to the physical, mental, and spiritual
welfare of humanity.[1] These include James Miranda Barry,
the first British woman doctor, who successfully served
the British government all her life disguised as a man;
Howard Brown, M.D., New York City's first health services administrator, the director of community medicine at
Fordham Hospital, and head of the Gouverneur Morris

72

Hospital Ambulatory Care Unit on New York's Lower East Side; Rosa Bonheur, a nineteenth-century artist; Erasmus (1466–1536), the greatest scholar of his age and editor of a Greek New Testament; James I of England, who commissioned the translation of the Bible that has come to be known as the *King James Version;* and Frederick the Great, who welcomed the persecuted Huguenots to Prussia and abolished press censorship and torture.

There are a host of others, among them poets Thomas Gray, Walt Whitman, Gerard Manley Hopkins, A. E. Housman, and W. H. Auden; authors Marcel Proust, Willa Cather, Henry James, and Edith Hamilton; educators Mary Emma Wooley, president of Mount Holyoke College for thirty-seven years and one of the first American women diplomats, and Carey Thomas, for many years dean and president of Bryn Mawr College; as well as such world famous and instantly recognized names as Leonardo da Vinci, Michelangelo, and Peter Ilich Tchaikovsky. Our lives are richer because of these same-sex-oriented persons and because of those thousands unnamed for lack of space.

Not Child Molesters, Not Recruiters

Demeaning as it may seem, you may have to reassure your parents emphatically that you are not a child molester, nor are you trying to recruit people to a same-sex orientation. If your parents have not already gotten the message that it is impossible to recruit people to a homosexual orientation, you may have to be blunt about this. The idea that children are in danger of being molested by all same-sex-oriented persons has been around for a long time. Anita Bryant's crusade in 1977 to repeal the Dade County, Florida, gay rights ordinance gave new visibility, impetus, and status to this already discredited supposition. Your parents need to know it is untrue that every homosexual person is a child molester or a recruiter.

You might also point out, if the occasion arises, that all the fears about homosexual teachers and others as role models for children tend to be exaggerated. Most homosexual children have grown up with heterosexual parents for role models, and many children know they are different (although they may not have a name to put to the difference) long before they reach adolescence or have had any sexual experiences. Approximately 90 percent of the population is heterosexual; thus nine out of ten of a child's role models are heterosexual.

What About Change?

What do you do if your parents talk about change?

First, remember this: *Stay calm.* Even though you may want to ride into battle immediately on this issue, with colors flying, *do not.* Ultimately, you will gain more by courteously listening to your parents than by trying to outargue them.

This does not mean you should agree to go into counseling. It means you need to understand the message underlying your parents' wanting you to change. They may be saying, in effect, that life would be simpler for you and for them if you were not same-sex-oriented. It may be a manifestation of the denial aspect of their grief—"Our child really doesn't *have* to be same-sex-oriented." They may, if they are religiously oriented, be concerned about the eternal damnation of your soul. (This is dealt with at greater length in chapter 9.)

Finally, there is the tantalizing shred of hope that holds—just out of reach—the possibility that same-sex-oriented people *can* change. William H. Masters and Virginia E. Johnson effected changes in some gay men and lesbian women, didn't they? And what about the ex-gay organizations that claim men and women have changed? Lawrence Hatterer, professor of psychiatry at Cornell University, has written about changing homosexuality in men.[2] Recently, a system of study called aesthetic realism has also been attracting attention with claims of having changed same-sex-oriented persons.[3] "See?" your parents are crying to themselves. "It is possible. *It is possible!*"

Possible, perhaps, but not necessarily probable. Years ago researcher Alfred Kinsey and his colleagues developed the Kinsey continuum, popularly referred to as the Kinsey scale.[4] Through research he and his co-workers discovered that besides those persons who were either completely heterosexual or completely homosexual there were those who could function with varying degrees of satisfaction and adequacy in either role.

Because one person can move from a same-sex orientation to an opposite-sex orientation does not guarantee that another person can; the two persons may occupy different positions on the Kinsey scale. One might be closer to the completely heterosexual position and thus have a considerable heterosexual component in his or her makeup, whereas the other might be close to complete homosexuality or else entirely same-sex-oriented.

Concerning Masters and Johnson's work in helping same-sex-oriented persons function satisfactorily in an opposite-sex-oriented way, one has only to read even sketchily in *Homosexuality in Perspective* to realize that they are not presenting a foolproof means for changing all homosexual persons to heterosexual.[5] Applicants for this therapy were carefully screened; the number of persons treated was statistically small; no claims were made that the persons treated were representative of the same-sex-oriented population as a whole. To generalize from their work that because one person could be treated successfully, all could is impossible.

In dealing with the claims of ex-gay organizations consider that there is no accurate way to confirm their glowing assertions. There is no follow-up five or ten years after change to ascertain whether the person is living exclusively as an opposite-sex-oriented person. Many times ex-gay means no more than that a same-sex-oriented person is living a celibate life.[6] Generally, ex-gay claims are strong on assertions of change and appallingly weak on reliable statistics.

As for Dr. Hatterer's statement that he has changed many persons, hopeful parents need to be aware of the earlier caution that because one person can change does not guarantee another can. They also need to know that such changes have necessitated large outlays of time, money, and effort as well as living in the proper geographic location—near a therapist effective in this area of work.

Parents need to be aware of still other considerations in the matter of change. What does it do to a person's self-concept to say, "I am unacceptable as I am; therefore, I must change" and then realize years later that he or she is going to have to remain "unacceptable" for life because change does not seem possible? Why should a young man or woman spend precious time and precious energy pursuing a goal that may be doomed at the outset? At the end of the years of effort he or she still has to do an about-face. Instead of fighting the same-sex orientation, the person now has to learn to live comfortably, productively, and happily with an unchanged sexuality. Is it fair for parents to force this difficult path upon a person?

There are many books, particularly religious books and articles, that can feed parents' dreams of changing a lesbian or gay child to heterosexual. If parents *must* read such books and articles, they would be wise also to read books with more scientific information, which present a less biased view of the possibilities of change.

Sexual Preference, one of the books in this area of concern, demonstrates the great complexity of possible causes of a same-sex orientation.[7] The reader who tries to follow and understand the path diagrams presented in the book will get a glimpse of the tremendously complex interaction

of a host of variable circumstances. The book also questions a number of ideas that have been seen as causes of a
same-sex orientation and shows that what has been assumed to be *causes* may in reality have *resulted* from a
same-sex orientation. For example, the supposition has
been that an unsatisfactory father-son relationship could
cause a homosexual orientation. Researchers raise the
question that if there is a biological basis for a person's
same-sex orientation, possibly the estrangement between
father and son may result from a perception (probably
unconscious) of the child's difference.

Your parents need the foregoing information if they are
serious about wanting you to change. Presenting the information to them without anger, as factual material, can give
them the opportunity to hear it without needing to defend
their ideas against heated attack. If you can keep your
feelings separate from the information you want to give
and can handle their and your emotions apart from the
giving of objective data, both you and they will have a
better chance of dealing constructively with the whole situation. Their dissatisfaction with your sexual orientation
is painful to you and may need to be addressed, but it
should be dealt with apart from the information that most
likely you cannot change.

Two sentences on the last page of *Sexual Preference*
should be repeated often, loudly and clearly: "It is possible
for both homosexuals and heterosexuals to enjoy mature,
constructive, and rewarding lives. Probably each orientation involves its own dangers, sacrifices, and compensa-
tions."[8]

Fears About Your Physical Welfare

Perhaps some of the apprehension your parents feel
may be related to your physical welfare. They may be
fearful for your health and safety. Almost surely they wonder if you are HIV positive, although they may not ask you

this. They may be so busy absorbing your news that they cannot deal with anything further. Or they may not want to know at this point whether you have the virus. If you do, the first chapter you may have turned to in this book is chapter 10, "Living with HIV/AIDS," and you therefore have some idea of how to deal with your parents' questions. If you are lesbian, it may not occur to them even to think you might be positive, because very little publicity has been given to lesbians with AIDS.

If your parents read newspapers and magazines and listen to radio or TV news, they may know that the incidence of sexually transmitted diseases other than AIDS is higher within the gay male community than within the straight community. In addition, they may be aware of the higher rate of violence against gay men and lesbians, whether carried out by those who hate same-sex-oriented persons or by the small percentage, heterosexual or homosexual, who are psychopathic and believe gay or lesbian persons should be eliminated.

Your parents' fears about disease and violence are not idle, and their concern for your health and safety indicates they care about you. If you can accept their concern and reassure them that you are doing all you can to maintain your health and protect your safety, you can contribute greatly to their peace of mind.

If you cannot do this, it might be indicative of several things. Your general relationship with your parents may be on such precarious footing that anything seeming to you to be parental meddling arouses angry, combative feelings of which you may not have been conscious, until now. If you become defensive, however, because you *are* doing the things they are concerned about, maybe it is time for you to take stock of yourself.

Let us face it: Sexual pickups can be dangerous because of the risk of contracting AIDS. Even the use of condoms promises only safer sex, not totally safe sex. In addition there is the risk of contracting other sexually transmitted diseases, as well as the risk of physical violence. Other practices destructive to physical and psychological health are common in the gay male community, such as the misuse of chemicals and drugs, including amyl nitrite and butyl nitrite, the indiscriminate use of antibiotics, and sadomasochism. Lesbians and gay men have often resorted to heavy use of alcohol to dull the pain of societal rejection. For this reason they have a higher incidence of alcoholism than a matching heterosexual population. If you indulge in any of these potentially destructive behaviors, perhaps you should take a look at yourself and ask why.

Why is there so much cruising and anonymous sex in the gay male community? Many gay men may be unaware of the underlying sociological and psychological reasons. Throughout history society has encouraged heterosexual men to form monogamous relationships with women in order to provide a secure setting in which to produce and raise children and thus perpetuate the human race. Society has been uninterested in encouraging stable, long-term relationships between same-sex-oriented persons for at least two reasons. One is that such relationships were, quite wrongly, considered a threat to the continuation of the race. Unconsciously, people must have believed that if same-sex relationships were allowed, these liaisons would prove so much more fascinating than heterosexual ones that most people would choose a same-sex partnership and population would therefore decline drastically. Stated baldly, the idea sounds ridiculous, as unconsciously held ideas often do. The other reason is that most people did not realize persons of the same sex could have loving, tender, bonding feelings for one another. The assumption was that sexual activity between persons of the same sex resulted only from lust so excessive it could not be satisfied heterosexually.[9] For these reasons neither society nor the church supported or even condoned same-sex relationships.

The same-sex-oriented population, duly indoctrinated with the wrong information it gleaned from heterosexual society, formulated its own behavioral standards. Because sexual contact between two men cannot result in pregnancy, the gay male community saw no reason to limit sexual activity. If it felt good, why not do it? There was no woman to hold back, tone down, or rein in the male sex drive. Interestingly, sexual activity within the lesbian community is quite different from sexual activity in the gay male community. Whether this reveals the difference between male and female socialization or represents different inborn instincts and drives is too complex a question to discuss here. The fact is there *is* a considerable difference.

But repeated, anonymous, or casual sexual stimulation can become a trap. It promises the warmth and real relationship that human beings yearn for, whether they are aware of this yearning or not. Yet this kind of sexual activity cannot fulfill its promise. For the brief time of sexual contact physical and psychological reactions take place that feel good. The brain releases endorphins, the body's own painkiller, producing a natural high. Emotionally, one's ego-boundaries fall and there is a fulfilling sense of oneness and sharing with the partner—for a moment.

Both these reactions may be deceptive. A person can get hooked on the euphoria produced by the endorphins and seek repeated sexual release in order to reproduce this feeling of well-being, never mind with whom. The oneness may be nothing more than an illusion that departs quickly. But if a person has no relationship in her or his life that is producing a *real* closeness and sharing, the temptation is to grab whatever feelings of closeness she or he can, however possible. When this type of fleeting liaison fails, in the long run, to produce a relationship of depth and extended duration, the tendency is to keep searching, thinking that one simply has not found the right person. And so the seeker keeps repeating a behavior pattern that cannot produce the results for which she or he is looking.

There are other reasons for seeking anonymous sex. "I finally realized that the times I went after anonymous sex were when I was really angry," a gay man told a group in a moment of self-disclosing honesty. "It was like I wanted to go out and shoot someone," he said, thumbs cocked and index fingers of both hands extended, as if he were firing two pistols. "Now when I feel like going out and having sex like that, I ask myself what it is I'm angry at, and I try to deal with the anger instead of going after sex."

Some deal with various other feelings by means of promiscuous sexual behavior. Because the true issues in the person's life are being bypassed, they cannot be resolved. Instead, the person repeats the behavior endlessly, always searching for a result the behavior will never produce.

The lesbian or gay man faces other pitfalls that result from her or his being part of an oppressed and mostly outcast minority.[10] To survive, such minorities develop their own rules. The collective gay community lore indicates that a gay man behaves in such and such a way. The lesbian community has also developed its own collective ideas about how a lesbian should behave. In this way minorities draw together and define their difference from the surrounding society that is hostile to them.

This drawing together and defining of differences is at once strengthening *and* detrimental to the individual lesbian or gay man. On the one hand, it clues her or him in on how a same-sex-oriented person of that gender behaves. On the other hand, it can severely restrict the gay man's or lesbian's choices of behavior to what are basically stereotypical reactions, even though they may be approved by the collective gay or lesbian community.

If you, as a lesbian or gay man, have been reacting according to collective prescriptions, sexual or otherwise, now is a good time to take stock of yourself. Are the choices you are making about your life-style the ones you want to make or are you unquestioningly following the herd? Are you dealing with your emotions and your body in a way that demonstrates caring and respect? Is your behavior constructive or destructive? Are you reacting with self-destructive behavior because of hostile messages from family or society?

Your reactions to your parents' concerns may open up these and equally soul-searching questions. Or your preparations for coming out to your parents may bring you face to face with such concerns. Do not evade the issues; they affect your life deeply. If you grapple honestly with these issues and stick with them until you have satisfied your needs constructively, you will have made giant strides toward a mature, creative, fulfilling life.

Is a Full, Satisfying Life Possible?

Another fear your parents may express is the belief that, because you will not marry and have children, you are doomed to a lonely old age. If your parents express such a fear, a frank and open discussion can help alleviate their dread. Marriage and children are not safeguards against loneliness in old age. A spouse can get a divorce or die. Children may precede their parents in death or may live hundreds of miles away when the parents are old.

Lack of an opposite-sex partner and children does not automatically sentence one to loneliness in one's advanced years. Your parents may not be aware that a long-term, committed relationship can exist between two same-sex-oriented persons and that many such enduring relationships are being maintained. Your parents also may not realize that many older gay men and lesbians, whether single or coupled, have built up a circle of supportive friends, just as older single and coupled heterosexual persons do. Because people are generally living longer, it is important for every person individually—heterosexual or homosexual, married, in a nonmarried relationship, or single—to make realistic plans so that old age is not a time of loneliness.

Your parents may also fear that you cannot possibly live a full, happy life because you will never have a heterosexual spouse and children. (Naturally, this fear will exist only if you have not already been married and had children.) This fear results, at least in part, from cultural conditioning. From the time your parents were children they have perceived marriage and family as the norm for adult life. Although this norm is being questioned vigorously by young adults nowadays, when your parents were growing up the assumptions were that everyone's goal was marriage and that, unless husband or wife was infertile, children would almost automatically follow. For this reason many parents find it difficult to imagine a full and satisfying life is possible on any other basis.

Your first reaction to this kind of thinking may be anger or, less intensely, annoyance: "*Of course* it is possible to have a good life built on bases other than heterosexual marriage and children. Marriage and family were *never* goals in *my* life, and what my parents think will bring me the greatest happiness *doesn't appeal to me at all.*" Is this what you are thinking? If it is, perhaps you should take a second look at this matter. Perhaps this is an area in which you, as a lesbian or a gay man, need to grieve with your parents.

This is not, as you may think, a typical heterosexist idea. It comes from Douglas Elwood, a gay man, a trained therapist, formerly a faculty member of the University of Minnesota School of Social Work and now an organizational consultant in human resources.

Because all children are assumed to be heterosexual, Elwood says, they are raised with the implied or expressed expectation that in time they will marry and become parents. When lesbians and gay men discover their same-sex orientation, face it, and work through to acceptance of it, they lose the role envisioned for them by society in general, by their parents in particular, and perhaps in their own thinking.

They also lose the approval society bestows on those who conform to its accepted patterns. Because both divorce and living-together arrangements are now prevalent, in the business world it may no longer be true that the unmarried male is considered unsuitable in many positions—provided he turns up with an appropriate female at business functions that require partner attendance. In addition, when there are casual exchanges among employees about what they did over the weekend, an unmarried man had better not say week after week that he and Joe, or Steve, or Michael, did this or that—unless he works in an enlightened environment. And though the unmarried woman may now have the advantage in business over her married female colleagues, within her family she may still be subjected to pointed questions about when she is going to get married. To the matchmakers among her relatives having even a live-in male partner may seem more desirable than having no man in evidence at all. A great deal of life is organized on the principle of two persons in a couple relationship—that is, a male coupled with a female, preferably by marriage. Those who do not conform to this pattern are penalized in subtle and not so subtle ways, and the greatest penalties are reserved for those who differ most from the established standard—same-sex-oriented persons.

Whether you, as an individual, wanted marriage and family or not, you are trading the secure societal role of a heterosexually oriented person for the more insecure position of a member of a stigmatized subculture. You are forfeiting many basic rights and protections that heterosexually oriented people take for granted: the right to live, eat, and go to school where you want; the right to enter any career for which you are educationally and temperamentally suited; the right to be judged by your knowledge and skill as a worker rather than by your sexual orientation; the right to equal protection under the law.

As you can see, you lose many personal and social rights and advantages as you face and accept your sexual orientation. Why should you not grieve at the heavy penalty exacted from you simply for being who you are?

Possibly the idea of such grieving does not appeal to you. Acceptance of your gayness or lesbianism may have been a difficult battle for you. Perhaps achieving peace with yourself came only after a long and determined struggle. Instinctively, you may fear that if you open the door to grieving for lost heterosexual privileges, you may loose such a flood of sorrow and self-pity that you will be inundated. It may seem better for you to keep the door shut tightly.

In facing and accepting your lesbian or gay orientation you are choosing to live in accordance with your real personhood, rather than attempting to live a hollow charade as a heterosexual person. You are choosing to be true to yourself, because you have realized that only in this way can you find wholeness and satisfaction in life. *Because* you want to live out your particular orientation it is necessary to grieve for the more socially approved avenues of life that are closed to you. In so doing you are not repudiating your given sexual orientation or your decision to live it rather than attempting the lifelong dishonesty and pain of pretending to be heterosexual.

Rather, by facing your loss, allowing yourself to feel it, and coming to a suitable closure you free yourself from wasting emotional energy in various forms of unproductive behavior. Out of such unacknowledged and undealt-with grief comes heterophobia, which may manifest itself in aggressive disparagement of heterosexuality, extreme defensiveness about homosexuality, and anger against anything perceived as a heterosexual value. Out of such unacknowledged feelings of loss may also come such things as alcohol or drug abuse, family problems, relationship problems, self-esteem problems, and ill health. If you have not allowed yourself to grieve, neither will you be able to allow your parents to grieve, and you will not achieve any real family closeness by coming out to your parents. Under such circumstances you may have chosen to come out to your parents in the unconscious hope that they could ease the pain of loss inside you.

A good deal of courage may be required for you to allow yourself to grieve along with your parents, and yet if you can share with them the anger and grief you felt as you faced your own loss, you can help them come to terms with their loss. You are giving them permission to be angry and to hurt because of *their* loss. In other words, you are telling them that their feelings are real and that it is all right for them to have these feelings.

Grief always has a paradoxical aspect. If you allow yourself and others to mourn a loss, you and they will recover from the loss and resume life more fully and healthily than if you repress or ignore your own and their grief. Bypassing grief only ensures your remaining in the process unhealthily and unproductively.

Winning or Losing Together

As you—both children and parents—may have gathered from this chapter, the essence of working through grief as a family lies in facing, acknowledging, and sharing your true feelings and then dealing with them realistically.

This is the ideal. Because we are less than perfect, it is not always possible to live up to this ideal. Somewhere along the way there will probably be some missteps—

raised voices, heated arguments, untenable positions firmly held.

There is a vocabulary that heals such breaches in family solidarity. It includes phrases like, "I'm sorry I lost my temper"; "I shouldn't have shouted"; "I've been thinking about what you said and it seems to make sense"; "Maybe we both need to get more information about this"; "In some cases I guess we have to agree to disagree."

Perhaps the foregoing material has given the impression that while working through grief, every encounter between parents and child must be a heavy emotional scene. This could be wearing. It could also create the suspicion that either or both parties, parents and child, are setting up meetings to hammer away at the other's point of view.

How much better it might be simply to have fun together sometimes, pleasant times when same-sex-orientation is put aside. If you and your parents have been going at it rather intensively, it might be helpful to agree ahead of time that the subject will not be discussed at the next encounter. If it seems uncomfortably formal or blunt to specify this ahead of time, the situation could be dealt with if the subject arises. A leading remark could be passed over (it is not *always* necessary to rise to the bait) or the subject could be put aside with the casual remark that perhaps it could be discussed at another time, that right now you are in the mood to have fun.

You may have noticed that many of the suggestions in this chapter will be easier to follow if you live in the same locality as your parents and meet each other in person from time to time. If you live a distance away, you will have to adapt the suggestions to your particular situation. If you are not in the habit of writing or phoning your parents frequently, it might be well to make more of an effort now to keep in touch. Such thoughtfulness and concern at this time could mean a great deal to them.

You and your parents are bound together in a situation

where all of you win together or all of you lose together. You cannot win at your parents' expense, nor can they win at yours. If together you can grieve for your lost role in society and in the family and together lay away the ideas of marriage, children, continuity with future generations, and a secure heterosexual niche in society, both you and your parents will be free to move on to shape an improved parent-child relationship and find the positive aspects of your life as a same-sex-oriented person.

Chapter 6

The Other Side*

If you are a parent reading this book, one week or one month or six months or a year ago you experienced a change in your world when your child told you he is gay or she is lesbian. In a matter of minutes one of the unquestioned assumptions you had made about your child—that he or she is heterosexual—disappeared. The discovery may have been a shock to you. Since then you may have been experiencing some of the feelings discussed in chapter 3.

On the other hand, the revelation may not have been a shock at all. You may have suspected—or perhaps were quite certain—about your child's sexual orientation and

*The material in this chapter, unless otherwise indicated, is based directly on "Coming Out Alive, A Positive Developmental Model of Homosexual Competence" by John Grace, manager of clinical policy development for Human Affairs International, a subsidiary of Aetna Health Plans (used by permission.) He was formerly coordinator of the Gay and Lesbian Family Counseling Program at Family and Children's Service, Minneapolis. His paper was delivered at the Sixth Biennial Professional Symposium of the National Association of Social Workers and is used here with the author's permission. The lesbian viewpoint was supplied in consultation with Jennifer Feigal, formerly of Family and Children's Service of Minneapolis, now in private practice in St. Paul, Minnesota. Both Mr. Grace and Ms. Feigal have helped in updating the original information.

were only waiting for him or her to bring up the subject. If this is the case, you may already know much of the information in the following pages.

For those who have moved through some of the most acute stages of grief, the time has come to discover what your child has been experiencing since his or her first inklings of difference. While reading the first part of this book, your child may have spent time trying to understand your life experiences and why you may have reacted in certain ways to the information he or she presented to you. For the sake of fairness—or more important, because of love for your child—it is time for you to reciprocate, to try to understand what your child has gone through in coming to terms with his or her sexuality.

The most obvious thing to do is to ask your child when he or she first realized the difference between himself or herself and his or her friends and peers. How did your child feel? How did he or she cope?

In all likelihood your child has gone through a fairly long period of trauma as he or she struggled with the realization of his gayness or her lesbianism. I have yet to meet a gay man or lesbian who decided one day that he or she was tired of being heterosexual and that it might be fun to try being homosexual. Many people think that at some point same-sex-oriented persons *choose* a homosexual way of life rather than one that is heterosexual. The choice is made, these people believe, because the homosexual persons wish to rebel against parents and/or society or because they have been influenced by some "evil forces" or because they were habituated into a homosexual orientation through early pleasurable same-sex experiences with persons of their own ages or with older persons (recruitment, or seduction).

These people have no idea of the years of pain and struggle that are often part of same-sex-oriented persons' realization of their identity as gay men or lesbians. The accounts I have heard all include the dawning awareness of some difference between themselves and their friends, an awareness commonly accompanied by panic or self-loathing and often by frantic attempts to convince themselves that they really are not perverts or monsters.

If there are twenty million homosexual persons in the country, there are twenty million different stories about how the truth was borne in on each one, often slowly and excruciatingly, that he is gay or she is lesbian. Although many stories are similar, no two are alike. The cold statistics are compiled from individual experiences, each one of supreme importance to the particular person who had to live through those experiences. Each person who is counted as an impersonal number in that twenty or so million is a living, breathing, feeling person struggling to cope with a situation that life, for some unknown reason, has thrust on her or him. These twenty million are ordinary people—your children and mine—who happen to have one characteristic that has made their lives considerably more difficult than you and I, as parents, had envisioned.

I think of a young man I met at a gay party. He had come because the latest in a long line of counselors had suggested that change was probably an impossibility for him and that perhaps, if he got to know some gay men, he might be able to reconcile himself to the fact that he is gay. He had struggled long and valiantly—and expensively—not to be gay, and it had not worked. Now he has found a measure of peace, has formed a circle of friends, and is active in a gay religious group. To a large extent he has accepted the person he is.

I think also of a woman named Debby.[1] As a teenager, she was active in her church. Suddenly, one day, because she admitted she had some feelings for another girl, she was not welcome at the church anymore. A few months later she had a nervous breakdown and spent eight months in a mental hospital.

When Debby was twenty-one she lost a job because her pastor would not give her a character reference after he heard a rumor—actually a false one—that she was sexually attracted to her female supervisor. At this point Debby was ready to kill herself. Later a Lutheran minister worked with her for two years, helping her to come to terms with herself, helping her realize that she could be both lesbian and Christian, even though many churches feel these terms are contradictory. It took Debby a long time to accept her sexual orientation but, fortunately, she succeeded.

I think of another young man I met. Obviously, he was in the throes of a tremendous crisis in his life. "I'm married," he told me, "and I love my wife, but I've discovered I'm gay. I want to stay married, but I don't know if I can." He and his wife had talked with several counselors. They were working on the problem that had engulfed them as maturely and responsibly as possible. Because I talked with this person only one time, I do not know the outcome of his and his wife's struggle. Clearly, if this young man had had his choice, he would not have chosen the situation in which he found himself.

I think of a twenty-nine-year-old woman who was married, with a baby daughter.[2] As she started working with women on women's issues she began to realize that here, rather than in her marriage, her emotional needs were being met. She also began to realize that in her life there had always been primary and intense relationships with women. Eventually, she made the difficult decision to divorce her husband because of her need to live as the person she had finally recognized herself to be.

Despite the fact that each person's story is different, lesbian and gay men usually go through certain definable stages as they become aware of their real sexual orientation and then begin to deal with it.

If you, as a parent, are cognizant of some of the stages

through which your child has passed or is passing, you can better understand why he or she is behaving in certain ways. Such understanding can help to alleviate the alarm you might feel if your child seems to be going against his or her upbringing. You may be more able to give understanding and love to your child instead of revulsion and condemnation. You may feel less need to break off your relationship, more able to talk openly with your child about your feelings, more able to listen to your child talk about her or his feelings. Particularly because of AIDS, maintaining a relationship in which you can talk candidly yet nonjudgmentally about sexual matters with your child can literally be lifesaving.

The coming-out process for a gay man can be divided into five segments: emergence; acknowledgment; crashing out, the search, or exploration; first relationships; and finally, self-definition and reintegration. Some psychologists and social workers reverse emergence and acknowledgment and prefer the term search or exploration to crashing out, which implies an explosive process. With some people the process *is* explosive. With others it is less dramatic or obvious.

For lesbians, there is often a preemergent stage, characterized by an empty marriage or promiscuity or by a feeling that they have been created asexual. Because they do not experience the feelings for men that other women describe, they assume that some sexual component was left out of their makeup and that they are incapable of experiencing the sexual aspect of life as others do. They have no idea that women will trigger the sexual feelings that men have failed to arouse. This happens because women may be unaware of their lesbian orientation until they are well into adulthood. Other lesbians, as with many gay men, know since their early years that their deepest attraction is to women. Emergence and acknowledgment for lesbians may be followed in some cases by a first relationship and only later by a version of crashing out or exploration that is not as exclusively characterized by sexual experiences as it is for their male counterparts.

Emergence

Most gay men go back to age four or five in order to pinpoint when they began to feel excited about other boys or men in their lives, such as a favorite uncle or family friend, a television or movie hero, a character in a novel, a teacher, an older brother's or sister's friend.

Some boys are lucky enough not to be ashamed or uneasy about these early attractions toward men. If no shame exists, possibly the emergence period can be relatively untroubled. One gay man was fortunate enough to be able to say, "As far back as I can remember, I always had feelings of love for other boys and men in my life. This included a lot of affection and physical and sexual intimacy during late childhood and throughout my adolescence. It wasn't until I was nineteen yeas old and away at college that I first realized all the other men in the world didn't feel the same way I did."

Usually, however, feelings of difference are discovered earlier than age nineteen for men and with more damaging consequences. Suppose, instead of such a comparatively calm acceptance of himself, the boy recognizes early, with shame and fear, that he is different from other boys.

Right here it is necessary to restate clearly where the shame—in both lesbians and gay men—comes from. It is a value judgment attached by society to same-sex orientation, rather than being inherent in the orientation itself.

Because of this fear and shame a vicious cycle develops. The fear and shame foster self-hatred and a feeling of worthlessness, which in turn make the boy—or girl—uneasy with both boys and girls his or her own age and with older people—parents, relatives, teachers, friends.

This awkwardness contributes to the self-hatred, and the cycle is off and rolling.

If the boy is unwilling to or cannot take part in the other boys' male activities, he is branded a sissy or, at best, shy. He discovers that he is "bad" no matter what he does. If he plays with boys and does not do it right, this is bad; but if he plays with girls, this is bad too. If his dad cannot make a man of him, he is bad; but if he makes up for this lack by being a good student and thereby gains recognition and acceptance, he is in danger of being labeled a teacher's pet, and this is bad.[3]

If he reacts to the stress of his confusion and fear by becoming sick, whether the sickness is pretend or real, he is bad. If he plays hooky to avoid being verbally or physically picked on, he is bad. If his mother, aware of his pain and frightened and confused by it, offers him support, comfort, and protection and he accepts it, he is bad and *so is she*.

Thus, perhaps even before he can put a name to his difference, he begins learning how to survive in a hostile environment. He learns to survive by pretending to be one person and presenting this public self, this mask to his family and friends and to the world at large. Yet underneath he has a secret, private, real self, the person he intuitively knows himself to be, complete with his sexual and emotional fantasies known, most likely, to himself alone.

The greater the difference between his public and private selves, the more likely he will experience confusion in his identity ("Who am I *really*?") and difficulty and distress in relating to the world. Logical reasons can be given for the large percentage of lesbians and gay men who are chemically dependent. This is true not because lesbians and gay men have weaker characters or are inherently worse than straight people, but because they have had to live with greater internal pressures and pain at younger ages than most other people. If your son or daughter is chemically dependent, understanding and love will help more than condemnation.

For lesbians, the emergent stage is considerably different. In the past, society has been more willing to accept tomboyish girls than effeminate boys. The girl was seen as aspiring to the "superior" status of the male—an understandable action—whereas a boy was seen as downgrading himself by taking on some of the characteristics of the "inferior" female. If a girl's interests lie in tomboyishness, people are not as inclined to suspect a connection between this trait and lesbianism as they are between a boy's sissiness and homosexuality. For this reason, lesbian girls are not nearly as likely to perceive themselves as different from their peers. This realization usually comes much later.

There are several other reasons why women are often considerably slower to recognize their same-sex feelings than men. One of these reasons is purely physiological. When a man has an erection he knows something has aroused him sexually. A woman does not have the same barometer of her sexual feelings, which are more diffuse. She can easily explain these responses to herself (if she even allows herself to be aware of them) as, for example, sisterly feelings, natural best-friend feelings, or admiration for a teacher, an older cousin, a female boss. Even if the girl or young woman is vaguely conscious that she is somehow different, often she is not aware of any sexual feelings in connection with this difference.

As a girl is growing up she is apt to be isolated if she does not date. So—she dates. Until recently, a woman's goal almost automatically was marriage. (If you had forgotten this fact, watch some of the old movies on television.) In the past it has been—and often still is—easy for a lesbian to marry, not realizing where her true primary emotional and sexual fulfillment lies. Sometimes a woman who is a lesbian engages in promiscuous heterosexual behavior, consciously or unconsciously hoping to find the right man, who never appears.

The heterosexual behavior of a woman who is lesbian can be confusing to her parents. How can they know that the heterosexual behavior is really a cover-up or a denial of their daughter's same-sex feelings? The daughter herself may not yet know, or she may be struggling by herself with her same-sex feelings. She is not likely to confide this kind of thing to her parents at this stage of her life, particularly if she has not yet dared to confide it to herself.

Some women who are really lesbians believe they are asexual and even incapable of experiencing love because men do not interest them. One woman I know, until she was twenty-five, believed she was asexual. Then she recognized that she had strong feelings for a woman, feelings unlike anything she had ever experienced before. She was confused until she read *Lesbian/Woman*, by Del Martin and Phyllis Lyon.[4] As she read she saw herself in the book. "Oh, that's me, that's me!" she kept saying. "I can really feel!"[5]

For all the above reasons the emergence stage is likely to occur later for lesbians than for gay men.

One aspect of the emergence stage applies equally to gay men and lesbians: It is possible for both men and women to have many emotional and/or sexual encounters with persons of the same sex, sometimes over a period of years, and still not comprehend that they are gay or lesbian. The human mind has a marvelous capacity to block out much that it does not care to acknowledge. The lesbians or gay men either do not see themselves as matching the lesbian or gay stereotypes or they simply do not make the necessary connections between their behavior and the popular derogatory definitions of lesbianism or gayness.

In addition, same-sex-oriented people have heard and

believed most of the erroneous platitudes society has developed concerning homosexuality:

"All children go through a phrase when they have attachments to the same sex, but they outgrow this."

"You can choose who you want to be."

"Homosexuals are sick."

"Queers (dykes) should be shot."

"All things are possible through prayer."

And, with an unintentional play on words, "Therapy will straighten you out."

None of these statements is likely to help a gay man or lesbian come to grips with his or her orientation. They either encourage the person to believe that what he or she is feeling is transient and will change or they fill the same-sex-oriented person with such dread that it is easy to deny what otherwise might be apparent.

Acknowledgment

In the case of gay men the acknowledgment of emotional and sexual attraction to others of the same sex typically begins at puberty. There can be wide variation, however; some boys know from late childhood on that they are gay, whereas some men do not allow themselves this realization until the middle years of adulthood.

How does a person deal with the knowledge that he is gay or she is lesbian?

One way, as said earlier, is to pretend that these lesbian or gay feelings do not exist. Some same-sex-oriented people work hard at manufacturing heterosexual personalities. (Much of this, if not all, is done on an unconscious level.) They apply themselves diligently to learning the correct behavior demanded of them as would-be heterosexual persons. And for a time this may work.

In addition, the same-sex-oriented person often retreats from close involvement with anyone—family, friends, peers, teachers, co-workers. She or he is acting a role, and the fear of slipping and revealing her or his real thinking is always there. Every word that is said must be considered and screened before being uttered. "We did so-and-so" must be changed to "I did so-and-so"—an example of the monitoring that must go on every day, endlessly, if the facade is to be maintained. During this time of his or her life the same-sex-oriented person exists in a pervasive cloud of fear before the ever-present possibility of revealing his or her true self through an inadvertent slip of the tongue.

Almost always some situation occurs that causes this carefully constructed life and personality to come apart at the seams. Either the person begins, in one way or another, to break out of the psychic cage she or he has constructed or the continual stress of trying to be someone she or he is not takes a physical toll.

For instance, one married man spent many years being treated for high blood pressure, impotence, bleeding ulcers, and migraine headaches. Then, when the man was fifty, his physician happened to attend a sexuality workshop, where something clicked into place for the physician in relation to his patient. He returned from the workshop and asked the man point-blank if he was homosexual. Even though the patient had never had a homosexual experience, he admitted that his sexual fantasies had always involved men. He was terrified even to talk about his gay feelings but finally acknowledged that he had always denied them. Whether physical or psychic, the cost of denying one's real feelings, one's real self, is always high.

In years past, many doctors, mental health professionals (who might have been expected to know better), and religious counselors have suggested that the way for a man to overcome unwanted homosexual feelings was to find a nice girl and marry her. In conservative Christian circles this "remedy" is still commonly applied. Those familiar with the gay community know that this "cure" seldom works. They know that a good marriage is not built on such a basis, that the woman is demeaned by being used as a means to an end, and that if there are children, the accumulation of anguish that is stored up over the years for all concerned is astronomically increased. Knowingly or unknowingly, many lesbians have also taken the route of marriage either because they believed the right man would make them forget their attachments to other women or because they had no idea men could not provide the deep emotional and sexual fulfillment they needed.

In general, lesbians are less likely to seek counsel and help for their same-sex orientation than gay men, probably because it is easier for a woman to hide her sexual feelings from herself than it is for a man. Besides, lesbians are first of all women, and therefore, as women, they have been subtly programmed to see themselves as second-class citizens, to endure rather than to make waves, and to turn their aggressions in on themselves. For this reason they have often adopted self-destructive means of dealing with their inner pain. Alcohol and drug abuse are two avenues many lesbians have taken as refuges from their real feelings, or they have chosen to remain in bad marriages to atone for the guilt they feel at the breakdown of the marriage.

Another method of dealing with one's lesbian or gay feelings is rationalization, or bargaining. The teenager in junior or senior high school, the young adult in college or on the job who has not yet come out to others hears people talk about queers, faggots, homos, amazons, lezzies, and dykes, knowing deep inside they are talking about him or her. Is it surprising that at this point many same-sex-oriented people panic, feeling as if the name-callers had looked right through them, as if their souls had been laid bare for all to see? Overcome with shame, they ask themselves, "Do I really have all those horrible characteristics?" And they begin to set up tests for themselves. Many of these tests or bargains are not consciously perceived. They are more like reflex actions that, if successfully carried out, automatically prove a point never clearly articulated.

For a gay man, the tests may go like this:

"If I'm a good student, I'm not gay."
"If I'm a good athlete, I'm not gay."
"If I date women, I'm not gay."
"If I'm a good Christian, I'm not gay."
"If I fool around with men only when I'm drunk, I'm not gay."
"If I work twelve hours a day, I'm not gay."
"If I marry and have children, I'm certainly not gay."
"If I'm really, *really* macho, how can I possibly be gay?"

The lesbian counterpart of these tests might include:

"If I'm a good student, I'm not lesbian."
"If I date men, I'm not lesbian."
"If I'm a good Christian, I'm not lesbian."
"If I sleep with a lot of men, I certainly can't be lesbian."
"If I marry and have children, I can't possibly be lesbian."

One of the most desperate bargains for men is, "If I beat up gay people, obviously I'm not gay." Because society has not approved of women using physical violence as the answer to their problems, women are more apt to take out their fear of their own sexual selves in other ways. For example, in the military services a lesbian may deflect suspicion from herself by joining wholeheartedly in a lesbian witchhunt. "If I expose a lot of women as lesbians, I'm certainly not a lesbian."

There are other ways in which same-sex-oriented persons try to deal with their sexual orientation during the acknowledgment stage of their development. One of these may be a search for a deeper religious experience in the hope that God can "cure" the person's homosexuality. Another may be depression and/or withdrawal from society.

Most gay men and lesbians make the first disclosure of themselves to another person during the acknowledgment stage. This takes courage. Suppose the confidant turns away in disgust. Suppose he or she says that the same-sex-oriented person is bad, sinful, or unlovable because of who he or she is.

Until recently, society has not provided a place in which young people are safe to explore their sexuality in helpful, nonthreatening ways. Ideally, this exploration should take place in the home. Children and young people should be able to discuss freely with their parents any and all sexual matters and to receive wise and helpful guidance and education in formulating their values. Almost everyone knows that this is a utopian dream. Churches, schools, and some community-based groups for young people may also provide settings in which they can explore their sexuality with the guidance of adults. In most cases it is heterosexuality that is explored.

Where can young people go to explore their suspected homosexuality and be dealt with understandingly, caringly, and nonjudgmentally? For many young people there are no such places, particularly if they live in rural areas, small towns, or even some urban centers in the conservative areas of the country. In such a setting acknowledging one's same-sex orientation is asking for rejection by family, friends, school, church, employers, landlords, and even those charged with protecting the public safety, police and sheriff's departments. Such attitudes may lead the same-sex-oriented person to split himself or herself into two parts, the public and the private self.

This is particularly damaging for adolescents. Because these young gay men or lesbians have no familial or societal permission to speak of same-sex attraction and feelings of love, they have no opportunity to put their inner experience into perspective. All they can do is struggle by themselves with the grim information society has given them about homosexuality and reach out tentatively to whoever promises help and understanding.

If a gay or lesbian person verbalizes his or her sexual feelings to someone else this may be a major breakthrough and may open the door to disclosures to other people. However, if the chosen confidant rejects the young person, this can lead to feelings of a blanket rejection by all of society and self-dissatisfaction or even self-hatred. The anger, sadness, and confusion—"What does all this mean?" or "Why me?"—that commonly accompany the realization of one's same-sex orientation can get twisted into anxiety and depression. Tragically, the intensity of these feelings sometimes reaches a suicidal level, and rather than face her or his real self, the same-sex-oriented person chooses to escape the crushing dilemma through death. It is no accident that gay and lesbian youths account for some 30 percent of all teenage suicides.[6]

Even those who do not resort to suicide often experience damage from their rejection by society both in their immediate community and in the larger context. In such cases these young people have a tendency to compartmentalize sex, cutting it off from the rest of their lives. Because sexuality cannot be integrated with the whole of their personalities or lives, it is easier in later years to keep it split off, and thus to view promiscuity and anonymous sexual encounters as separate actions unrelated to other facets of life. Because of such adolescent repression, these gay men and lesbians have no way to measure the success of the relationships they may form.

Fortunately, today the climate for same-sex-oriented young people—indeed, for older gay men and lesbians as well—is not quite so bleak as it was in past years. Television and radio talk shows have, it seems, explored every possible type of sexual expression. Sometimes their emphasis on all kinds of sexual behavior seems excessive; but it may also reassure lesbian and gay young people to know that the latitude of sexual activities carried out in our society is very wide. Lesbian or gay characters occasionally appear in prime-time television programs or movies, sometimes as the main protagonists—but not always in a favorable light.

Magazines at times carry articles about gay men and lesbians, and news magazines periodically deal with same-sex-oriented issues. In 1992 the *Detroit News* began carrying a weekly column on gay issues, written by Deb Price. The column has appeared in other newspapers as well, including *USA Today.* Bob Bernstein, an articulate member of P-FLAG, the national organization of parents of lesbian daughters and gay sons, has written columns that have appeared in a number of newspapers around the country.

Some organizations have sponsored local or statewide groups to provide safe places for homosexual young people. Massachusetts has formed a Commission on Gay and Lesbian Youth. Minnesota's P-FLAG organization and the Minnesota Task Force for Gay and Lesbian Youth have instituted an annual youth award ceremony to honor outstanding gay and lesbian young people. Every high school in the state receives information about the awards.[7]

Initiating a neutral discussion of television programs, movies, articles, or organizations can be a way parents may open up dialogue with their child. Or the child may be the one who initiates the conversation as a means of sounding out where the parents stand on such matters.

In earlier days gay, and at times lesbian, bars were the only places to make contact with other same-sex-oriented people. Now computer bulletin boards provide another means of communication with lesbian and gay persons. Contact by computer has the peculiar advantage of not being associated emotionally with feelings of shame, as some other means of contact might be. Computer bulletin boards devoted to a wide range of specialized interests have become a socially accepted way of meeting people, at least electronically, around the country or even around the world (see Appendix 3 for resource information). It is possible to have "dates" by computer or telephone. Some of these services feature fairly explicit sexual conversation. Such contacts can provide an odd, compartmentalized way of dealing with one's sexuality, but satisfying relationships sometimes do begin in unusual ways. There is even the possibility of using the mail to establish contact with another person.

In a day when all sexual relationships are fraught with the danger of possible infection and death, intimate conversation via phone, computer, or letter may be a risk-free outlet. Such conversation, of course, need not concentrate on sex. It can be used as a means of developing friendships with other like-minded people. In recent years, gay and lesbian communities have relearned the difference between overtly sexual relationships and the more general concept of intimacy, which may or may not include sex, but certainly includes a far greater range of caring and closeness.

Such varied means of communicating with other like-minded people can facilitate all of the stages through which lesbians and gay men pass as they deal with their sexual orientation.

Gay Men and Crashing Out, or Exploration

The next two stages of the coming-out process—crashing out, or exploration, and first relationships—differ in some important aspects for gay men and lesbians. Let us look at the male pattern first. Because the lesbian counterpart of crashing out often occurs after a first relationship, it is considered here in that context.

The gay man's main objective at this point usually is to make up for lost time. His straight friends have been dating for years while he has wondered (suspected and dreaded to face) what was "wrong" with himself because he was not interested in dating girls. Or he may have dated but did not experience the same feelings about girls that his friends described.

And now at long last he has come into his own. He has found others who share his feelings. Is it any wonder he may go a little wild? Even if he is twenty-five or thirty or forty, well established in his career or vocation, dealing with all other aspects of his life on an adult level, he may find himself acting socially like an irresponsible teenager. "What's wrong with me?" he may wonder. "I seem to have lost my senses." This is not true; he is simply making up for the time when, chronologically, he should have been reacting in this way but could not.

A gay friend in his early thirties told me that for six months he was at the bar every night. "I *had* to go," he said. "I would almost go crazy if I couldn't get there." He hinted delicately that the point of going to the bar was a compulsion to pick up a bedmate for the night. "All of a sudden that ended," he continued. "It was over, done with. I couldn't believe that I had ever done what I'd done. I haven't been to the bar now for months."

This man was behaving in a compulsive manner because unconsciously he was compensating, in a typically male-prescribed way, for his lost adolescence.

If your gay son is in this stage of coming out, you may be distressed by indications of promiscuity. What can you do about it?

First, recognize that the sexual morals many parents grew up with are, to a large extent, things of the past, whether we are talking about heterosexual or homosexual behavior. Pressure to refrain from premarital sex used to be the norm. Today pressure is almost as great to be sexually active before marriage, and even in adolescence. (Not that previous generations *did* always refrain, but they were not as frank and open about it.) Television and movies today continually send the message that being sexually active is the normal way of living.

Add to this the fact that because the gay community has existed outside the pale of society for centuries, it has developed its own behavior patterns. If you tell people often enough that they are immoral and worthless because of who they are, many of them are going to believe this. While straight society exerts pressure to uphold the institution of marriage, same-sex-oriented people have no means of proclaiming a committed relationship that is recognized and supported by society. There are many more-or-less committed relationships within the gay and lesbian communities, and today, through the influence of such groups as the Metropolitan Community Church, Evangelicals Concerned, and other lesbian/gay religious groups, there is a movement toward honoring and supporting these relationships with such services as Holy Union, the Blessing of Relationships, or the covenanting of two people to be life partners. In the wider community, however, there is no ethical or legal support for such unions.

In addition, men have been socialized according to a double standard. A man is thought to be most masculine when he is a sexual tiger. Traditionally, he has been *supposed* to be the initiator, the pursuer. *He* has been the one who sees how far he can go, and the woman has had to hold the line and say, "This far and no farther." While awareness of this double standard has grown, it is far from disappearing entirely.

In an all-male community where the men behave with other men according to the ways in which they have been socialized—and according to the newest ways popularized by the sexual revolution of the past decades— sexual interaction is likely to be a strong feature.

Because of the prevalence of AIDS, such an attitude has led to a remarkable amount of confusion. On the one hand the pressures to be sexually active are still there, either because of the natural response to the body's hormones or because movies and television continue to portray guilt-free, AIDS-free, unprotected sexual activity. On the other hand, articles in newspapers and magazines constantly warn about AIDS and the dangers of unsafe sexual activity and advocate new types of sexual outlets.

Because the religious community has often washed its hands of same-sex-oriented persons—except perhaps those who are living celibate lives—it has cut itself off from having any ethical input into lesbian and gay communities. In the light of the accumulated evidence, is it any wonder that these communities have formulated their own values and that some of these values do not contribute favorably to the development of the whole person? Lesbian communities are probably better able to foster the healthy development of the whole person than gay male communities, largely because women have been socialized to be more concerned with relationships, more nurturant, more intuitive, and sexually less aggressive.

There is another aspect of your son's crashing out stage. Because crashing out, or exploration, for gay men—no matter what their chronological age—is a stage comparable to heterosexual adolescence, this may have been—or may now be—a chaotic period of emotional highs and lows for your son. If he does not clearly understand what he is looking for in any given situation where he gathers with other gay men, or if he does not understand that he may be looking for intellectual, spiritual, or emotional intimacy rather than sexual intimacy, he may invest all his needs in sexual intimacy, thinking this will supply everything he is looking for. When it does not he may assume that sexual intimacy with the next person *will* provide these things. In this way sexual activity can become a compulsive cycle that never satisfies if he is unaware of what he is looking for and how to find it.

Many gay men *are* looking for something more than sex. A number of them have said to me, "Well, the sex is OK, but what I really like is when a man holds me close." All human beings have a need to be touched. The enthusiastic embracing that goes on in Lutheran, Episcopal, and Catholic gay communion services at the passing of the peace is perhaps one way of satisfying this hunger nonsexually.

Suppose you feel your son is too active sexually. What are you going to do about it? If he is an adult and you no longer have control over his life as you did (or thought you did) when he was growing up, is there anything you can do? If he is not yet legally an adult, what can you do?

You, as a parent, need not remain silent in either case. What *is* of great importance is the manner in which you talk with your son about the sexual activity that concerns you. If you issue directions as an all-wise parent to a naughty child or dwell only on the evils (as you see them) of such behavior or state *your* feelings without taking time to listen to what he has to say, you are certain not to make any headway with your son. He will tune you out and erect a wall between himself and you.

In dealing with this situation be honest with yourself about your aim in talking with your son. Do you want to impose your values on him? Or do you want to *talk over* the situation as one adult to another, *exchange* ideas? *Talk over* and *exchange* mean that ideas are going in both directions. Listen (and I mean *listen, hear*—not simply be silent until it is your turn again to talk) as well as set forth your views. You *can* express your feelings, your puzzlement, your values, your need for clarification of the situation, your willingness to listen.

"I don't understand why you're being so active sexually," expresses your *feelings* rather than being a heavy-handed condemnation of your child. "It's different from my values."

You may think your feelings about your son's sexual activity are related to his gayness. Yet if you knew a straight son or daughter was very active sexually, you probably would feel the same way. Express these thoughts to your son, that you are not viewing this as a gay issue, but rather as an issue of general sexual values.

"I don't like what's going on," you can say. "I need to understand your values about sexual intimacy and what you really want out of such intimacy."

In talking with my children about sexual values and behaviors I have discovered the tremendous difference between the somewhat Victorian atmosphere in which I grew up and the increasingly permissive sexual climate in which they have come of age. I have discovered that they have difficulty envisioning the influences that shaped my values. For my part, I had greatly underestimated the prevailing influences with which society had surrounded them as they were growing up.

If your son is confusing emotional intimacy with sexual intimacy, talking it over with him (*not* arguing, *not* condemning) may open the door to a different perspective for him. If it does not, you may have begun to understand his viewpoint—even though you may not approve of it—and he may have gotten a new perspective on your values. The end product of your conversation(s) may not be agreement between the two of you, although that might seem to be the end you desired. Knowing that his parents have listened to him, have been honest about their thoughts and feelings, and have not tried to coerce him may have a powerful effect on your son, an effect you may not necessarily be aware of. Such an exchange says to your child, "The door is open between us. We can be honest with each other without always having to agree." It says, "You are an adult, responsible for your own life, and I care about you enough to allow you to be a person in your own right, not a parental appendage who must agree with me on every point."

Most important, by raising such issues you may have challenged him to search for new and more constructive values.

First Relationships, Lesbian and Gay

For gay males, the next stage in the coming-out process, after crashing out, is probably the development of a first relationship. For lesbians, the development of a first relationship may occur immediately after the acknowledgment stage.

Generally, a gay man seeks out the gay community upon acknowledging his sexual orientation. He may take some time getting around to his first relationship because he is so busy in the exploration stage. A lesbian may follow one of two patterns when she acknowledges her orientation. She may move directly into a relationship with the first lesbian she encounters who is open to establishing such a relationship. Often these partnerships are formed in isolation from any type of lesbian community. This is likely to happen if the woman lives in a rural area or a small town or in a politically and religiously conservative area where there is not much if any lesbian community. The partner is not chosen for suitability from a number of eligible friends and acquaintances, because in this circumscribed situation no such group exists. She simply falls into a relationship with the first available woman.

If the woman lives in a more liberal area or in a progressive urban setting, she has more options and is not as likely to settle into the first relationship that presents itself. There may be lesbian bars where she can meet potential partners. There may be coffeehouses and nonalcoholic bars, gay/lesbian religious groups, women's sports teams, as well as women's groups, which often include both heterosexual women and lesbians with a wide spectrum of interests. There may be lesbian/gay publications to alert her to related groups. The general press and television coverage in the area may present news about lesbian groups and activities, and the public library may provide information about these activities. Under these circumstances the woman is not as likely to settle for the first relationship that presents itself. She may be too busy exploring her newfound community to be interested in an exclusive relationship at this time.

If, however, she is past her first youth, she may be more likely to accept an early relationship that is less than ideal, simply because she knows that in competition with younger women she may not have a great deal of choice.

Even though the partners in relationships formed because of limited choice may be hopelessly mismatched, some of these couples remain together for years. This may be attributable in part to society's emphasis on permanence in relationships involving love and sex and the cultural prescription that maintaining permanence is the woman's duty. The fact that this prescription usually applies to heterosexual relationships makes no difference. Women think they must make a relationship work, and they feel a deep sense of failure if they cannot.

Sometimes there is a secondary reason for remaining in the relationship; this is true for gay men as well as for lesbians. Fear grips the partners: "If I break up this relationship, will I find someone else?" Having a poor relationship may be preferable to not having any relationship. Although some of these relationships do endure— whether they deserve to or not—many founder within a few years.

The end of a first relationship is as painful for a same-sex-oriented person as the breakup of a heterosexual first love affair (whether it has included sexual activity or not) or a marriage. If you want to be of real assistance to your child in a difficult period of her or his life, you will listen, you will acknowledge the grief and pain your child is experiencing, and you will withhold any condemnation. Heterosexual or homosexual, when a love relationship falls apart your child *hurts*.

You hope your child learns and grows from this experience. In all likelihood your son will move on to the stage of self-definition and reintegration. Your daughter may also, although if she has not yet gone through her stage of crashing out/exploration, she may now move on to this phase of her development.

Gay and lesbian youth are particularly at risk for one type of relationship. Because of their emerging realization of their sexual orientation, they frequently feel themselves isolated from their peers and indeed from the community as a whole. In such cases, an unscrupulous adult who senses a young man or woman's struggle can involve him or her in an exploitive relationship. A teacher or high school coach of either sex, for example, can lead a young person of the same sex into a sexual relationship. In recent years many such relationships between Catholic priests and altar boys have been uncovered. It is possible for *any* leader of youth, heterosexual or homosexual, to indulge his or her penchant for such unequal relationships. The harm in these liaisons stems from two factors. One is the inequality of the relationship. The young person may have difficulty saying no to an adult, particularly if the older person is charismatic and attracts the admiration of young people. The young person is therefore *used*, exploited, to satisfy an unhealthy need in the older partner. The other harmful aspect lies in the breaching of the boundaries of the young person's sense of self. In becoming an extension of the older person's ego, the younger is laid open to continued exploitation by others. The damage thus inflicted can last a long time, and the exploited person often requires therapy to eradicate the painful and destructive effects.

Crashing Out, or Exploration, for Lesbians

Whether your lesbian daughter crashed out before she entered into a first relationship or after, she is less likely to have as many sexual encounters as a gay man, and the encounters will probably not be as impersonal. Because society has trained women to be more responsible for relationship building than are men, few lesbians are much interested in casual sexual encounters for any prolonged period.

Whether or not your daughter has been through a first relationship that foundered, in the crashing out stage she explores the possibilities for dating other women and finding a partner. If she has been through an unsatisfactory relationship, she may eventually *choose* another partner with more care and discrimination, rather than falling into the first alliance that becomes possible.

Also at this point your daughter's evolution may include involvement in the lesbian political, cultural, and social community, rather than involvement in many and promiscuous sexual encounters. This may mean joining a coming-out group, a lesbian softball team, or a lesbian chorus; hanging out at lesbian bars and coffeehouses; and in other ways expanding her connections to meet other women who may be available for friendships, dating, and relationships.

During the period of first relationships and crashing out many lesbians choose primarily women—and especially other lesbians—as friends. Most parents interpret this as isolationism or man-hating on the part of their lesbian daughters. "If she'd give herself a chance, she might find she liked men," the parents think. Or they believe other lesbians are out to get and brainwash their daughter.

What parents do not realize is that such exclusiveness is a way for the lesbian who is trying hard to find her way in new and unfamiliar territory to develop support in a generally hostile world. It is also a way for her to have comfortable social relationships, because many heterosexual persons are not comfortable with lesbians. Lesbians must guard their behavior in heterosexual public places. They may not hold hands as heterosexual couples do; nor may they dance together. For this reason lesbians feel freer and more at ease in lesbian places and seek these places in preference to those that are heterosexual.

The same is true of gay men. When they seek out gay friends and gay areas they are looking for support and the opportunity to be themselves. They have not been subverted or brainwashed, as many parents think.

Self-definition and Reintegration

The final stage of your homosexual child's development into a whole human being with a same-sex orientation is self-definition and reintegration. Your child, lesbian or gay, now has a variety of experiences as a same-sex-oriented person to serve as background material against which consciously to shape her or his life. Your child is also in a better position to evaluate goals, short and long term, and make informed and careful decisions about how public to be with her or his private self. Your child is ready to make these decisions in the light of a healthy self-interest, personal pride, and self-respect, rather than reacting out of fear, shame, and desperate need for approval or acceptance. And because life is a process of change, new situations will continue to provide challenges to your child in assessing the risks and benefits of sharing her or his lesbian or gay identity with others.

During the self-definition and reintegration stage—which is less a stage than an ongoing learning process—your child's life will expand much like any person's life expands, whether hetero- or homosexual. New feelings about oneself continue to emerge, and one learns to understand these feelings and integrate them into life.

Your child will find and explore new groups, new friends, and perhaps, of necessity, new primary relationships. Your child will return to the acknowledgment stage each time a decision is made to share her or his true identity with a family member, employer, colleague, or friend.

Because unconsciously all of us as young people see ourselves as immortal, we possess a kind of shining vigor that grows progressively dimmer as we advance into adulthood. The process of becoming adult has been defined in part as a process of disillusionment with youthful viewpoints, a loss of the quality of innocence with which we all are born and which we lose as we grow older. Some of this loss is inevitable and right—but we don't want to fall into jadedness and cynicism. The ideal combination would maintain a balance between the wisdom of experience and the unspoiled invincibility of youth.

You, as a parent, have presumably gained some wisdom in this area. How then can you help your same-sex-oriented child in this state of change and growth, including the stages simply of maturing, as well as of self-definition and reintegration? The answer, of course, is to do the same things you would for your heterosexual child. See him or her as a responsible, mature person. Respect his or her individual personhood. Everyone needs to be dealt with and appreciated as a unique person.

Coping with the Idea of Your Child's Partner

People who compile dictionaries will tell you that our language is constantly evolving. A gay or lesbian person's significant other used to be called his or her lover. The word often carries a somewhat disreputable connotation, and some parents were uncomfortable with it. "Isn't there some other term?" they would ask.

Parents may be relieved to know that today partner and companion are preferred to lover. To call the person one is living with one's lover is now seen as a slightly dramatic declaration that overidealizes the relationship. With a somewhat more realistic attitude toward people who live in love relationships with other people, whether heterosexual or homosexual, newspapers and magazines now use the term companion or longtime companion. Especially when there has been a service to bless and confirm the relationship between two same-sex-oriented persons, the term of choice is life partner. Indeed, I have seen this used for heterosexual couples, with no indication of whether this connotes a married relationship or simply a bond of personal commitment between the two parties.

Terminology aside, parents often find that what really bothers them is the idea of their child having sex with a person of the same gender. There may be a horrified curiosity (many times unacknowledged) about how they do it. Frequently it is a jolt for parents to realize that their child, of either sexual orientation, is "having sex." Why parents should find the normal course of human maturation distasteful in this one area must say something about our culture's love-hate relationship with sexuality.

For many parents the thought of sexual activity by a heterosexual son or daughter outside of marriage is bad enough. In a same-sex-oriented child sexual activity outside of marriage somehow seems much worse. Often parents cling to the idea that the only kind of sexual activity sanctioned by God occurs within marriage. There may be a number of underlying hang-ups that such a statement camouflages.

"Why can't they just be friends?" the parents wonder. The question is a naive attempt by parents to shut their eyes to their child's kind of sexuality. It may be illuminating to realize that the same question is hardly ever asked about an unmarried heterosexual couple who are living together. Society accepts that there is a strong urge between a man and a woman to consummate their love relationship in a sexual way. Yet the idea that two men or two women may feel the same strong urge toward their partner of the same sex seems "unnatural."

Yet homosexualities—Morton and Barbara Kelsey use the plural to indicate the many possible origins, multiple kinds of possible manifestation (dreams, fantasies, emotional climate, or actual bodily contact), and greatly varied methods of expressing these inner realizations—are "empowered with the full energy of the reproductive instinct; they fall into the same category with regard to their potency as the drive for food and self-preservation. They have deep unconscious roots and take the same heroic strength to control as heterosexual desires. . . . There are as many variations of physical gratification of the homosexual urge as there are of heterosexual desire."[8]

Many parents refuse to deal with a child's partner. "You can come home, but not your friend," they say. They would not think of saying to a married daughter or son, "*You* may come home, but don't bring your husband (wife)." (It is even doubtful that you would tell your heterosexual child not to bring his or her friend.) In your child's eyes the partner occupies the same relationship as the spouse in a heterosexual situation. You may not see it this way. If you do not accept the partner, you are likely to lose more than you gain, because you have weakened your relationship with your child.

Perhaps you have difficulty accepting your child's partner because of the fantasy pictures your mind paints about homosexual intercourse. These pictures may be so repellent to you that you do not want anything to do with your child's partner. You may feel the partner has seduced your child. This can be especially true if your son or daughter is young and the partner is much older. Yet the mechanics of same-gender sexual activity includes little that is not done at some time by many heterosexual couples. Our uneasy feelings about this activity are rooted in our more pervasive cultural problems with sexuality in general.

In spite of the obvious fact that we use sex to sell all kinds of products, we are really not at ease with the sex in sexuality. It is, as the Kelseys have pointed out, one of the several powerful instincts built into human beings in order to perpetuate the human race. The "deep unconscious roots" they refer to probably incorporate many attitudes propounded by various religious bodies over a period of thousands of years. These attitudes found their way into the cultural mainstream even though the ideas often rested on expediency or faulty information rather than on sound psychological footings.[9]

Because of the hold sexuality has on us at the same time that we fear its power and often far-reaching consequences, we find it easy to displace these feelings onto homosexuality. Sexual attraction to people of the same gender seems to us to represent something totally "other"—quite opposite to what we suppose are "natural feelings"—and yet also to mirror any feelings we may have of sexual attraction to people of our same gender. In addition there is an emotional need to defend *our ideas* of what constitutes masculinity and femininity, the vulnerability of sex-role performances, and a traditional Western fear that any loss of individual or social control will lead to loss of controls in general.[10]

Your perception of homosexual sex as abhorrent because it is "unnatural" may be a smokescreen for feelings you are unaware of and would rather not deal with. Yet these unrecognized feelings may be robbing you of a close relationship with your child.

Psychologically, it is untrue that what you do not know cannot hurt you. What is buried in your unconscious can be detrimental to your peace of mind and well-being. Begin by going back over your sexual autobiography. What ideas about sex were inculcated in you as a child? What ideas did you absorb from your parents and the other adults who surrounded you? What ideas did you absorb from your peers? What were your childhood and adolescent sexual fantasies and experiences? How did you feel about these experiences, or the lack of them? If such introspection generates an undue amount of fear, shame, and distress, you may want to seek counseling in dealing with your own sexuality.

"But I was handling my sexuality just fine until this happened," you may be thinking. "Why should I go for counseling when it's my child's 'unnatural' sex that is at fault? Let *him* (*her*) get the counseling."

True, you may have been getting along fine until you learned of your child's homosexuality. Now the whole equation of your life has changed. This is not your child's fault; nor is it yours. No one is at fault. New information—your child's same-sex orientation—has come into your life, and you cannot cope with it. This hurts you and your relationship with your child. Either you curtail or cut off the relationship with your child or you take steps to grow in order that you may maintain a loving and noncondemning relationship with your child. Making your child choose between you and her or his partner can only result in hurt for everyone.

You may feel your child has hurt you deeply. You may be in deep pain because of your child's same-sex orientation, especially as you come face to face with the outward manifestation of this orientation—your child's partner.

The pain is *yours*, and you cannot deal with *your* pain by trying to change someone else. You can deal with this pain only by exploring its dimensions, only by heading into it and through it to the other side. There are no bypasses around pain. When one tries to bypass it one finds it waiting up ahead, and in the meantime it has become more formidable, having "earned interest," so to speak, along the way.

Some people can head into their pain and work through it by themselves. Others need help—a wise friend, an understanding doctor or minister. If such a helper is not available to you, search out a professional mental health counselor to serve as a sounding board and to offer guidance as you plow through this painful territory.

If you are to understand your child and his or her relationship with a partner, there are some things it might be helpful for you to know. First, the problems your child and his or her companion may face are most likely to be of the human variety rather than specifically gay or lesbian problems.

Your son's or daughter's first relationship may be fragile. Often lesbians and gay men enter into relationships before they are ready for such experiences. The miracle of being in love has burst on them. They desperately want to find persons with whom they can share their whole selves. Possibly, they have been so starved for love from persons of the same sex that they latch onto the first ones who offer themselves. This is the love of the century, they think, not realizing they may be in love with love rather than with the person the partner really is.

What is going on between your child and partner is not so different from what happens in millions of heterosexual relationships. Often the dynamics of the relationship between the two partners could just as well go on between heterosexual partners.

Let us expand this idea. The same dynamics can occur between brothers and/or sisters or even between two unrelated people who decide to live together in a nonsexual relationship. The situation of an unmarried friend opened my eyes to this fact. Her parents had died, leaving her and an unmarried sister to share the family home. As time went on it became apparent to my friend that she could not live with her sister and avoid a nervous breakdown. One of the most difficult tasks she ever faced was to tell her sister she was moving out and then actually move.

The facet of her story that interested me the most was that the problems within the relationship between her and her sister almost duplicated some of the problems that had caused my divorce. Although there was no sexual aspect to her and her sister's relationship, the similarity in other respects between her situation and mine was uncanny. Right then I realized that a large percentage of problems in marriage and in living-together relationships have no connection with sex. They are interpersonal problems that can occur in any relationship where two (or more) people occupy the same living quarters. If there is a sexual aspect to the relationship, the strains may be evidenced in sexual as well as other ways. But most of the stresses do not originate in the sexual connection; they originate in the human connection that occurs when people share living space.

For most of her or his life your same-sex-oriented child has had to cope with society's hostile evaluation. Every day your child must cope with misunderstanding and discrimination. Perhaps you can begin to recognize how important it is for you, as a parent, to obtain accurate information about homosexuality and to continue to love your lesbian or gay child. She or he has enough difficulties to contend with in everyday life, difficulties resulting not from a willful choice or from bad parenting but from the circumstances life has handed her or him—and you.

This is why it is so important for you to make the effort to understand your child and your child's sexual orientation. It is natural for you to be upset, to fall back on the ideas and beliefs about homosexuality with which you grew up. These beliefs and ideas have collided with the information that your child is same-sex-oriented, and this collision is causing you to experience pain, disorientation, a sense of loss, and grief.

Can you deal with the intense feelings your child's coming out has aroused in you? Will you be able to reconcile all the different feelings you are experiencing? Is it worthwhile making the effort to accept (not necessarily approve) your child's sexuality and maintain a close and caring relationship with her or him?

Each person's answer, of course, will be different. But thousands of parents *have* made the effort and have found it more worthwhile than they believed possible.

Nobody—or almost nobody—says it is easy. Occasionally, I talk with a parent to whom his or her child's homosexuality presented no particular problem. Most parents, however, have considerable difficulty dealing with the same-sex orientation of their children. Perhaps a glimpse at some of the dynamics of parenting will help you understand why this is so and will offer a way of living with this fact of your life.

Chapter 7

Letting Go

Tom Braden, a newspaper columnist, has captured the essence of changes in family relationships that come as the children in the family grow up.[1] He first became aware of the change after his children had returned to college from a Thanksgiving vacation. During their stay at home he began to realize that he was no longer the final source of authoritative information for his children. He discovered that when his "facts" were tested against "facts" given by other people, his turned out to be "what people 'used' to think."

He also discovered that, as father, he no longer controlled his children. One evening after dinner the children, both male and female, went out. They didn't ask permission, nor could he recall afterward that they had even bothered to tell him they were going. They simply went. One of them, without calling home, spent the night at a friend's house. He had had a few beers with his friend Bill and decided to stay all night. A year or two before, Braden says, this could not have happened, or if it had, there would have been a family row about it. Now the son is 21 and, Braden writes, "he knows I disapprove. I wonder whether I should disapprove."

Braden concludes the column with the question: "Why

didn't somebody tell me that there would come a time when I would be stripped of my powers and when the word 'father' would mean not much more than 'old friend'?"

Mothers also face pitfalls as their children mature. At age eighty-two Florida Scott-Maxwell, an author, dramatist, and analytical psychologist, wrote with great insight about the unconscious feelings that cause mothers to react in seemingly odd ways:

> A mother's love for her children, even her inability to let them be, is because she is under a painful law that the life that passed through her must be brought to fruition. Even when she swallows it whole she is only acting like any frightened mother cat eating its young to keep it safe. It is not easy to give closeness and freedom, safety plus danger.
>
> No matter how old a mother is she watches her middle-aged children for signs of improvement. It could not be otherwise for she is impelled to know that the seeds of value sown in her have been winnowed. She never outgrows the burden of love, and to the end she carries the weight of hope for those she bore. Oddly, very oddly, she is forever surprised and even faintly wronged that her sons and daughters are just people, for many mothers hope and half expect that their new-born child will make the world better, will somehow be a redeemer.[2]

Nobody sets out to be a mother or father who smothers. We may have the best intentions in the world of being marvelous parents, but somehow along the way something trips us up. Or we may have assumed that knowing how to be a mother or father is an instinctive skill that surfaces when the baby is born. Birds and dogs and horses and cats know how to be parents—or at least mothers. But we are not birds or animals, and therefore, we have considerably different mental equipment. The instincts that enable nonhuman living creatures to survive by doing what comes naturally, without conscious thought, do not operate in human beings within the same restrictive limits. True, we do carry within us some ideas of how to be parents. But a great deal of our human action depends on how we learn to act.

We learn to be parents in a number of ways. One is by imitation of our parents. If we had good parents, we have a head start on our own parenting. If we had examples of deficient parenting as we grew up—abusing parents, to cite a glaring example—we are more likely to become deficient parents ourselves than we otherwise might.

We also learn a great deal about being a father or a mother by what society tells us a father or a mother should be. Much of our learning is unconscious. We absorb by osmosis, from the air around us, ideas of how a mother or a father behaves. We are not even conscious that we are receiving and retaining these ideas. Often when we become parents we act in certain ways without knowing why.

In addition, the particular culture in which we grow up influences our actions. The ideal Victorian mother would behave totally differently from the ideal mother of the 1990s. An aboriginal mother would behave quite differently from a mother in a civilized Western culture.

One of the ideas about motherhood acquired from the culture around us is the feeling that a mother's love is instinctive, unquestioning, and total. In the beginning a baby is almost helpless. The mother does everything for the child without asking anything in return. Because of this, mother love is considered to be the most sacred of all emotional bonds.

What have not been so well publicized are other important aspects of a mother's love. During the first months and years of a child's life a mother gives and gives and then gives some more. We forget that the essence of a mother's love, as Erich Fromm has pointed out, is

> to care for the child's *growth,* and that means to
> *want the child's separation from herself.* . . . The moth-
> er must not only tolerate, she must wish and sup-
> port the child's separation. It is only at this stage
> that motherly love becomes such a difficult task,
> that it requires unselfishness, the ability to give ev-
> erything and to want nothing but the happiness of
> the loved one.[3]

Note that in the beginning the mother's unselfishness demands that she do everything for her child. The time comes, however, when her "unselfishness, the ability to give everything and to want nothing," no longer means the total immersion in her child that unselfishness meant in the child's early years. Now the unselfishness means that she lets go, withdraws, no longer tries to control and direct.

For a mother to want this separation of the child from herself is not always easy, although I believe it is easier for some women than for others. Some mothers find the helpless-baby stage more endearing and rewarding than their children's older stages, and for these women it may be more difficult to want their children to be separated from them. This may be why some women look forward so longingly to grandchildren.

Personally, I have had the opposite difficulty. I had never been around young children and was not comfortable with the baby stage. I looked forward almost desperately sometimes to the day when I could relate to my children in more adult ways. I was ashamed that I was not more enthusiastic about my children as helpless little bundles, toddlers, and preschoolers. Something must be wrong with me, I thought, until one day I discovered that a friend, the mother of *six* teenage and young adult children, had had the same feelings. "Oh, I enjoyed my children much more when they started to grow up than when they were babies," she said—and a load rolled off my mind.

It is not always easy to know how to shift gears in parent/child relationships as our children grow. We may not recognize that we are still smothering our children. It may be painful suddenly to discover that our children are making their own decisions without even telling us what these decisions are. But presumably, this is what fathers and mothers have been aiming for all along.

A father's love, according to Fromm, "should give the growing child an increasing sense of competence and eventually permit him to become his own authority and to dispense with that of father."[4]

That it may be no easier for a father to let go than for a mother is evident from what Braden writes. Certainly it is difficult to be demoted from the position of father, the source of wisdom and authority, to not much more than the position of old friend. And yet how fortunate if a father can in fact become an old friend to his children. Perhaps this is the basic goal toward which we, as parents—father or mother—need to aim as our children grow up. No longer are we the commanders, the authorities, the people without whom our children would have difficulty surviving. The parent/child relationship must become much more that of good friends—adult to adult—and rich are the rewards if such a relationship of mutual respect and mutual caring can be achieved.

It is not only we parents, however, who may have difficulty making the transition from a parent/child relationship to an adult/adult relationship.[5] From the moment of birth and for many years thereafter our children have been dependent on us for care and sustenance. Unconsciously, they have come to perceive us as powerful persons. As mother or father, we govern, modulate, and control almost everything that happens to our children in their early years.

As our children mature, they continue to carry, deep within, an unconscious perception of us as "big" (powerful) and of themselves as "little" (powerless). The conscious mind knows this is not an accurate perception. Yet unconscious ideas exert great power, a fact of which we are all frequently unaware.

Even though our children may now be adults they may continue to relate to us as if we were still the directors, the caretakers. Within our children may still be a residue of the child-to-parent relationship rather than an adult-to-adult relationship. Often a conscious effort is necessary on the part of one or both sides to move out of the parent/child habit patterns into adult-to-adult patterns.

What is an adult-to-adult pattern? How can we relate to our children, how can our children relate to us, in an adult mode without sacrificing love and caring? Can it be done?

Florida Scott-Maxwell, expressing herself as a mother, writes: "I have learned the hard truth a mother learns slowly, that the quick of intimacy she has known becomes hope for loved strangers."[6]

Erich Fromm, speaking more dispassionately, characterizes mature love as "union under the condition of preserving one's integrity, one's individuality."[7]

How can one define the union Fromm speaks of? To me, the word caring could replace union and the sentence would mean the same thing. "Mature love is *caring* under the condition of preserving one's integrity, one's individuality."

The extreme importance of these last two conditions—preserving one's integrity, one's individuality—was graphically illustrated to me a number of years ago. I was attending an open-ended Christian therapy group with friends. At one point during the session a middle-aged woman, with tears running down her cheeks, said she was experiencing great pain and difficulty in her life, because often when she passed strangers on the street she felt a desperate hate for them.

"What's wrong with me?" she sobbed out. "How can I hate them? I don't even know them!" That she was a Christian and therefore felt under a moral imperative to love rather than hate brother and sister human beings contributed to her distress.

I looked closely at this woman. She wore a shapeless, nondescript tweed suit. A button was missing from her suit jacket and the bottom of her skirt sagged on one side where the hem had come loose. Her hair was pulled untidily into a knot on top of her head, and she wore no makeup or jewelry. Her stockings were wrinkled about her ankles, and her shoes were "sensible" and homely.

"Who is she?" I whispered to my neighbor.

"You won't believe this," my neighbor whispered back, "but she is the head of the research department of a large corporation. She is a brilliant, capable woman," he continued, "but she lives at home with her parents and they treat her like a four-year-old."

It was suddenly clear to me why this woman "hated" strangers. The impossible role demanded of her at home had resulted in a tremendous amount of hatred and anger within her toward her parents. Her inability to free herself from her parents' domination had also resulted in overwhelming anger and hatred toward herself, hence her careless appearance. Apparently, she did not think she was worth fussing over. Because she seemingly did not dare to face and deal with her unacceptable feelings, she was unconsciously projecting her anger and hatred onto strangers, rather than dealing with her feelings and her circumstances more maturely and rationally.

This is an extreme example of what can happen when we do not allow our children to grow up, when we do not trust them more and more out of the psychological nest. It does, however, point up the fact that once a person has reached maturity agewise, she or he has also passed a psychological and spiritual checkpoint in life. As parents, we cannot choose whether or not we want to allow our children to pass this checkpoint, just as we cannot choose whether or not we want to let our babies grow physically out of babyhood or our children out of childhood. This is something that happens, and there is no stemming the tide. Neither do our children have any choice in the matter of growing up into adulthood. Peter Pan may have successfully managed to escape maturity, but no one else has been able to pull it off.

If we try to keep our children under our authority after they have reached the late teens, we are severely crippling them in their ability to deal with life. If, as emerging adults, they cannot make their own choices and decisions, even though these may be at variance with our wishes, a great deal of pain and difficulty is likely to await them five, ten, or twenty years in the future.

It seems part of the very structure of life that if a grown man or woman allows himself or herself to be dominated by one or both parents, he or she will end up hating both parents and self. If does not matter whether the adult child has clung to the domination of the parents or has inwardly rebelled against it, even though allowing the domination to continue. The result is the same. Something deep within the center of each person knows instinctively that the psychological umbilical cord to the parents must be cut. If this separation does not take place, the child becomes emotionally crippled to a greater or lesser extent.

If a relationship of mature caring between parents and child is to exist, there first has to be some sort of psychic separation, a letting go on both sides, a learning to live independently of the other. The paradox of real closeness between two persons lies in the ability of each to exist independently of the other. Only as grown children learn to exist independently of their parents and the parents of their grown children can each side be free to care about the other, to allow the other person to have his or her own feelings and not be too threatened by these feelings.

Up to now everything in this chapter applies with equal force to *any* adult child and his or her parents, not only to those family groups where one member is oriented toward same-sex relationships. Too often both parents and lesbian or gay children think, "If it weren't for the homosexual factor in our family, we would not have to deal with these problems of relationships."

Of course this is not true. The problem does not arise because one family member has a different sexual orientation. The same problem exists in families where all the children are heterosexual. It arises because the family is a community of human beings who must grow and change through the various stages in the lives of both parents and children.

There *is* one particular problem you as a lesbian or gay child must face that your straight sisters and brothers are not called on to cope with. Chapter 6 deals with your public self versus your private self, and chapter 4 with the fact that, as you were growing up, your mother and father parented only your public self. You lived with an un-spoken fear: "If they knew who I really was, would they still love me?" The person for whom your parents did things was a false self. Their care of you, their concern, their guidance, their support materially and emotionally, their understanding of you, their affirmation of you—all these things were given to the boy or girl, young man or young woman who you were impersonating; they were not given to the real you.

Part of the reason you have come out to your parents may be that you still want and need most of these things from them, and unconsciously—or perhaps consciously—

you are hoping your parents hear your cry of need and respond. Even if you have reached the age where you no longer need their physical care, their guidance, and their material support, you may still long for their concern about you, their emotional caring and support of you, their understanding, their affirmation of the person you really are.

Right here may be the crux of the matter for you and for your parents. You may be crying desperately to them, "Mother, Dad, please, *please, PLEASE* love me as I am." And they may be crying back to you just as desperately, "You have threatened my inmost self so strongly that I can't love the gay or lesbian you."

What can you, as a son or daughter—what can you, as parents—do in the face of such an impasse?

This book attempts to help you, both parents and children, discover what can be done. The resolution of the problem boils down to several things: being patient (time often *does* help, at least to an extent); coming to a new and deeper understanding of yourself, whether children or parents, because you cannot reach out to others if you do not understand yourself; struggling toward mature forms of love and caring.

But suppose, as parents, you cannot give what your child wants. Your values are too deeply embedded for you to change. How far *can* you go with your child? What *can* you offer? Can you at least say, "I want to keep in touch with you. I want to know about your job or your career. For the present I don't want to talk about your lesbianism (gayness), but I'd like to keep the door at least ajar between us"? Can you go this far? Can you be frank with your child about the limitations of what you can handle? I have found in dealing with my children that if I am honest with them about my real feelings, they can handle that much better than if I try to pretend I am feeling something I am not. My pretense puts a distance between us. It says,

"This is something we daren't touch or talk about." To breach this kind of silence later is difficult.

What you cannot do is ask your child to change so you will be comfortable. You may want your child to live a celibate life, or you may want him or her to become heterosexual. Psychologically, one cannot make oneself comfortable at the expense of another person without in some way destroying a part of the other person.

Looking at the impasse from the other side, what will you, as the gay or lesbian child, do if your parents cannot accept your sexual orientation?

You will have to learn to accept your parents as *they* are. This is not easy. And it happens to many children in many different situations that have nothing to do with sexuality, so you are not alone—for whatever this is worth to you. As I stated earlier, I spent at least thirty years trying to change my mother before I finally realized that I had to accept her as she was and do whatever was necessary to protect myself from her desire to dominate me—which she tried to do even at a distance of a thousand miles!

What can you do in order to live with the situation? You may need to allow yourself to experience all the grief and rejection you are trying to avoid. In this effort you may find considerable help in the chapter "Finishing" in Judy Tatelbaum's book *The Courage to Grieve*.[8] You deal with the situation by working with yourself, or you may need some help from a trained counselor. Whatever else you do, *do not* put your feelings aside, thinking they will go away if you pay no attention to them. You can play ostrich for fifty years, providing you do not have a nervous breakdown or develop ulcers, arthritis, or some other physical manifestation that forces you to confront the psychological pain. When you pull your head out of the sand the pain will be right there, as fresh and as agonizing as it was fifty years earlier. You may as well work it through now and then get on with living.

Some lesbian and gay people, as well as some parents, terminate the parent/child relationship. A number of parents have done this, but I know of only one same-sex-oriented person who has terminated the relationship with his family—not because they could not accept his sexual orientation (he has not come out to them), but because other aspects of the relationship were so hurtful to him he could not remain in the relationship. Perhaps other children have separated themselves from their parents because of the way the parents were dealing, or not dealing, with the same-sex orientation.

I am filled with the hope that, as a parent, you can accept the person your child really is. "Accept" does not necessarily mean "approve." No parent approves of everything his or her child does, and no child approves of everything his or her parents do.

Coming back to the definition of mature love, can you *care* about the other while still leaving him or her, parent or child, free to be himself or herself? As a grown child, you cannot "go home again" in the sense of returning to emotional dependence on your parents. If you try it, you end up hating yourself and your parents. As parents of a grown child, you cannot keep your child in the same dependent relationship that existed during his or her growing-up years.

Again, this does not mean parents and grown children cannot maintain warm relationships with each other. This does not mean grown children cannot talk over things with parents and get the parents' ideas and perspective on a job change, a proposed move, investment of money, or anything else. Happy are the adult children who have parents to whom they can go for advice and counsel, knowing that the parents will share what wisdom they may have on the subject and yet not try to coerce their children into something they do not want to do. Happy are the parents whose children feel comfortable turning to them—as well as to other adults, both peers and older friends—to talk over a matter that is important in their lives.

Happy also are the parents who can turn to their children and talk over their—the parents'—problems and decisions. Personally, I find it a continuing joy to be able to go to my children and discuss my concerns with them. I appreciate their listening and offering their ideas, even though I may not always take their advice or suggestions, just as they do not always take mine. It is exciting to me that the babies I nurtured and raised are now responsible people with whom I can have adult-to-adult interchange.

Real togetherness comes not from coercion. Rather, it can grow only in the soil of the freedom that comes from letting go of the other person. We, as human beings—parent or child—cannot ultimately satisfy our deepest needs through relationship to another person, no matter who this person is—child, parent, spouse, significant other, friend, mentor, therapist. We can satisfy our deepest needs only by being in touch with our deepest selves. It is out of our deepest selves that we discover the strength to give, to love, in a nondemanding way.

Letting go of parents by adult children and of adult children by parents is therefore not a destruction, an ending. Rather, it is a creative rearrangement of relationships that promises new and satisfying associations between parents and children. One of the marvelous facts of life is that every ending carries within itself the potential for a new beginning.

Chapter 8

Parents Also Come Out

Some years ago I visited my hometown. I was in the process of finding a publisher for my book *My Son Eric* and realized that if the manuscript were accepted for publication, it would only be a matter of time before my friends there learned that my son is gay. Before I went I decided, with Eric's approval, that whenever the opportunity arose I would say that Eric is gay.

The experiment provided me with some interesting insights. Mainly, I discovered that most people did not want to talk with me about my son's being gay. It seemed to be an uncomfortable topic for them. *I* may have been ready to talk about it, but they were unprepared to deal with the subject on such short notice.

In looking back on this experience I realize that, because of my desire to come out as the parent of a gay child, sometimes I may have introduced the subject inappropriately. Another side of the matter is that if one waited to come out until people were ready to receive the information, there would seldom be any coming out.

The last thing you may want to do at this point is come out to *anyone* as the parent of a lesbian or gay child. Or, the matter of your parental coming out may not be a big problem for you—but in that case you are probably not reading this book.

"Do I *have* to come out as the parent of a gay or lesbian child?" you may be wondering. "Can't I go through life without saying anything about this to anyone?"

To make things more difficult, your child may not understand why you do not want to acknowledge to others that your son is gay or your daughter is a lesbian, and he or she may be eager to push you toward such an open acknowledgment. If each of you has some understanding of the conflicting dynamics in the situation, this understanding may help you resolve the tension between you.

A parent's thoughts are apt to run something like this: "What will *my* parents, my brothers and sisters, my other relative, my friends, my minister or priest or rabbi, my coworkers think about me? They'll think I was a bad parent, that I did something wrong in raising my child. They'll think there is something wrong with my marriage, that it's a failure. Maybe they're right about all these things. I must have failed somewhere along the line or this wouldn't have happened."

The more unsure you are about yourself as a person or as a parent, the more terrifying may be the thought of standing revealed before others as the father or mother of a same-sex-oriented child. This is not merely an impersonal fact you are considering passing on. This is information that could confirm others' suspicions that you are an inadequate person, a stupid or a bad person, even a dismal failure. You may not be conscious of any of this, much less be able to express it. All you know is that *at all costs* this information about your child must be kept secret.

To your son or daughter, however, this need for secrecy may seem like betrayal. "My parents are ashamed of me. They are denying before our relatives and friends the person I really am. If my parents really loved me, they would let people know I'm lesbian (gay)."

When these two sets of attitudes meet, a collision is bound to result. To make matters more difficult, maybe neither side can express what each is really feeling. You, as parents, know only that your child is trying to force you to do something you are determined not to do, and your child knows only that you are being stubborn about something that is absolutely necessary to him or her. Each feels that the other "can't possibly love me or she or he (they) would do what I (we) ask."

Impasses like this are hard to break; being honest about one's deep inner feelings is not easy. Only when one is willing to endure the pain of expressing one's fears, when one musters the courage to do this, can any progress be made.

If you, as parents, could dare to verbalize your fears that your child's same-sex orientation results from your failure as parents, you would open the way to discovering that this is a false belief, that you are torturing yourselves needlessly. If your child could express the rejection she or he is feeling because of your refusal to tell others, you would at least have the opportunity to reassure your child that you love her or him and to ask for patience until you, too, are ready to come out. You could remind your child that it probably took her or him a while to decide to come out to others.

If you, as parents, do decide you are ready to come out, another question presents itself: "May I give this information about my child to anyone I want or should I check with my child first?"

No one answer applies to all situations. It is important to work out with your child both your and your child's real feelings in each particular situation. Whom do you want to tell or not tell? Why? Whom does your child want to tell or not tell? Why? Both you and your child may have to bring all your love, forbearance, courtesy, and patience to these discussions, as well as honesty about what each of you is really feeling. These discussions may be times of tension, but the tension can be constructive if both parties remember that words can wound, and strive to control tempers. "*I* feel pressured (threatened, unhappy, scared)" is always better than "*You* don't understand (care, love me)."

Tense as such discussions may get, they can result in greater understanding on both sides. They may not always result in complete satisfaction for you and your child. Almost by definition, family situations demand concession and compromise.

To understand why you do or do not want to tell a family member is also important. Rather than saying, "I can't possibly tell Grandpa," try to discover why you feel you cannot. Of course, you *can*—are physically able to— tell Grandpa. What you mean is, "I *choose* not to tell him." You may have excellent reasons for not sharing your information with him, and it will help you if you understand what these reasons are.

Too often we give away our power over circumstances unnecessarily, because we fail to understand the destructive impact of imprecise thinking. When you say, "I *can't* tell Grandpa," you are encouraging yourself to think of him as strong and of yourself as helpless. You may *choose* not to tell him because he has demonstrated a closed mind on the subject of homosexuality and you do not care to mount an assault on his prejudices at this time. You may need your energy for activities that are likely to be more productive. Or you may feel the information would close a door between you and a relative who may die within a few years, and you want to keep this door open. Be realistic about what you can deal with and what you do not care to deal with at this time, realistic about the reasons for your decision.

The difference between feeling you cannot tell and choosing not to tell may seem like a minor point to you, a game with words. Yet your phrasing can have an impact on whether you view yourself as a victim without control of the situation or as a responsible person who has control and can therefore look at the options and make a decision. All of us at various times in our lives are victims of happenings we have not chosen, that have been imposed on us by circumstances beyond our control. What we *do* control are our responses to the circumstances. When you confront a situation realistically you can decide whether you are willing to pay the price of the action you propose to take. If Grandpa is very old and has a serious heart disorder, you may choose to say nothing of your child's sexual orientation. You have weighed the factors involved and have made a choice.

If you believe that telling a close friend about your child's lesbianism or gayness would be the end of the friendship, you need to assess, realistically, this person's value to you. Why is he or she important to you? What do you get from the relationship that you do not want to sacrifice at this time? Whenever you feel helpless in the hands of another person you need to examine the hidden dynamics of the relationship if you are to remain healthy emotionally. Unconsciously, you may be giving the person power over your life that it is not necessary or desirable for you to give.

Conversely, you need to be aware of the realities of your situation. Is your job at stake? Is your friendship with a particular person very meaningful to you? Why? Is your position in a group—whether in church, in an organization, or in the community—at stake? Any of these situations is possible, and genuine wisdom would counsel you to keep your mouth shut in such a case.

Undeniably, there *are* obstacles to coming out, both for parents and for the lesbian or gay person. Society may exact a heavy penalty through job loss (or at least lack of advancement), through social rejection and ostracism, and through other forms of discrimination. Count the cost *be-*

fore taking action, rather than after. If you are not anxious to be a hero or heroine at this particular time in your life, you can *choose* not to be.

Also recognize that no one should try to choose the heroic role for another. I think especially of two different sets of parents of two gay men. Both sets of parents live in small towns and belong to theologically conservative churches. The father of each of these men is in a business that could be severely affected by community attitudes toward him. There are younger children in each case whom the fathers want to see through college, and each man is heading toward retirement in several years.

Should these men come out before their small communities as the fathers of gay sons and possibly jeopardize their businesses, their ability to provide for their younger children's education, their and their wives' social and religious life in the community, and their security in retirement? In cases like these, both parents and their same-sex-oriented children need to consider carefully all aspects of the situation. The heroic gesture is easier to make when one is younger and can more easily get another job or when one has no dependents. It is considerably more difficult to assume a heroic role when one has spent a lifetime in a particular community and has a standing it is important to maintain in order to cope with life. If you, parent or same-sex-oriented child, are going to be open about yourself, count the realistic cost beforehand, and be willing to pay whatever price may be exacted of you. If you decide not to make any disclosure at this time in your life, you need not condemn yourself or accept condemnation from another. Obviously, there are realistic reasons for remaining semicloseted, or else writing and reading books like this would not be necessary. You are treading a circular path: It is difficult to come out because of society's present attitudes, and yet society's attitudes are not likely to change until more people come out.

Both you and your lesbian or gay child should keep in mind that, although you may not be ready to come out now in a particular situation, this does not necessarily mean you will never be ready. Perhaps a year or two from now you will be able to do what seems impossible today. And if you are never ready, this is your privilege as a self-directing person. For your child to try to force you to do something is no more acceptable than for you to try to force your adult child into a particular course of action.

A different situation may arise if your child is an activist and appears in the media, making statements concerning gay and lesbian issues or marching in Gay Pride Week parades or taking part in picketing or sit-ins. In this case you may not have much choice as to whether or not you are going to come out of your parents-of-a-homosexual closet. Under these circumstances, if you are having a great deal of trouble dealing with your forced expulsion from the parental closet, you may want to consider seeking help from a trained counselor. It is surprising what good things can result sometimes from situations that initially appear dire or threatening. If you have been kicked from your comfortable berth, make every effort to come to terms with your particular problem, and retrieve all you can from what may seem, at first, to be a disastrous situation.

Seeking professional help is not easy. Perhaps one of the most difficult and courageous acts a person can perform is to pick up the phone and make an appointment for counseling. There is something within everybody that stubbornly resists such a step. Making an effort to reach out for help, however, is a positive choice that indicates strength rather than weaknesses. Sometimes the only means of moving away from the dead center of indecision is to say, "Right or wrong, I'm going to do this. If it turns out wrong, I'll try something else." Do whatever is necessary for you to come to terms with your circumstances.

What if you or your child is not ready to come out to aunts, uncles, cousins, grandparents, and so on, and yet these people periodically needle you and your child with questions about when Joe or Joanne is going to start dating or get married?

One of the best ways of dealing with such questions comes from a lesbian whose mother spoke of it on a nationwide television program. The young woman's grandmother had been asking her when she was going to get married. Her reply to her grandmother's question went something like this: "If I could be happy without being married, would you be happy for me?"

The basic approach of this answer can be adapted to many different situations. Two things are implicitly stated: The answer perceives caring on the part of the questioner and appreciates it, but what makes one person happy does not always do the same for another.

If you and your child decide to come out to other family members, remember that these family members may experience some grief reactions. They, too, are having a piece of disquieting information given to them that asks them to rearrange their perceptions and confront a sexual orientation with which they may be uncomfortable. Remember also that their initial reaction will not necessarily be the same as the feeling they may have later.

What about gatherings of the extended family at holidays and other occasions? Because such gatherings can present problems for the family with a lesbian or gay member who has a partner but is not yet "out" to the wider relationship, the Families of Gays and Lesbians group to which I belonged once planned a meeting around the topic "Can holiday family gatherings be happy—and gay?"

The group zeroed in on the subject from four angles:

1. If the gay or lesbian person has a partner, can he or she join the family group?

2. How does one explain the partner's presence to Grandma, Grandpa, Aunt Beth, Uncle Tom—or even to younger siblings and cousins?
3. Do you (as parents) even *want* your child's partner to join the celebration?
4. How might your lesbian or gay child feel if you do not want the partner at the festivities?

Although you may not have been aware of it before, suddenly you realize that these traditional family get-togethers are governed by unwritten but rather inflexible guidelines that do not include those unrelated by blood or marriage. You may feel that including a "friend of Joe's (Joanne's)" is the same as announcing your child's sexual orientation. (Possibly you are supersensitive about this and others might not draw this conclusion.)

The patterns that are "always" followed at such get-togethers can impart a sense of compulsion. Carl Whitaker remarks in *The Family Crucible* that it is difficult to be unfaithful to the rules of one's family, even though these rules may be largely unspoken.[1] What you "always do" on such occasions carries with it its own enforcement, and you may find it exceedingly difficult to break out of established patterns. Obviously, a different course of action will have to be taken, difficult as it may seem to you.

Your problem may be that the extended family is unaware of your child's sexual orientation—or it may be that the family is only too aware and does not want her or him at the gathering, much less her or his partner.

Whatever course of action your immediate family takes should be a joint decision, and as I have noted repeatedly, joint decisions are not arrived at easily, because they involve honesty about each person's real feelings. To say, "It doesn't matter to me," when it does matter, or "That's fine with me," when it really is not, only lays the groundwork for more difficulties in the future.

Whatever your family's situation there *is* a solution: It begins with honesty to yourself about your wishes and desires and a real listening to the honest feelings of other family members. Silent martyrdom has no place in a situation like this, nor does an uncritical feeling that you are in a trap from which you cannot extricate yourself.

Whenever you feel you have to conform to the pattern of previous years it is time to investigate why you feel this way. What are the unconscious pressures you are experiencing? Try to dig them out. What alternative arrangements can be made? If you follow a certain course of action one year, you do not necessarily have to follow it another year. You can decide (as a family) that "this year we will do what Mother and Dad want," and next year you will celebrate in the way the children want. You can decide that this is the year to take a short trip over Christmas. Maybe this decision *is* running away from the problem. What is wrong with that if it gets you through the holiday season? By the time next Christmas rolls around you may not need to run.

Perhaps the time has come to make a bold decision. One mother I know, who is a widow, has chosen to celebrate holidays with her son and his partner, neither of whom is welcome at the holiday gatherings of her other children and their families. Her straight children are not happy with her decision and have suggested that it would be fairer to celebrate some holidays with them and some with her gay son. She is a woman who knows her own priorities. She has told her straight children that they have their spouses, their siblings, and their children at holidays, and that until they include their brother and his mate, she will celebrate holidays with these two. Despite this one point of contention she maintains a good relationship with her other children and their spouses and sees them and her grandchildren at other times.

It *is* possible to break with traditional patterns, but often it is not easy to do so. Much depends on where you, as parents, are in terms of dealing with your child's sexual orientation. What you find impossible to do this year may be possible in a year or two. Situations that are very difficult now may one day be not nearly so difficult.

Coming out for your child has probably been a long, slow, step-by-step process. It is not likely to be much different for parents.

Chapter 9

Religious Issues and a Same-Sex Orientation

Although many parents have trouble accepting their child's lesbianism or gayness, religion may not be the primary issue. In some cases, however, as in mine, religion is—or seems to be—the most important consideration.

This chapter deals to some extent with various Jewish viewpoints and in a more extended fashion (because I am more familiar with this), with an evangelical-fundamental-charismatic theological position, which, for the sake of brevity, I generally refer to in the chapter as a conservative viewpoint.

The chapter is divided into six sections: Some Jewish Viewpoints; What Does the Bible Say About Homosexuality?; What Some Conservative Writers Say About Homosexuality; Can Same-sex-oriented Persons Really Change?; The Bible, the Church, and AIDS; and Is My Child Lost for Eternity?

Several listings in "For Further Reading" provide more detailed information on Jewish viewpoints.

At the end of this book are also listed several books written from a Christian viewpoint that throw a different light on the biblical passages generally believed to deal with homosexuality. Although these interpretations differ from the usual conservative stance, it is helpful for Christians to understand that there are various interpretations, made by earnest, dedicated Christian scholars.

For both Jewish and Christian parents, I call attention to the wisdom of Gamaliel, which he set forth in a situation totally unrelated to homosexuality. Nevertheless, the principle is valid in dealing with religious issues: "If this plan or this undertaking is of men, it will fail; but if it is of God, you will not be able to overthrow them. You might even be found opposing God!" (Acts 5:38–39).

Some Jewish Viewpoints

Many Jewish parents, depending on the way they interpret the Jewish scriptures, feel great anguish about a child's same-sex orientation because of their religion. Some of these parents deal with their pain over this issue by saying Kaddish (the prayer for the dead) for a lesbian or gay child. Are other Jewish responses possible? If so, what might they be?

In order to find out I contacted a number of Jewish persons and groups concerning the subject of a same-sex orientation and received diverse responses.

My question about their position on homosexuality to the Lubavitch—a group of the Hasidim, who themselves are a group within the Orthodox Jewish tradition—brought the quick, firm reply, "Homosexuality is taboo."

The Union of American Hebrew Congregations

As early as 1977 the General Assembly of the Union of American Hebrew Congregations (UAHC), representing the Reform Movement in North America, adopted a resolution regarding the human rights of same-sex-oriented persons. This body called for equal protection under the law and opposed discrimination in areas of opportunity, including employment and housing. It affirmed the belief that private sexual acts between consenting adults were not the proper province of government and law enforcement agencies, and urged its constituent congregations to conduct appropriate educational programs for youth and adults to provide greater understanding of the relation of Jewish values to the range of human sexuality.

In 1987 the UAHC General Assembly called for the full inclusion of gay and lesbian Jews in all aspects of synagogue life. However, while that resolution urged congregations not to discriminate in employment, it did not specifically address rabbinic employment, pending a report from the ad hoc Committee on Homosexuality and the Rabbinate of the Central Conference of American Rabbis (CCAR).

By 1989 the UAHC had admitted to membership four synagogues with an outreach to gay and lesbian Jews. Hundreds of men and women who had once felt themselves alienated from Judaism and unwelcome in mainstream congregations joined these synagogues, thereby adding strength and commitment to the Jewish religious community. In 1989 the UAHC reaffirmed its commitment to the work for full inclusion of gay and lesbian Jews to membership, as singles, couples, and families. It also commended the CCAR for its "sensitive and thorough efforts to raise the consciousness of the rabbinate regarding homosexuality." It further urged the CCAR to "pursue its own mandate with vigor and complete its tasks as soon as possible in order to respond to the communal and spiritual aspirations of gay and lesbian Jews."[1]

The Federation of Reconstructionist Congregations and Havurot

In January 1992 the board of directors of the Federation of Reconstructionist Congregations and Havurot, the lay arm of the movement, adopted the report of the Reconstructionist Commission on Homosexuality. The Reconstructionist Rabbinical Association passed the following resolution in March 1992:

We affirm all previous statements, policies, and resolutions of the Reconstructionist movement with regard to issues of homosexuality.

We endorse the spirit and intent of the document entitled *Homosexuality and Judaism: The Reconstructionist Position* and applaud its courage.

We return this document to the Reconstructionist Commission on Homosexuality and instruct the Commission to direct rabbis and their communities to study, discuss, and respond to the document with the intention of seeing that it be adopted in substance by the Reconstructionist Rabbinical Association and the Federation of Reconstructionist Congregations and Havurot in 1993.[2]

By March 1993 the Reconstructionist Rabbinical Association had unanimously adopted the report with minor changes of wording, not of content. Because of these changes, the report was resubmitted to the Federation of Reconstructionist Congregations and Havurot for final approval, a necessary matter of procedure, although approval without objection was anticipated. The rabbinical association also passed a set of seven guidelines to aid congregations in their use of the material.[3]

The document named above represents a thorough, scholarly approach to homosexuality and Judaism. The thirty-nine page document includes a section titled "Discussion of Values Fundamental to Reconstructionism That Undergird Our Stance on Homosexuality," values such as human dignity and integrity, holiness, equality, stable family and community life, and justice. Other sections deal with contemporary scientific understanding, Jewish sources in the light of science, and a Reconstructionist understanding of homosexuality. This approach "must be consistent with our experience, with our fundamental values, and with the knowledge available from contemporary science."[4] The Reconstructionist process of reintegration "should extend to issues that pertain to the inclusion of all Jews who are seeking to find religious fulfillment within our community." Reconstructionist groups see this as an issue of social justice as well as of Jewish survival.[5]

The report notes that in many states "legal protections such as those that protect other minorities do not exist. Legally, homosexuals are excluded from the civil right to marry one another, and they face major obstacles in child custody cases. The laws of some states ban a variety of sexual activity between consenting adults, including same-gender sex."[6]

The report goes on to say that committed same-sex life partners are denied the basic rights granted legal marital partners, such as access to joint tax filing and insurance policies, as well as the lack of visitation and control in the custodial care of a seriously ill partner. It further notes that in its most extreme form, bias resorts to violence, resulting in assaults against gay men and lesbians. Such violence is not clearly and consistently condemned and is even sanctioned by some people and groups. At the time the report was written, violence against same-sex-oriented people was on the rise.[7]

The report further labeled as anti-gay bias the fearful popular misconception that gay men and lesbians would sexually molest others, especially children. It compared this misconception to similar harmful negative myths about Jews during the Middle Ages.[8]

Although many individual persons and bodies within the Reform movement could not agree on an affirmation of committed same-sex relationships, the Reconstructionist approach to homosexuality states:

We affirm the importance of loving, caring, intimate relationships as a primary source of companionship and comfort. . . . We affirm the qualities of mutual respect, trust, care, and love in committed relationships regardless of sexual orientation. Gay and lesbian partnerships embody these values no more or less than do heterosexual marriages. As we celebrate the love between heterosexual couples, so too do we celebrate the love between gay or lesbian Jews. As we affirm that heterosexual marriages embody *kedushah* [holiness], so do we affirm that *kedushah* resides in committed relationships between gay or lesbian Jews.[9]

Traditionally, the Jewish community has believed that all its members should be married and create families. The Reconstructionist statement now acknowledges that there may be valid reasons for the decision by people—lesbian, gay, or heterosexual—to remain single, and that such people should be treated as equally valued members of the Jewish community.

Furthermore, it encourages "individuals of both sexual orientations to create permanent family units and to raise children," an undertaking "significant to personal growth and satisfaction." Such family units should be committed to the human dignity of all members. In addition, Jewish communities should welcome and support individuals and families regardless of their type of family structure and do everything within their means to enable them to find comfort in belonging.[10]

The Reconstructionist Commission on Homosexuality has also issued a study and discussion manual, *Homosexuality and Judaism: A Reconstructionist Workshop Series*, a 119-page publication with comprehensive material for eight workshops, together with five appendices.[11]

Conservative and Orthodox Movements

The Conservative movement attempts to balance a concern for the rights of the individual with fidelity to the stance held by the historical Jewish sources. During the 1990 Convention of Conservative Rabbis, the Rabbinical Assembly passed a resolution in support of civil rights for gay men and lesbians, while affirming and recommending the traditional life of heterosexuality. This resolution "welcomed gay and lesbian Jews in Conservative synagogues, deplored anti-gay violence, and called on the Conservative movement and its affiliates 'to increase our awareness, understanding and concern for our fellow Jews who are gay and lesbian.'"[12] Nevertheless, the discussion about the resolution indicated clearly that the Conservative movement is far from ready to accept openly gay or lesbian rabbis, or to give gay men and lesbians equal status within the leadership of congregations or the movement."[13]

When the Executive Committee of the National Jewish Community Relations Advisory Council (NJCRAC) met in the fall of 1992, it adopted a policy statement on discrimination based on sexual orientation. Consistent with the NJCRAC's "longstanding and deeply-held position in opposition to discrimination," the council "opposes discrimination based on sexual orientation in employment, housing, public accommodation, and education; supports legislation to bar discrimination in these areas; supports the incorporation in such legislation of exemptions, that may already exist in other civil-rights laws, designed to protect the right of religious institutions to carry out their religious purposes."[14]

The Union of Orthodox Jewish Congregations of America, a part of the NJCRAC, abstained from voting on this issue. It has stated that it is opposed to discrimination and vigilantism against any individual or group, yet because the Halacha prohibits homosexual activity, it cannot join in a statement that could be misinterpreted to imply other-wise. The NJCRAC notes that several community member agencies also abstained.[15]

Two Personal Viewpoints

In preparing to write the first edition of this book I asked a Jewish lesbian who understood the Jewish religious community in some depth about its position regarding homosexuality. The gist of her reply (not quoted verbatim) is as true today as it was then:

> There is no one position that all Orthodox, Conser-vative, or Reform Jews take concerning homosexu-ality. Even within the three traditions there is no unanimity. It depends on who is doing the inter-preting of the scriptures. If you find that your rabbi or the people in your synagogue are rigidly anti-homosexual, find yourself another group of Jewish people who will accept you. There are some. As far as parents are concerned, many use their professed religiosity to maintain their anti-homosexual beliefs. In other words, they use their religious beliefs to rationalize a cultural prejudice.

Rabbi Moshe Adler, formerly of the B'nai B'rith Hillel Foundation at the University of Minnesota, offered wise counsel that can speak to the hearts of parents whose religious beliefs and family affections may be at war. He pointed out that rabbis perform two functions: the magis-terial function and the pastoral function. The magisterial function refers to the authoritative teaching of Jewish law and ethic, seeking to define what is right and what is wrong. The pastoral function refers to caring for the needy and the hurt, regardless of their level of religious belief or practice. Rabbi Adler said:

> When same-sex-oriented persons or their families come to a rabbi, the rabbi should deal with them

primarily in a pastoral way, acting out through his own compassion the love of God. Gay or lesbian people and their families come to the rabbi because they want to know that God still loves them and that their own religious community will not cast them out.

You know, God gives us laws as disciplines to holiness, not as mere exercises in obedience. Because God is both just and compassionate God's laws must be construed to reflect that balance of justice with compassion. For this reason, I believe, God's law does not demand heterosexuality of a person for whom this is an impossibility. It seems to me that, in this matter as in all others, the Torah's directive presupposes a person's ability to make a moral choice in full freedom and not under duress. Someone who can choose to "swing" either way, sexually speaking, can meaningfully be commanded to limit his or her "swinging" to one way and not another. It is within the justice of God that he command us and expect our freely given compliance. Here, as in the dietary laws, for example, the commandments discipline our appetites by requiring that we satisfy them in a manner sanctioned by the Creator. Where, however, homosexuality is not simply a matter of satisfying one's appetites, but is the only manner in which a person is able to give and receive adult love and thereby make a loving commitment to another human being, it cannot, I would argue, come under the Torah's prohibition.

Rabbi Adler went on to point out that the community is often selective about the sins for which it excludes people.

Many people violate the Sabbath, but nobody is thrown out of the synagogue or kept from positions of community leadership because of it, even though

Sabbath observance is, by both scripture and tradition, the central covenantal institution of Judaism. There's got to be some emotion other than religious zeal behind this anti-homosexual bias.

When the parents of a homosexual person come to me I encourage them to talk at length about their concerns, and then I say, "Before we start looking at any scriptural or Talmudic passages, can you talk about what's really bothering you? What prevents you from accepting your child?" Usually, they're not really talking about religion. The reason they are finding it so difficult to deal with their child's homosexuality is that they themselves have hang-ups about sexuality and sex roles.

Conventional ideas about the roles of men and women make it very hard for a Jewish family to accept a gay or lesbian child. The family, traditionally regarded as the nuclear unit of Jewish life, still tends to assign conventionally sex-based roles to its members. The man is expected to be a tower of strength. The woman is expected to enable the man to come across as this impossible tower of strength, to pick up the pieces when he comes apart under the strain, and to keep herself together lest the family unit collapse. In such a structure a gay son will be seen as effeminate and therefore powerless—not a real man; a lesbian daughter will be seen as masculine and therefore dominating—not a real woman. In either case, parents and children are apt to feel they have failed each other. Mother and father ask, "Where did we go wrong?" Gay son or lesbian daughter asks, "Even though you don't approve of my life-style, can you not love me?"

One of the best things the family can do is go into family therapy and work the whole thing through *together*. The family rabbi can make the referral and continue supplementing the therapy in his pastoral and supportive role.

And what of the Torah? People so often seem to forget that, in addition to prohibiting things, the Pentateuch also commands, "You shall love your neighbor as yourself." Jesus didn't make that up; he was quoting from the Torah. There is a story of a man who came to a Hasidic master and said, "My son is straying. What shall I do with him?" The master replied, "Love him more." This is essentially what I tell parents whose child has just come out to them: Love your gay son or lesbian daughter more, because with all the problems society will put in your child's path, he or she will need your love more urgently than ever.

What Does the Bible Say About Homosexuality?

When I learned about Eric's sexual orientation all my ideas about why homosexuality is unacceptable focused on what I believed the Bible had to say on the subject. I believed in the inerrancy of the Bible, that it is without error in all that it affirms and is the only infallible rule of faith and practice.

How can one argue with a statement like this? It sounds so simple, so irrefutable, so right. If one is going to believe the Bible, one has to believe *all* of it. One cannot pick and choose what one is going to believe or one empties the Word of God of all meaning.

The Bible, however, is not a simple, self-evident book. Let us look at several of the problems encountered in understanding the Bible.

1. *Most of us read from translations of the Bible, rather than from the original Hebrew or Greek manuscripts. For this reason one translation of a passage may state one thing whereas another*

translation states something different. This may happen because the translators have worked from more ancient and therefore, presumably, more accurate manuscripts. This also happens because translators are not automatons, and inevitably, they incorporate their own theology and ethics into their translations. Their choice of the English words they use grows out of their particular theological and ethical position and can represent a particular viewpoint.

John Boswell has put his finger on another difficulty we need to be aware of as we read the Bible.[16] He says that the passage of thousands of years often obscures, sometimes beyond recovery, the exact meaning of words in the languages of ancient people whose experiences and life-styles were very different from ours.

In addition, the original manuscripts physically present many problems. Parts of them may be disintegrating, with the result that words crucial to the meaning of a passage may not be there, gone forever. Hebrew texts were originally written without vowel marks, which were only later introduced to minimize ambiguity. Thus even the most conscientious scholars often have difficulty in making a translation that accurately reflects what the original writer was saying.

While some conservative scholars and many conservative Christians believe God has given us an inerrant original text, God certainly has not given us inerrant translations. In fact, the process of providing us with a Bible would appear, humanly speaking, to be hit and miss. From our finite point of view there would seem to be less possibility of errors creeping in if God had given the biblical message engraved on tablets of stone or cast on gold plates to ensure its survival in one form and one form only.

Yet we find God risking the use of perishable skins, cryptic writing, necessity of translation hundreds or thousands of years after the writing—and not even a sure and certain designation of which manuscripts were the inspired Word of God and which were not.

None of this is intended to indicate that the Bible is *not* God's word to us. This does mean that often the meaning of a particular passage is difficult to nail down. Why, we might wonder, was the Creator so casual in the methods used to provide us with the Bible?

Divine Truth Versus a Literal Interpretation

2. *Those who say the Bible is the infallible word of God cannot mean that every word of the Bible is historically accurate*, as many conservative biblical scholars believe. Francis Schaeffer spells out the dilemma: "What sense does it make," he asks, "for God to give us true religious truths and at the same time place them in a book that is wrong when it touches history and the cosmos?"[17]

With minimal research one realizes that this *is* what God has done. In Genesis 1 and 2 two different accounts of creation are given and they do not agree. Which account is correct? And although each of the four Gospels tells the story of Christ's life, they differ in many significant ways. In the first three Gospels the Last Supper takes place at the Passover meal. In John's Gospel Jesus is crucified on the day the lambs are sacrificed in the temple for the Passover meal. So in the fourth Gospel the Last Supper takes place before the Passover day. Which account is correct?

John Marsh, in discussing the difference in historical facts among the four Gospels, makes the point that these manuscripts were not written as historical records, but as theological treatises, to highlight particular aspects of God's message through Jesus Christ to humanity.[18]

In commenting on such differences in the Bible, C. S. Lewis has written: "The very *kind* of truth we are often demanding was, in my opinion, never even envisaged by the ancients."[19]

Those who say, "Every word in the Bible must be true historically and scientifically as well as spiritually" are afraid that if people can say parts of the Bible are not accurate in these ways, they can then go on to say, "Why should I believe that Jesus Christ rose from the dead? You can't prove it."

It appears to me that this is why God has gone about giving us the Bible in such a seemingly casual way and has allowed material to be included that is not necessarily historically accurate in every instance. (There are undoubtedly many other reasons. I make no claim to having any direct revelations from God on this subject. I speak as a human being making human deductions from study, observation, and experience.)

"Now faith is the assurance of things hoped for, the conviction of things not seen" (Heb. 11:1). I do not believe God intends to prove the reality of the divine Selfhood in the ways we humans would go about proving it. I therefore believe that the Bible presents to us *divine truths*, which is not the same as saying that every word of the Bible is scientific and historical fact. Moreover, we often have to dig to understand what these truths are; many are not self-evident.

Nor does the Bible contain the answer, in easy prooftext form, to every problem that may arise in anyone's life. Let us look at one well-known example.

For many years the Bible was used to prove that slavery is an acceptable way of treating human beings. Now Christians are using the Bible to show that slavery is incompatible with the Christian view of life. Christians have had to study the message of the Bible as a whole and make deductions from a variety of biblical principles in order to arrive at this conclusion. Not even such a dominant and authoritative figure as Paul made any definitive statement against slavery. Instead, he sent a runaway slave back to his master, accompanied by a letter that is now known as the Epistle to Philemon.

Interpreting the Bible's Meaning

3. *If the interior meaning of the Bible is so difficult to discern, and if we have to work so hard, how can we be sure* what *God intended?* Such indefiniteness does not seem fair to us human beings who are trying, with finite minds, to understand and obey an infinite God. It may even threaten us. If we cannot be precisely sure of what God is saying, how can we know we are doing what God wants us to do? How can we *know* we are saved?

I offer a few thoughts in relation to the above questions. First, it appears God preferred to give us a book that would offer enough material to keep the wisest person occupied for a lifetime without ever coming to the end of what the Bible has to offer. In the Bible, God has provided an inexhaustible supply of treasures. These are presented in a form that requires us to read, study, wrestle, think, and pray and that necessitates interaction between God and ourselves in order to understand what any particular passage of the Bible is saying.

Furthermore, there are different levels of meaning. One verse or passage may speak to us truly but superficially at one point in our lives, and at another time we may find this same verse or passage speaking to us more deeply. "Why didn't I ever see it in this light before?" we wonder, because now the truth of which we are suddenly aware seems almost self-evident. The deeper insight comes, of course, because *we* are ready to perceive it, not because the message has changed or because God was not ready to impart it to us before.

Then there is the problem of whether we should interpret the Bible in light of the conditions that prevailed at the time each particular book was written or whether we should accept the precepts contained in the Bible as a message given once but applicable as it stands to all eras.

It is difficult to make a good case for the latter position without getting into many problems. We cannot take every statement in the Bible at face value and try to put it into practice or, among other things, we would be putting people to death for adultery (Leviticus 20:10); no person born out of wedlock—or for that matter that person's descendants for ten generations—would be allowed in church (Deuteronomy 23:2); and the roof of every house would have to have a railing around it (Deuteronomy 22:8).

4. *We cannot understand what the Bible is saying to us today* until *we understand what the conditions were at the time those words were written, and therefore what those words really mean. Only then can we understand what* underlying truths or principles *we should apply to our present-day situations.* Otherwise, we arrive at erroneous conclusions as to what we should or should not be doing. Even those who believe in the "literal" interpretation of the Bible have to rationalize their nonadherence to many of the Bible's directives.

It is enlightening that present-day careful research into Paul's writings reveals Paul in a new light with respect to the position of women. If we read 1 Corinthians 14:34-35, for example, against the background of conditions in Paul's day, we discover that the Greek word translated as speak is *lalein*, which "refers primarily to utterance rather than meaningful communication," according to Richard and Catherine Clark Kroeger.[20] The writer of an ancient dictionary defined the term as "to talk nonsense." Knowing that in certain pagan Greek rituals "frenzied shouting was expected from women and considered a necessary ingredient" of worship, one begins to realize that Paul *was* speaking to specific difficulties that occurred, because his congregation was made up of newly converted pagans.

In further clarification of the passage the Kroegers say that "women were encouraged to question their husbands at home, since the women had usually been denied an opportunity for education." "For it is shameful for a woman to speak in church," Paul wrote, in 1 Corinthians 14:35. If he was referring to gossip or meaningless pagan shouting, this throws a new light on the real meaning of the passage.

Gang-Rape, Idolatry, and "Shameless Acts"

Some theologians and scholars feel that, at times, Paul was in error in what he said, that his wisdom was not infallible. Certainly we know that in some instances Paul makes a distinction between his human instructions to a congregation and specific ones he has received from God (1 Corinthians 7:10, 12, 25; 2 Corinthians 11:17).

But if we might have *misinterpreted* Paul's teachings about women, might we also have misinterpreted the biblical passages dealing with homosexual acts? Notice that I did not say *homosexuality*. The Bible does not deal with homosexuality in the sense of giving guidance for those who have a same-sex orientation to life. The Bible speaks only of certain same-sex abuses: attempted gang rape (Genesis 19 and Judges 19), lust as an expression of idolatry (Romans 1) and what seems to be exploitative and extortionistic homosexual prostitution (Leviticus 18:22; 20:13; 1 Corinthians 6:9; 1 Timothy 1:10). The Bible says nothing, as Virginia Mollenkott points out, about a *same-sex orientation* or about homosexual *love*.[21]

Reread the story of Sodom and Gomorrah and you will notice the following points:

- The men of Sodom wanted to *gang-rape* the two visitors to the city. (Homosexual gang-rape was a standard practice in those days by which conquering armies humiliated their fallen foes.)

164

- One would not suppose the whole population of Sodom was homosexual, or why would Lot have moved there in the first place, why would two of the men be betrothed to Lot's daughters, and why would Lot have offered the men his daughters to distract them from demanding his guests?
- What the men of Sodom were proposing was the *gang-rape of God's messengers.* This introduces the dimension of attempting to degrade the Hebrew God.

The real sins of Sodom, according to Ezekiel 16:49-50, seem to have been "pride, surfeit of food, and prosperous ease"; not aiding the poor and needy; and being "haughty" and doing "abominable things" before God. Strong's *Exhaustive Concordance of the Bible* gives "idolatrous actions" as one of the meanings of the Hebrew word translated as "abominable things."[22]

In the New Testament Jesus refers to Sodom and Gomorrah in connection with the rejection of his message in various cities (Matthew 10:15; 11:23-24; Luke 10:12). There is no connection between Sodom's sexual behavior and Jesus' condemnation of these cities. Rather, he appears to be referring to Sodom's violation of the almost sacred ancient Eastern code of caring for the wayfarer within a city's gates.

Here we should note that the English word sodomite, used in some versions of the Bible, is not a translation of a Hebrew word. Instead, it is a word which encapsulates and perpetuates a cultural misunderstanding. "No Hebrew or Greek word formed on the name 'Sodom' ever appears in the biblical manuscripts on which these versions are based," says Victor Furnish. In every instance in the *King James Version* where the word sodomite is used, "the reference is to male prostitutes associated with places of worship." He further points out that the Old Testament text attacks male prostitutes, not because they had sexual relations with other males, but rather (as also in the case of female prostitutes) because they were serving alien gods.[23]

In Leviticus 18:22 and 20:13 there is no doubt that the writer is condemning homosexual acts. Or is there? John Boswell points out that the Hebrew word translated as abomination "does not usually signify something intrinsically evil, like rape or theft," but rather something that is ritually unclean for Jews, like eating pork or engaging in intercourse during menstruation.[24]

That the act described in Leviticus 18:22 could be connected with the worship of idols is also indicated by the fact that the previous verse prohibits the sacrifice of one's children (*Revised Standard Version* translation) to Molech. In the *King James Version* "children" is translated as "seed," leading Boswell to comment that "the prohibition of homosexual acts follows immediately upon a prohibition of idolatrous sexuality. . . . 'And thou shalt not let any of thy seed pass through the fire to Molech.'"[25]

Again, Strong's *Concordance* provides us with a different understanding of "abomination," giving "idolatry" or "an idol" as meanings. In fact, it says, "especially idolatry."[26] If we read verse 22 with this translation—"You shall not lie with a man as with a woman: it is idolatry"—we get a different understanding of the verse, especially taken in conjunction with verse 21.

In Romans 1:18–32 the main drive of the passage is that the Gentiles (pagans) ought to have recognized God's sovereignty and holiness because they could see it all around them in nature. Instead, they foolishly worshiped idols. Because of this, God gave them up to lust. An example of this lust is given in verses 26 and 27, and then Paul reverts to his main argument that because the Gentiles did not acknowledge God, the Creator gave them up to a base mind and improper conduct. Interestingly, in the intensive catalog of their sins that Paul lists in verses 29–31, homosexual acts are not mentioned. In fact, in those verses he does not allude to any sin of a sexual nature. The passage as a whole focuses not on homosexual acts but on idolatry.[27]

Several points about verses 26 and 27 should be noted. First, this is the only passage in the Bible that mentions homosexual behavior of women, calling it unnatural but not amplifying this further.[28] Paul is more explicit about the men, who are "consumed with passion for one another," committing "shameless acts" with men "and receiving in their own persons the due penalty for their error."[29]

Furnish throws some interesting light on the "shameless acts." In biblical times, he says, homosexual acts were seen as the overflow of a heterosexual lust so fierce that intercourse with women could no longer satisfy it. He demonstrates this clearly with two quotations from ancient writers. One is Dio Chrysostom, a first-century Roman, who wrote that when a man finds there is no scarcity of women (especially prostitutes) and no resistance to his advances, he will feel contempt for such easy conquests and scorn for a woman's love. Such a man "will turn his assault against the male quarters," believing that there "he will find a pleasure difficult and hard to procure."[30] The other quotation is from Philo Judaeus, a Jewish philosopher of Alexandria and a contemporary of the apostle Paul: "Not only in their mad lust for women did they violate the marriages of their neighbors, but also men mounted males without respect for the sex nature which the active partner shares with the passive."[31]

Two other New Testament passages deal with homosexual acts: 1 Corinthians 6:9–10 and 1 Timothy 1:10. Or do they? John Boswell points out that one of the two Greek words, in 1 Corinthians 6:9, *malakos*—which in a number of translations has been coupled with the other Greek word and translated as homosexual—means, basically, soft. It is used in Matthew 11:8 with this meaning and elsewhere in the New Testament as "sick" (see Matthew 4:23; 9:35; and 10:1).

"In a specifically moral context," Boswell writes, "it very frequently means 'licentious,' 'loose,' or 'wanting in self-control.'" He goes on to point out that "the word is never used in Greek to designate gay people as a group" or even to refer to homosexual acts as a type of behavior. Often, he says, it occurs in other writings from the same period as Paul's letters in reference to heterosexual persons or activity.[32]

The second Greek word is *arsenokoites*, which appears in 1 Corinthians 6:9 and in 1 Timothy 1:10. It is made up of two words, *arsen*, meaning male, and *koite*, meaning bed. What is not clear is the action the male is performing. The phrase means simply "lying [with] a male" or "one who lies with a male." The word could mean a male prostitute who serviced women or men. General usage of the word in Paul's day referred to prostitution and did not denote homosexuality.[33]

Preserving the Integrity of Scripture

Robin Scroggs' book *The New Testament and Homosexuality* greatly amplifies the situations suggested by Boswell's translation of individual words. Scroggs has made an exhaustive study of the New Testament passages that are seen as dealing with homosexual acts. If we dare sum up in one sentence the contents of Scroggs' book, it is that the homosexual acts referred to in the New Testament dealt with pederasty, slave prostitution, and idolatry. Of course, such a stripped-down statement doesn't begin to do justice to the wealth of careful research Scroggs has done, the various shades of meaning in different passages, and the background against which the passages were written.

Among the conclusions Scroggs draws are two that are vitally important for the present-day church: "*The context today must bear a reasonable similarity to the context which called the biblical statements into existence"* (Scroggs considers this so vital that he italicizes the words) and "Paul's judgments may . . . be eternally valid but can, nevertheless, be *valid only against what he opposed.* If he opposed something specific, then his statements cannot be generalized beyond the limitations of his intentionality without violating the integrity of the Scripture. Thus New Testament statements can be applied only to situations which are similar to those addressed by the New Testament" (again, Scroggs' italics).[34] Scroggs then turns his statement around, saying, "If the contemporary situation is not reasonably similar, then biblical injunctions cannot become answers to contemporary questions. If the situation proves to be noticeably different, then it is the proper course of action not to use such injunctions to decide contemporary issues, *however much the believer considers the Bible to be authoritative"* (his italics).[35]

Despite these assertions, the conservative church continues to quote these scriptures to prove that the Bible condemns a same-sex orientation. Because few of us are knowledgeable enough to interpret the Hebrew or Greek of the original manuscripts, we have to rely on what the translators think most closely approximates the original meanings, and as pointed out earlier, translators do have biases. We also must rely on what church leaders and scholars tell us. In the end we accept a translation on trust—trust in the person or persons who have made the translation, trust in the people who interpret the scriptures to us. We can do nothing else.

By now it must be clear that there are many possible ways of translating and interpreting the biblical passages dealing with homosexual acts. Usually, we tend to read only those authors whose theology coincides with our own and will therefore reinforce our beliefs. We may be willing to concede that the others have done a great deal of research, but we cannot believe that they really know the Lord. How could they and still write the things they do?

But perhaps we are not allowing the real message of the scriptures to come through. Perhaps we are putting God in the box of our own prejudices and biases. Uncomfortable and threatening as this idea may be, you owe it to yourself and your gay or lesbian child to try to read with an open mind. Such scholars as Scroggs, Furnish, Boswell, Rev. John McNeill, Letha Scanzoni, and Virginia Mollenkott carefully document the reasons for their interpretation of these passages.[36] It is impossible to make an intelligent appraisal on any subject without looking at both sides of the question.

There is *no perfect interpretation* of the Bible, just as there is no perfect translation. You can choose to believe the conservative writers who hammer away at the idea that a same-sex relationship is sinful because it is a same-sex relationship. Or you can choose to believe what would seem to be a more accurate understanding of biblical manuscripts. God has given no one person or group a complete and unerring interpretation of the Bible from beginning to end. Had God wanted to give such an interpretation, this could have been accomplished. It would seem, instead, that the divine intention is for human beings to struggle with the biblical material, to learn and grow as they interact with it in the light of new knowledge, both religious and scientific, and thus to move continually onward in humankind's struggle from the Garden of Eden to the New Jerusalem.

What Some Conservative Writers Say About Homosexuality

At the time that I wrote the first edition of *Coming Out to Parents*, I discussed a number of books by conservative writers that were on the market at that time. Most of these books are no longer in print. Two of them, however, are

still available: Tim LaHaye's *The Unhappy Gays*, now retitled *What Everyone Should Know About Homosexuality*, and
surprisingly, an extremely right-wing, hardline book by
Greg Bahnsen, *Homosexuality: A Biblical View*.

Although LaHaye's book has been retitled, nothing in it
has changed. My original objection was that it contained
much misinformation and wishful thinking without including documentation about how the author arrived at
his conclusions.

"No one is born homosexual, nor is it something over
which he has no control—unless he *thinks* he has no control over his sexual direction," LaHaye says, without giving any evidence to support this conclusion.[37] The trouble
with refuting such a misleading sentence is that the information to disprove statements of this kind is based on
scientific studies, and these resist short, bumper-sticker
summaries.

Over the years there have been many studies that show
in one way or another that people indeed may be born
homosexual, that the only control they have is their degree of sexual activity, not the objects of their sexual desire. For instance, a three-year study by James Weinrich
and Richard Pillard of the Boston University School of
Medicine found that gay men are five times more likely
than heterosexuals to have a gay brother, suggesting that
homosexuality runs in families. Pillard concluded that
"being a gay male is a familial trait. It isn't just randomly
distributed" and that the findings are "compatible with the
genetic theory."[38]

Unreliable "Facts"

A number of LaHaye's assertions indicate a lack of understanding of human nature. For instance, he states that
every counselor he interviewed acknowledged that "homosexuals are unquestionably more miserable than
straight people."[39] Wouldn't you be miserable if you were

unaccepted by society, in fear for your job, and in general treated by society, the law, and religion as a second-class citizen? LaHaye also writes: "Angry people are not happy people, and it seems that homosexuality foments a hostile way of life."[40] Apparently it does not occur to him that gay and lesbian persons may be angry—justifiably—at the way in which society devalues their personhood.

LaHaye believes that people choose to live as gay persons because they have been fooled into thinking that a gay life-style implies a more cheerful, high-spirited way of living than heterosexual people have.[41] "Anyone considering homosexuality as a life style ought to face the realistic fact that it is extremely conducive to rejection"[42]—as if the gay or lesbian person is not thoroughly aware of this!

"Every country and civilization that has endorsed homosexuality as an optional life-style has seen an increase in homosexuality."[43] Thus LaHaye sweeps hundreds of sociological and anthropological studies into one brief misstatement. Apparently he does not realize that throughout history roughly 10 percent of the population has been gay or lesbian. When a same-sex orientation is proscribed by law, very few people publicly acknowledge their sexual status. When the laws are not so strict, more men and women come out of their closets, but homosexuality itself does not increase.

LaHaye ends his book on a paranoid note: "Some people believe that an international network of homosexuals has been working its way into governments for years."[44] The probable basis for this statement indicates that nothing is too farfetched or outdated for anti-homosexual persons to seize upon. In Germany in the first years of this century a scandal involving Friedrich Krupp of the Krupp armaments company broke into public print in a periodical published by Maximilian Harden. Harden ran an editorial claiming the imperial court was controlled by a clique of "catamites" and that homosexuals formed an international conspiracy that created a bond across all barriers of creed, state, and class, uniting "the most remote, the most foreign. . . . All rally together against the common enemy."[45] Why is LaHaye so gullible—or so eager to use anything as ammunition for his cause—that he takes the unsubstantiated claim of a publisher made almost a century ago and presents it as a present-day threat?

Because LaHaye is still a popular figure in the conservative church, the unwary reader may be influenced by what such a supposed authority says, without understanding that LaHaye's "facts" have been filtered through his need to make them conform to his prejudices.

Austere and Uncompromising

Greg L. Bahnsen's *Homosexuality: A Biblical View* is written from the standpoint of theonomy, his overall philosophy that our country, and indeed the world, should be ruled according to the laws laid down in the Bible, particularly the Old Testament. To say that Bahnsen's position is stringent, harsh, stern, austere, and uncompromising is hardly an exaggeration.

> Christian ethics does not have its source in human research, evaluations, plans, or authority, but rather in the revealed Word of God. . . . Because God is omniscient, because He has created man with his specific nature, because He sovereignly governs every event of history, God does not depend upon man's modern research to make His law applicable or relevant to man's every historical situation. . . . God is not threatened with obsolescence; He and His law are relevant to every moment of finite man's existence. . . . It also needs to be underscored that the necessary, unquestionable, and relevant law of God is absolute—there are no ex-

ceptions that go beyond the text of revealed Scripture.[46]

Furthermore, Bahnsen writes, "The moral law of God forever binds all persons, believers or not, to obedience. God's commandments are established forever; indeed, every one of His righteous ordinances is everlasting. Consequently, nothing can be subtracted from God's law or ignored."[47]

I hardly need add that, while Bahnsen does not say so explicitly, governing by means of biblical law would require putting gay men to death. "If . . . the moral code of Leviticus 18–20 is not received as inspired by God, then it is superfluous to debate its binding character."[48] Such binding would include putting adulterers to death (Leviticus 20:10), not rounding off the hair on one's temples or marring the edges of one's beard (Leviticus 19:27), not letting one's cattle breed with a different kind, not planting two kinds of seed in the same field, and not wearing clothing with two kinds of fibers (Leviticus 19:19). There would also presumably be sacrifices for peace offerings and guilt offerings (Leviticus 19:5, 21).

It is not surprising to find Bahnsen stating near the end of his book that "God does not—and has not been found to—contradict His clear message in Scripture by information revealed through nature, history, or any realm of creation."[49] If we follow this line of reasoning to its logical conclusion, the Bible is the ultimate historical and scientific textbook. But as C. S. Lewis said, "The very kind of truth we are demanding was often never even envisaged by the ancients."

Change or Celibacy

For a time conservative and mainline Christian writers played theological Ping-Pong with the issue of whether or not homosexuality is a sin. When one side came up with a new argument to support its contentions, the other side would discover a further argument to discredit its opponent. This would be duly refuted, and a new slant added to the well-worn arguments. Since both sides were dealing with at most a dozen verses of the Bible, it became increasingly difficult to find new information to keep the argument going.

Because all conservative religious writers start with the same basic premise—that the Bible says homosexuality is a sin—they must therefore establish that this is what the Bible actually states. They must prove that, one way or another, a homosexual orientation to life can be changed to heterosexual. Failing that, the authors need to prove that celibacy can be made to work for any and all homosexual people, since even a committed sexual relationship with a person of the same sex is, they believe, unacceptable to God.

Two works selected more or less at random indicate the direction many books and articles are now taking. Joe Dallas, president of Exodus International, the "ex-gay" umbrella organization, writes in *Desires in Conflict* with a disarming reasonableness. He makes no hardline arguments, as Greg Bahnsen does. He understands therapy-speak and the logical approach. He shows how it is presumably possible to change. At the end of his book he includes a brief appendix, "Answering Pro-Gay Theology."[50]

The other book, *The Broken Image* by Leanne Payne, details how gay men, lesbians, and "others suffering from similar sexual identity crises can be healed and reoriented toward normal sexuality by the power of the Holy Spirit working through healing prayer."[51]

It is always thrilling to hear of such healings. There is an aura of mystery about them. How can this be? We too want to experience such a miraculous event in response to whatever needs we may have. It certainly seems a lot easier than working through normal channels to accomplish whatever it is we want to accomplish. In some cases it may

be the only way healing will come to people such as quad-
riplegics, for example. Unquestionably there have been
real healings through prayer and anointing, through prayer for the healing of memories, perhaps even through ex-
orcisms. Not all such prayers are answered. The late Kathryn Kuhlman said that she did not know why some of
her prayers for healing for others were answered and
some weren't. She cautioned against assuming that a person's faith was deficient. She understood that God is not
our genie who must accede to our every demand.[52]

Agnes Sanford, whose healing ministry lasted many
years, said with wisdom and humor:

> Yes, I know all things are possible with God, but all
> things are not as yet possible with Agnes. . . . I am
> not as yet a wide enough channel for the full flow
> of the power of the Holy Spirit. No one born lame
> has as yet stood upon his feet and run and leaped
> by the mere stretching forth of my hand in the
> name of Jesus Christ. Therefore, one of the first
> works of wisdom is to decide when to stretch forth
> my hand and when to abstain.

Sanford cites the example of Jesus at the pool of Bethesda,
where, out of a multitude of sick folk, he healed one
man—and one only.[53]

C. S. Lewis, in *The World's Last Night*, says: "Prayer is
request. The essence of request, as distinct from compulsion, is that it may or may not be granted." He goes on to
comment that, although some passages in the New Testament seem "to promise an invariable granting of our prayers," we have only to look at Christ in the Garden of
Gethsemane to realize that this cannot be what those passages really mean. "The holiest of all petitioners prayed
three times that a certain cup might pass from Him. It did

not. After that the idea that prayer is recommended to us as a sort of infallible gimmick may be dismissed."[54]

Can Same-sex-oriented Persons Really Change?

The matter of change is more complex than many conservative writers care to admit. Who are the persons who have been "cured"? Had they lived as same-sex-oriented persons for some time? Had they had only a few homosexual encounters? (Alfred Kinsey found that more than 33 percent of the male population had had homosexual encounters.[55]) Had they had homosexual fantasies but never a homosexual encounter? Do they fall near the center on the Kinsey scale, indicating that they are not exclusively homosexual, although they find same-sex encounters provide greater emotional and sexual fulfillment than heterosexual encounters?

And those who claim high rates of cure—what do their follow-up statistics look like? Is the person still satisfied with his or her new heterosexual orientation five years, ten years, fifteen years after treatment? Before I can accept that the new heterosexual orientation is permanent, I need to know the person's track record over a period of time. Then I will believe in the reality of that person's change-over.

It is all too easy, if one is sufficiently motivated, to repress one's homosexual desires into the unconscious, to consciously choose heterosexual reactions, and thus to believe that one has been healed, changed, and cured. If one has grown up in a church that declares homosexuals to be "seriously disordered," as the Catholic church does, or that declares homosexuality a sin and the gay or lesbian person's soul therefore lost for eternity, it may be possible for a time to imagine oneself changed. There is strong pressure for a person to perform the psychological sleight-of-hand that will enable a gay man or lesbian woman to believe he or she is no longer subject to homosexual desires.

The number of people who once headed so-called ex-gay ministries, which purport to move people out of homosexuality and into heterosexuality, is not encouraging. (See Appendix 2.) In addition, the definition of "overcoming homosexuality" varies greatly and is acknowledged to be "a long and complicated process" in which there is "a high rate of backsliding into homosexual practice within the ministries," according to Alan Medinger of Regeneration ministry.[56] Joe Dallas himself said on a radio program in Los Angeles that ex-gay does not mean ex-homosexual. "He explained that 'ex-gay' is more convenient than having to spell out each time that 'ex-gay' is a quick way to speak of 'Christians who have homosexual tendencies who would rather not have those tendencies. . . . It just rolls off the tongue better.' "[57]

Mario A. Rodriguez of the Dallas-based Alternative Identification Ministry (AIM) went even further when he said, after spending two years in AIM: "I never saw anyone 'cured' of their homosexuality. Instead, I saw many people hurt by AIM's message that a fundamental part of their being was immoral."[58]

"Using" Marriage

In the past, one of the ways some counselors suggested to facilitate a conversion in sexual orientation was for the gay or lesbian person to marry. Presumably what the same-sex-oriented person really needed was the love of and sexual experience with a person of the opposite sex. Indeed, some lesbian and gay persons did undertake marriage in response to such counseling or chose marriage on their own because they believed or hoped it would effect a change. It seldom worked. Heterosexual marriage cannot and should not be used as a method of "curing" a same-sex orientation.

First, if the person has a true same-sex orientation, marriage cannot change it. I am told by those who have experienced it that even though complete fidelity may exist within the marriage, there is an area of unfulfillment. The actions within the marriage may be completely heterosexual, but the inner climate of the gay or lesbian person has not changed. He or she still longs at times for the fulfillment of a same-sex relationship. One married gay man expressed his feelings clearly when he said that in heterosexual intercourse he does not experience the letting down of ego boundaries, the sense of spiritual oneness with the partner that he does in intercourse with another man. Another gay man told me that, although his marriage remains intact, he and his wife live together as a brother and sister might. Although the wife wants sexual interaction, the proper stimulus for the husband (another man) is lacking, and he cannot get or maintain an erection. Dr. Ralph Blair, who has studied ex-gay organizations and claims intensively, says that ex-gay people don't see marriage as necessarily including genital sexual activity. He believes that most of these marriages are convenient living arrangements that do not satisfy the need for erotic intimacy.[59]

Another reason why marriage should not be used as an attempted cure for a same-sex orientation lies in the word used. A marriage undertaken on such a basis can bring nothing but heartache to both partners. It is difficult enough to make marriage work without adding such a risky burden.

The whole idea that same-sex-oriented people can or should change presents us with another dilemma. Some conservative writers believe that homosexuality itself is enough to bar a person from the reign of God. Others are content to accept the fact that same-sex-oriented persons cannot change their orientation and are not condemned by God for it, as long as the person lives a celibate life. It is the homosexual *acts* that are wrong, not the orientation. Again, we are faced with a need to choose what interpretation of biblical passages—or which proponents of varying views—we accept. Which school of thought *really* represents what God intends?

Celibacy and Salvation

The idea that to be acceptable to God a lesbian or gay person must refrain from any genital expression within a committed same-sex relationship carries its own problems. What we are really saying is that the person's salvation depends on celibacy. This sounds unpleasantly like, "By works are you saved." Paul wrote in Ephesians 2:8–9: "For by grace you have been saved through faith; and this is not your own doing, it is the gift of God—not the result of works, so that no one may boast." The framework of belief and salvation could be significantly altered by trying to make celibacy the touchstone of a person's (another person's!) salvation.

On a less theological level, I wonder how long celibacy would remain an issue for these writers if the situation were reversed. If other-sex-oriented persons knew that their kind of sexual relations would prevent them from going to heaven, that only homosexual relations were approved, I wonder whether they might not decide to let their eternal salvation take care of itself and live as they saw fit now.

Celibacy is not something we dare *impose* on someone else. It can only be freely chosen by the person who will have to live out the choice. Donald Georgen, a Dominican who has studied at the Kansas Neurological Institute and the Menninger Foundation, has had the task of counseling with those who are in the process of deciding whether or not to commit themselves to a celibate life. The questions he asks them to consider carefully throw a new light on the matter of celibacy.

180

Here are some of the questions:

What is it about celibacy that you find attractive? Why would you choose to be celibate? What does celibacy mean to you? What does the notion of "call" mean to you? What are the practical problems raised by a celibate life-style? Are you willing to undertake these? . . . Are you personally capable of the commitment celibacy requires? . . . How do you want to use your celibacy? How can you increasingly integrate it into the person you are coming to be?[60]

There is a stronger and more positive reason for embracing the legitimacy of same-sex genital expression. James B. Nelson has expressed this position in his book *Embodiment*, summarizing the position taken by theologian Norman Pittenger: "God's abiding purpose for humankind is that in response to divine action we should realize our intended humanity as human lovers—in the richest, broadest, and most responsible sense of the term. Our embodied sexuality is the physiological and psychological base for our capacity to love."

Abnormality or deviance, Pittenger feels, should not be measured statistically, but rather against the

norm of humanity in Jesus Christ. Gay persons desire and need deep and lasting relationships just as do heterosexuals, and appropriate genital expression should be denied to neither.

Thus, the ethical question which Pittenger poses is this: what sexual behavior will serve and enhance, rather than inhibit, damage, or destroy the fuller realization of our divinely-intended humanity? The answer is sexual behavior in accord with an ethics of love. This means commitment and trust, tenderness, respect for the other, and the desire for ongoing and responsible communion with the other. On the negative side, an ethics of love mandates against selfish sexual expression, cruelty, impersonal sex, obsession with sex, and against actions done without willingness to take responsibility for the consequences. Such an ethics always asks about the meanings of acts in their total context—in the relationship itself, in society, and in regard to God's intended direction for human life. Such an ethics of sexual love is equally appropriate to heterosexual and gay Christians. There is no double standard.[61]

Can same-sex-oriented persons change? Conservative religious writers are hopeful that they can. These writers need to be optimistic. The entire basis of their faith lies in a particular interpretation of the Bible. If it is possible to pick and choose which passages to believe and obey, they say, then we undermine belief in the resurrection of Jesus Christ, and the Christian faith becomes void. The idea that it is necessary to view scriptural passages in the light of social and cultural conditions at the time those passages were written seems to them to deny the truth of scripture. If scripture was inspired by God, these writers say, then God knew the beginning from the ending, and the Bible's message is for all time. They are unable to view the writing of scripture in a more realistic way and to acknowledge that the Bible does not speak specifically to many situations that, as C. S. Lewis said, were never even envisaged by the ancients.

Can the Christian Church Support Committed Same-sex Relationships?

Of course the kinds of same-sex practices dealt with in the Bible were wrong. They still are. Nowhere does the Bible speak to the matter of loving, committed same-sex relationships. The fact that the only approved sexual acts take place within the context of heterosexual marriage does not necessarily reflect an enlightened ethical under-standing of relations between men and women; rather, rules about sexual practice and marriage were dictated by concern for male property.

In ancient Israel women and children were men's prop-erty. Adultery bore more relation to theft of property (the man's wife) than to betrayal of trust between two commit-ted partners. Fornication robbed a father, who owned his daughter until she became a man's wife, of an asset—a sexually pure woman who could be given to a man in marriage to enhance her father's position. The other many sexual sins spelled out in Leviticus, for example, all had to do with invading the property rights of the head of the family. In the tribal way of life, anything that damaged the head male damaged the whole extended family. Anything that contributed to his success contributed to their collec-tive success. The individual was of little importance. It was the collective family and tribe that mattered.

The increase of the tribe was of great importance. A Hebrew man's duty was to marry and beget children. To this end semen was precious and should not be wasted. It was thought that the whole child was contained in the semen[62]; the woman simply supplied the incubator. Un-der such circumstances there could be no thought of wast-ing semen in such unproductive acts as sexual activity between two males. Nobody gave much thought to sexual activity between females, because women counted for very little, no semen was spilled, and no child would re-sult from such activity.

In the New Testament, when Jesus denounced the di-vorcing of a wife by her husband (a woman could not divorce her husband), he was not so much protecting the sanctity of marriage as destroying the hierarchy of male privilege. In Matthew 19:4 Jesus reminded his hearers that God had created the female as well as the male in the image of God (Genesis 1:27), and in the second creation narrative they were to become "one flesh," implying, again, equality of male and female. William Countryman points out that "the family structure in ancient Israel did not, in fact, acknowledge either an equality between male and female or a complete unity of flesh between married persons. The wife, though she was in some ways an extension of her husband and was an important part of his household, did not become truly and fully a member of his family and was certainly not his equal."[63] Jesus' redefinition of adultery to include the man's role—heretofore, under provisions of the Torah it had been impossible for a man to commit adultery against himself—created the possibility for the male to be as liable to this sin as the female. Jesus forbade the man to divorce his wife, thus giving her a permanent and indissoluble claim on him as sexual property. "Henceforth," Countryman says, "his sexual freedom was to be no greater than hers."[64] In effect, Jesus was instigating a reevaluation—even a revolution—in the hierarchical sexual structure of Jewish society.

We read into New Testament passages dealing with sexual matters our own traditional preconceptions, Countryman says. "Sex is not a primary concern in the New Testament writings nor is physical purity an accepted principle there. To those who read the New Testament in the light of modern Western Christianity this will always be difficult to comprehend or accept, for a long history of pietism, both Protestant and Catholic, has made physical purity a major principle and sex a primary concern among us."[65]

These understandings will seem to many to undermine completely the principles of Christian morality. In reality, they shift the base of such principles from a blind acceptance of an incorrect interpretation of scripture to a need to formulate our own ethical understandings of relationships between men and women, standards based on caring, rather than merely sexual, love, commitment, integrity, trust. These same standards may apply to the relationship between two people of the same sex. It therefore becomes entirely possible for the church to bless such a relationship, to give it the same support it gives conventional marriage, and in time, perhaps, to bring legal status to same-sex relationships in the same way that the law gives status to opposite-sex relationships.

In the matter of committed same-sex relationships, the Catholic stance provides a note of sad irony. A person who has spasmodic sexual encounters with someone of the same gender can go to confession, perform a penance, and thus remain in a right relationship with the church and thus by presumption with God. The person who is in a committed, monogamous relationship with a person of the same gender, however, does not have access to forgiveness unless he or she agrees to foreswear any sexual activity within the relationship. The peculiar unintended result of such a position is to give a kind of approval to the very activity that is most detrimental to the person's physical, emotional, and spiritual well-being.

We have traveled far from the original question: Can a same-sex orientation be changed? If we understand the Bible in the light of the times in which the various books were written, we have a lot of rethinking to do. Drawing on the great themes set forth in the Bible, with the Holy Spirit's help we should be able to formulate ethics that speak to the issues of our day in a reasoned, responsible way, rather than as children adhering unquestioningly to parental rules. We will have grown beyond the stage of needing "spiritual milk" into the stage where we are mature enough to want the "solid food [of] those who have their faculties trained by practice to distinguish good from evil" (Heb. 5:12–14).

The Bible, the Church, and AIDS

There are still denominations and churches whose main message about AIDS is one of condemnation, unless the person with AIDS is an "innocent victim"—that is, an infant born with AIDS, someone who has contracted AIDS through a blood transfusion or other accidental means, or a spouse infected by a partner who, unknown to the spouse, has AIDS. Such bodies base their condemnation of same-sex-oriented people with AIDS on an interpretation of the scriptures that condemns homosexuality as sinful. Therefore, because people with AIDS have brought their disease upon themselves through their sinful actions, the church is not obligated to minister to them except perhaps through evangelism.

Many other denominations and churches also base their attitude toward people with AIDS, no matter how the disease has been contracted, on biblical principles. In this case, however, they point to Jesus as their model. In Luke Jesus announces his mission to minister to the outcasts of society (4:18). Never does he inquire about the possible misdeeds of those whom he heals, nor does he require a statement of faith before he ministers to them. In fact, he seems to go out of his way to help those whom Jewish society had ostracized.

William E. Amos, Jr., indicates that Jesus did not grade some sins as being worse than others. "He wanted to make clear that it is the person involved in a situation who is important."[66] Amos says the whole Bible is consistent in its attitude toward sin: Sexual sins are no more condemned than are such transgressions as idolatry, thievery, drunkenness, slandering, and swindling. "We [Christians] are woefully inconsistent in our response to people and situations," he says.[67]

Amos points out that what we are doing is passing judgment upon certain people and certain sins. "In regard to AIDS," he says, "our judgment of others often comes from an emotional frame of reference rather than a theological one. What we do not understand or like or even admit the possibility of in ourselves is usually that on which we pass the harshest judgment."[68] To pass judgment is not our task, but God's. Furthermore, in ministering to people with AIDS, a heavy emphasis on evangelism can only alienate. Simply to be available to the person and to listen and help where possible is what is most needed, Amos says. Sooner or later religious issues will very likely surface, though perhaps not in the form we had envisioned. Spiritual counseling may have to deviate from preconceived formulas for salvation. "Whatever our concern about a person's relationship with God, a sensitive pastoral presence will provide more than enough opportunity to deal with any aspect of this issue."[69]

Finally, Amos emphasizes what may seem to be a very small matter: touch. Jesus was not afraid to touch people, to have physical contact with them.[70] AIDS is a disease that in the eyes of many people turns the ill person into a modern-day leper. Although we have been assured that we cannot catch AIDS from casual contact—a handshake, a hug, a hand on a fevered brow—many people want to keep their distance from a person with AIDS. Being willing to touch such a person can say more to him or her than a thousand words or protestations of love and goodwill.

Parents in particular need to be aware that no words about repentance and renunciation of life-style are likely to help their ill child. If parents truly want to demonstrate a Christian attitude they will forget their attempts at evangelism and concentrate on demonstrating unquestioning love and acceptance of their daughter or son. In his parables Jesus tells about the Samaritan who helped a man who had been robbed and beaten on the road to Jericho. Very probably the victim was Jewish, and Jews and Samaritans did not associate with each other—literally, Jews did not even use dishes Samaritans had used.[71] In the great parable about the end of the age (Matt. 25: 31–46) Jesus indicates that service to the hungry, the thirsty, the stranger, the naked, the ill, and the imprisoned is service to

Christ. There is no standard of righteousness that the one ministered to must fulfill. The need is the standard.

Whether you are physically able to care for your child or not (we will deal with this in the next chapter), your love for your child will mirror the love of Christ and speak to his or her heart in ways that no amount of preaching or attempts at evangelism could ever do. As Rabbi Adler's earlier story about the Hasidic master makes clear, your child as never before needs demonstration of your love and caring, not theological pronouncements.

"Is My Child Lost for Eternity?"

Recently, the parents of a gay man came to see me. All three—father, mother, and son—are fine, intelligent, well-educated, sensitive Christians. I had met the son previously and he had asked if his parents could meet me.

After the parents and I had talked for a while, the young man's mother voiced the urgent question many Christian parents have: "If the Bible says that homosexuality is an abomination before God and that no homosexual person will inherit the kingdom of heaven, is my gay or lesbian child lost for eternity?"

If we are to be realistic, we need to recognize that the Bible does not necessarily say what we think it says on the subject. To me, the evidence that the Bible is speaking of certain homosexual acts—which it is right in condemning—is far stronger and more believable than the idea that God condemns those who have not chosen their sexual orientation and who are unable to change. Neither can I believe that such persons are commanded to live a celibate life. Those who have included the option of celibacy in the framework of their religious lives understand that it must be a freely chosen vocation, not a forced servitude.

I believe that all persons, heterosexual and homosexual, are called by God to live sexually responsible and loving lives. Millions of married heterosexual persons are not living sexually responsible and loving lives within their marriages, as the statistics on infidelity, battering, and incest reveal. Police blotters and more formal statistical studies show that a high percentage of prostitutes' clients are married. The statistics are perhaps less accurate on the clandestine homosexual activities of married men, but gay men speak of the high percentage of married men who cruise in gay areas and pick up free homosexual sex or else hire male prostitutes. Obviously, heterosexual men and women do not always behave with impeccable morals.

I believe it is possible for lesbians and gay men to have loving, responsible, committed relationships that include genital sexual activity, and I believe that these relationships are as acceptable in God's sight as loving, responsible, committed heterosexual relationships. At present it is more difficult for gay and lesbian people to do this than for straight people, because, generally, same-sex-oriented couples receive no support for this type of relationship from either the church or society—and then we criticize them for a promiscuous life-style, which we often assume is the only type of life-style they live. In the case of gay men, not even the gay community provides much support for such a relationship. As we have seen, the lesbian community is more likely to provide support for stable, long-term relationships than does the gay male community.

Virginia Ramey Mollenkott speaks of evaluating homosexual relationships on the basis of quality of relating rather than on the basis of the "object" with whom the relating is done. What she says is of great importance to parents of same-sex-oriented children:

> Constitutional homosexual orientation is a *state of behaving* . . . in which the individual's most authentic and therefore deepest and holiest love-feelings flow naturally toward persons of the same rather than the other sex. To treat these love-feelings on a

par with gang rape, adultery, prostitution, and acts of flagrant exploitation is to defame and deny homosexual personhood.[72]

Concerning covenant relationships between persons of the same sex she writes: "Many church leaders persist in comparing such unions to sicknesses like alcoholism, or violations of covenant like adultery, or exploitation like bestiality. Such insensitivity fills me with rage and pain on behalf of the people whose highest love nature is being treated with contempt."[73]

The idea that sexual activity is sinful without the sanctification of marriage may be so ingrained in some parents that even a loving, caring, faithful same-sex relationship can never be acceptable to them. Or it may take them a long time to learn to live with such an arrangement for their child. If this is the case, they need to learn the truth that God does not always ratify our decisions.

Saved by Grace and by Choice

The question parents ask—"Is my gay or lesbian child lost for eternity?"—is probably emotionally the most highly charged question that could be asked. *They want to know that they will meet their child in heaven.*

The fear voiced by conservative Christians is that "sloppy agape"—love that accepts and approves of anything and everything—does not in reality help the same-sex-oriented person. They believe that if Christians do not take a tough line concerning homosexuality as sin—at least concerning homosexual acts as sin—they are encouraging actions that will exclude such a person from heaven and thus, in the long run, they are being cruel because they are condemning the person to eternal punishment.

I understand the cry in the heart of conservative Christians: "If we do not maintain a hard line against sin, it will engulf our world. Our churches will crumble. Our civilization will be swept away. God expects us to maintain biblical standards of righteousness." Yet surely there is a difference between compassion for persons and the condoning of every type of sin. The truth is that only love can open and unfold the human spirit.

Many conservative Christians have said, in this connection, that one should love the sinner but hate the sin. The trouble with this idea is that so often it is difficult for the "sinner" to understand the finely tuned message about whom Christians love and what they hate. And if Christians are hating a "sin" that seems to be almost an inborn condition—or at least one that the experts tell us seems to be well set by about age five—they may find themselves dealing too harshly with some of God's children.

Because I have participated in many services of lesbian and gay religious groups, I have seen at close range their need and desire for an intimate relationship with God. I wonder what would happen if churches did not discriminate against same-sex-oriented people, did not try to label them "sinners." What would happen if churches put into practice some words written by the Rev. Ann G. Suzedell?

When we read through the scriptures we cannot help but notice that divine love for the people of God as promised in the biblical narratives is not careful, not calculated, not distant. It is extravagant, risky, intimate. "When you pass through the waters, I will be with you." When you walk through fire, I will be with you. When you grieve, when you hurt, when you laugh, when you rejoice, I will be with you. "For you are honored, and precious in my sight, and I love you."[74]

The promise does not say: "I will cure everything that ails you." It says, "I will be with you, I care for you, I love you."

She goes on to quote what Henri Nouwen writes in *Out of Solitude*:

> What we see, and like to see, is cure and change. But what we do not see and do not want to see is care, the participation in the pain, the solidarity in suffering, the sharing in the experience of broken- ness. . . . Cure without care makes us into rulers, controllers, manipulators, and prevents a real com- munity from taking shape. Cure without care makes us preoccupied with quick changes, impa- tient and unwilling to share each other's burden.[75]

Nouwen has laid his finger on the churches' dilemma in relation to homosexuality: *Heterosexual Christians want to see cure and change.* Often they do not want to participate in the pain the homosexual person experiences when he or she finally acknowledges his gayness or her lesbianism. Heterosexual Christians do not want to feel solidarity with the suffering of their lesbian sisters and gay brothers as an outcast minority. Heterosexual Christians want to cure or ostracize, but they do not want to *care.* They do not want to listen, to hear, to understand what is going on in the heart and mind and life of a gay man or a lesbian. Far easier to label such persons sinners and pass them by on the other side if they cannot meet the church's standards of change or celibacy!

No one can *know* about the afterlife in the same way we can know about this life. No one, therefore, can give you total assurance that your lesbian daughter or gay son (or for that matter you yourself) will enter heaven at the close of life here on earth. Even change to heterosexuality or celibacy cannot guarantee this for your homosexual child.

I believe a same-sex oriented person has as much chance for salvation as anyone else. Each of us is saved by grace and by choice. Each of us is born with a spark of God's spirit within us. Some nurture this spark and learn to live in the spiritual dimension as well as in the physical. Others continue to deaden the spark until any vestige of the spiritual is either extinguished or put in the service of total evil. One's sexual orientation does not determine one's entrance into heaven; one's relationship to God does.

A fundamentalist friend who had read *My Son Eric* sat down with me to discuss the book. At one point in our conversation he said, "Mary, have you given serious thought to the fact that because of what you say in your book many gay and lesbian people will not make any effort to change and will therefore be lost?"

"Yes, Michael," I answered, "I've given the matter *very* serious thought. But have you considered that because of the church's idea about a same-sex orientation millions of lesbian and gay persons may be kept from a close relationship to God and that on Judgment Day the church may be called to account for this?"

Establishing a Relationship with God

In his book *Healing the Pain of Everyday Loss* Ira Tanner writes of a young woman who, after her husband had divorced her, prayed that God would reconcile her and her husband. Then the thought came to her that she was asking God to give her what she wanted. She realized she was not praying but begging. "She changed her prayers," Tanner says, "from begging to simply talking with God, asking him to help her through the crisis."[76]

Within your particular circumstances as the parent of a same-sex-oriented child what will you pray for? You can focus your prayers narrowly: "Oh God, heal my daughter (son)." Like a child, you are simply crying for what you want.

The real purpose of prayer, its real essence, is to establish and maintain a relationship and a dialogue with God, to learn the mind of the Creator, to experience redemption again and again, in each situation of our lives as it arises.

193

What does redemption mean in this context? It means deliverance, rescue, liberation, extrication, release from a particular situation.

God has many ways of releasing us from a situation. I have often been struck by the fact that in a particular crisis I see only one way of resolving it, and if I were directing the action, I would head straight for this point. God does it so differently. God seems to have in mind another way of resolving the crisis, one that leads out into broader vistas than I, with my finite tunnel vision, could have imagined.

At this point you feel that you are in a straitjacket. Fighting the straitjacket is not going to get you out and will probably tangle things tighter. As you fight, panic rises within you, increasing your inner tension, which drives you to flail harder, which only tightens the straitjacket around you still more.

Only as you begin to relax, to be quiet, to wait, to listen, will you hear the quiet voice give instructions, a few at a time, telling you step by slow step how to exit from the straitjacket of fear and perhaps loathing in which you are trapped.

When you pray, then, say, "O God, please show me why this has happened to me, to my family. What do you want me to learn in this situation? What is the promise hidden in this event?"[77] You can add, "Thank you for the answers you are giving me." You may not have seen any answers yet, but in saying this you are indicating you do expect God to answer. You are acting out faith.

Some time ago I received a beautiful letter from the father of a gay man that illustrates so perfectly what is stated above.

I gave my heart to Jesus when I was fourteen years old. I have a lovely Christian wife, and we have three beautiful Christian children. All of them are active in the church and the community. We are

Baptists and raised our children in the best Christian home we knew how to give them. We love our children, but our eldest son is our special joy. Of the three he is the most thoughtful, the most helpful, the most concerned about us. Perhaps we actually love him the most. Surely he needs our love more than the others. You see, he is gay. Living in today's world he needs all the love we can give him.

It was a shock to us when he told us, now almost three years ago, though the two younger ones had apparently known for some time. He told us one evening as we gathered for family prayers more or less in this way: "I want to tell you something, and I want you to pray for me. Don't pray for God to change me, because there can't be any change. God made me this way. Pray that God may use me even in the way He made me." And then he told us he is gay. For a few minutes we just sat in silence. Then I kneeled and began to pray aloud that God would lead us, that He would open our hearts as well as our minds to His will.

The answer did not come at once. Nor did it come easily. It came gradually and came in part through the positive Christian attitude of the younger two. We listen to our children. We discuss things with them and weigh what they have to say. We have always made it a policy never to act in haste or anger with our children. And so the answer came gradually. We observed no outward change in Peter, except that he seemed even happier than usual, if that were possible. He was always a good boy, and we realized that he is still a good boy. He is, in fact, still the same fine person he was before we knew. We soon realized that his habits had not changed. He still had the same friends. We still knew whom he went out with, where he went, and when he would come home. He was still a good influence in the church and in the community. We continued to pray for God's guidance, and eventually the answer came. We at last knew that God was saying to us, "This is your son. He is the way I made him. Love him. Love him the way he is." We know in our hearts that this is the answer God has given to us.

We told Peter by our actions that we continued to love him. Finally we told him with our words and family prayers that since God made him gay we believe that God made him that way for a purpose. My wife and I had wondered if Peter had any gay friends, but we did not want to pry into his privacy. That was another question we had to wait to have answered. One evening two of Peter's closest friends were with him at the house. When it came time for family prayers, Peter asked if they might join us. As we sat discussing what things needed to be prayed for, Peter's friends told us how happy they were that we have accepted Peter the way he is. Then Jim requested that we pray God's blessing and guidance upon his and Peter's love for each other and on their relationship. And so we prayed. Now we feel that in addition to our own fine three sons God has added two more. Truly our cup of joy runneth over. But we still pray daily that God may protect them from a hostile world and use them in His own way.

The most important words in this letter are near the middle: "The answer did not come at once. Nor did it come easily. It came gradually." The answer the letter-writer received is also important, because it is probably the beginning of your answer too: "This is your child. He (she) is the way I made him (her). Love your child. Love your child the way he (she) is."

God is waiting to open new insights, new adventures, perhaps even a whole new life to you, not despite your child's sexual orientation, but because of doors that open to you through a closer listening, a deeper relationship to God. There *is* a promise, a world of promises, hidden in this event.

Years ago—long before I learned that Eric is gay, long before my divorce—at a moment of extreme anguish, God placed in my hands a pearl of great price. I was on my way to an emergency appointment with my psychiatrist in the early days of a deep depression into which I had fallen. In my agony I cried out to God, "Why do I have to suffer so?" And then, having discharged a small amount of my pain and desperation, I added, "If it helps somebody, sometimes, it's all right."

Immediately, clearly, words were in my mind in answer to my cry: "Nothing that is given to me is ever wasted." This was the first time that God had spoken to me in such a way that I realized God was giving me a definite message. I was sure it was God speaking to me, because if I had been talking to myself, I would have said, "Nothing that is given to *God* is ever wasted."

For some reason I was comforted. The agony was still there, but it was not as sharp. The touch of deity on my life had brought a new dimension to my suffering. My pain had a purpose. We are willing to suffer if we know the suffering is not purposeless.

Then I said, "God, I give you my suffering," and I went to my appointment, having turned a significant corner in my life. Complete healing waited a long time, but I had been given a lifeline to hold on to that would pull me through many dark days ahead.

In the intervening years I have learned that the most important offering we can bring to God is not our strengths, our good points, our talents. What God wants from us is an offering of our individual pain, our weakness, the worst parts of ourselves, the worst things that happen to us. Until we offer these things God cannot begin to deal with them and transform them from loss into gain.

We never learn or grow by running away from those things within ourselves (fear, anger, temper, hatred, lust) that we do not want to admit, even to ourselves, or by running away from situations that we do not want to deal with. These things are transformed only as we summon our courage to look them in the eye, acknowledge their existence—and offer the situation to God. What God wants most of all, it would seem, is a way into the fortresses of our souls to begin the process of transformation.

Do not look for quick and easy answers. Many times this is not the way God chooses. You are starting—or perhaps continuing—on a pilgrimage. Often pilgrimages are made on foot, and hiking is not the fastest or most luxurious mode of travel. But because you proceed slowly you will learn many things along the way you would not have discovered otherwise. The goal is not to move you from here to there as quickly as possible, but to open your eyes to the beauties, the vistas, the truths, the marvelous possibilities of the land through which you travel.

Do you feel nothing good could possibly come of your daughter's lesbianism, your son's gayness? Do not keep yourself in this straitjacket. At this point in the development of the human race, change for your child is probably not a viable option. Open yourself to the many other possibilities God is offering you. Open the door, right where you are. One simple sentence—"God, I give you my concern over my child's sexual orientation"—will set your feet on the path.

It may be slow. Continue to pour out your thoughts and feelings to God; then wait and listen for those slight pressures on your spirit, those rare insights, the messages that may suddenly come to you as you are still and expectant before your creator. You are starting on a pilgrimage with God, and although there may be deserts and mountains to cross, do not give up. The end will be worth it.

Chapter 10

Living with HIV/AIDS

As if coming out to your parents weren't difficult enough, now you may face an added dilemma: telling your parents you are HIV positive, or else that you have AIDS. HIV, of course, stands for human immunodeficiency virus, and AIDS for acquired immune deficiency syndrome. A person who is HIV positive may in time develop AIDS, a more serious involvement of the immune system.

Michael Callen, author of *Surviving AIDS*, tells of reading the first description of AIDS cases in the *New York Native* in the spring of 1981, when the problem was still referred to as GRID, gay-related immunodeficiency.[1] There was never any doubt in his mind, he says, that he would get it. "I retain a clear image of myself on a subway platform at rush hour, frozen in place, reading for the first time about a new, lethal, sexually transmitted disease that was affecting gay men. I remember feeling disoriented by the knowledge that life was going on all around me, oblivious to the fact that my world had just changed utterly and forever."[2]

There's no doubt about it, living with HIV/AIDS is different from simply living.

It may have come as a real shock to you when you discovered that you were HIV positive or had AIDS. You may inadvertently have discovered your positive status much as pro basketball player Magic Johnson did, in one of the most well-publicized situations in recent times, when he applied for health insurance. You went to the doctor for some other reason, and, totally unexpectedly, you discovered that you are HIV positive. You feel as if a bombshell has burst in your life, bringing with it panic and turmoil.

Conversely, you may have had inklings that you were positive. You may have had some of the telltale signs—unexplained fever, tiredness, swollen lymph nodes, night sweats, diarrhea, some weight loss, perhaps only a general sense that all was not well within your body—that sent you to the doctor or a clinic for a blood test. Perhaps you had no symptoms, but because you knew your previous behavior put you at risk, you periodically had blood tests. You were pretty certain the virus would show up eventually and have been preparing yourself for the news for some time. Still, the certain knowledge that you are HIV positive (which may or may not have advanced to AIDS) can change the whole complexion of your feelings. As long as there is doubt, you can tell yourself that you will be one of the lucky ones, or that you have an unrelated health problem. Now there is no doubt, and you experience a much more intense range of feelings.

What should you do? How can you handle the powerful emotions that assail you? One man, who had strongly suspected he was HIV positive, told me that he sat down with an AIDS counselor the day after his diagnosis to explore his physical and emotional options. He was wise to do this—but he is the exception. Most people react in much less focused ways.

Before we go any further, we need to recognize the fact that lesbians can and do get AIDS. They contract the disease in the same ways that anyone does: through blood and sexual fluids. The virus can enter the body through unprotected sex with an infected person, sharing of needles and contaminated sexual appliances, contact with infected blood, and so on. However, because many more gay men than lesbians are HIV positive, the personal experiences in this chapter come from gay men or their families, and the designations used are masculine.

When you first learn you are hosting the virus, you may go into maximum denial. The body and the self have ways of shielding us from the enormity of a knowledge so devastating that in the shock of discovery it could incapacitate us. If denial continues too long, however, you cut yourself off from learning helpful ways of dealing with this disease.

On the other hand, you may decide that you are going to survive, no matter what. Or you may ricochet between certain knowledge that you are going to die and certain knowledge that you are going to survive. You have found yourself on a roller coaster with tremendous hills and deep valleys. Some days you may ignore the whole problem, burying yourself in work, pleasure, TV, or more damaging means of blanking out the problem: alcohol, drugs, or even intensified sexual activity. You are, of course, experiencing acute grief reactions. As we saw in chapter 3, these include denial, anger, guilt, blaming, bargaining, depression, acceptance—with some fear, shame, and self-pity thrown in.

From the Gay Person's Side

Gather Information

One of the essential things you must do when you discover your positive status is gather as much information as you can about the medical aspects of HIV/AIDS. What are the manifestations of the disease? What medical treatments are available? What alternative holistic treatments may help to strengthen your body and your immune system? What spiritual practices can help to remove stress from your life and reorient your outlook? What precautions must you take to protect others from the disease? What precautions must you take to protect yourself from infections to which you may be more susceptible because of your weakened immune system?

For several years after the appearance of AIDS, having the virus was regarded as a speedy death sentence. That is not the case today. An encouraging number of people have survived four, five, even ten years or more with HIV positive status, often because they have made conscious efforts to do things that contribute to their health and well-being.

Many excellent books and articles can answer the questions listed above as well as others you may have. Several books are listed at the end of this book in "For Further Reading." Check with your library or the resource organizations listed for other sources of information.

Grief Reactions

Denial and Bargaining

You have just learned you are HIV positive. You walk down the street and you feel as if everyone who sees you knows you are sick, and knows how you got the disease. You feel like a walking illness. One man told me he felt like a slime monster, totally toxic. He was overcome with horror that there was a thing in his body that was capable of killing other human beings. Why should we be surprised that people go into denial and refuse to believe the diagnosis when they first learn they are HIV positive?

If you are in denial at this point, you may be going about your daily life as if nothing has happened. You may be vowing passionately to yourself, "I'll never have sex again." Or you may be frantically living it up. You may in effect be saying to yourself, "If I go out every night, if I'm enjoying myself, that means I'm not really HIV positive. Look at my vitality!"

Such thoughts and behavior represent aspects of denial. They may also be a form of bargaining. Sudden interest in being "the best little boy in the world" may be another form of bargaining. Astonishingly, you are in church, temple, or synagogue every Sunday, although previously you had not entered such a building for years. You suddenly accept the condemnatory statements of conservative religion: You are indeed a miserable sinner who is reaping the rewards of your ungodly and profligate way of life. Or you may suddenly and frenetically embrace service to others in a nonreligious context. There is certainly nothing wrong with making a new start in faithful attendance at religious services, in an honest change in beliefs, or in altruistic endeavors. What matters in each case is motive. If you are bargaining with God or with life, you are fooling yourself. Bargaining is an attempt to buy yourself out of your situation, and it is doomed to failure.

Denial may be a necessary phase of coming to terms with the fact that you have HIV/AIDS. If it causes you to indulge in harmful behaviors such as excessive drinking, drug-taking, or promiscuity, while ignoring those actions that would contribute to healthful living, denial can be a serious, even deadly matter.

Young People, Denial, and Destructive Actions

If you are a young person, you probably do not think about the fact that you—along with everybody else in the world—will someday die. Death probably seems like something that will happen only when you are very old. Because you are young, you may feel that nothing can touch you, nothing can stop you. No matter what you do, "it can't happen to me." Such an attitude can be a deadly forerunner of many problems: "I can drink without becoming an alcoholic"; "I can do drugs without getting hooked"; "I can drive fast without having an accident"; "I don't need to practice safe sex *because I won't get the AIDS virus*"; "I won't die, period."

This is denial before the fact, and it can destroy you and the wonderful promise of the life ahead of you. Because your behavior affects your staying alive as well as the quality of that life, you can literally save your life by becoming aware of your real vulnerability to the dangers of alcohol, drugs, wild driving—and AIDS. It definitely can happen to you.

Denial may not be the only reason you behave in ways destructive to your health and well-being. Such actions may also stem from a lack of love for yourself. An inner voice may keep telling you in a variety of ways that you are of no account, that you don't deserve to receive good things. If as you read this you find yourself saying, "Yeah, that's me," start examining your ideas about yourself carefully. Who, in your childhood or growing-up years, told you you were stupid, that you couldn't do anything right, that however good your performance, it was never good enough?

As we grow up we get our ideas about ourselves from those around us, particularly from the adults in our lives. If those adults tell us we are worthless, we internalize those ideas. That must be true, we think. And because we believe we are worthless, we see no reason to place a high value on our self-protection.

Don't believe those negative voices. You've probably seen the posters and bumper stickers that tell us, "God don't make no junk." That may be a cliché—but it has become a cliché because it's true. No matter what you have been told, no matter what your behavior is or has been, simply because you are alive you deserve the best break you can give yourself. You are not junk—never have been, never will be. Take care of yourself. Don't let a lack of self-esteem rob you of your life.

Anger, Blaming, Self-pity, Guilt

One of the strongest of the grief reactions you feel may be anger, accompanied by an almost automatic desire to blame somebody—anybody—for your ill fortune. Why did God, or whatever force you believe governs the universe, allow this to happen to you? You may feel like shaking your fist at God, expressing your rage with obscenities and curses. In my life I have found that when I was *really* angry at God, if I allowed myself actually to swear and express that anger in strong terms I was better able to listen to what God wanted to tell me through my inner spirit. Rather than trying to ignore my real feelings because "good people don't get angry at God," I expressed them, holding nothing back. This meant I no longer had to expend psychic energy repressing those feelings. There was no longer a roadblock between me and my inner voice. I also discovered that, much as a wise parent does not punish a little child for a temper tantrum, God did not punish me for such expressions of anger.

Instead of being angry at God, you may be angry at the person who gave you the virus—so angry, in fact, that you could kill, if it would help. "*He* gave it to me," you may be saying to yourself in rage. If that someone is your partner, both you and he are in a potentially explosive situation. If you value the relationship and do not want to shatter it, find a neutral person such as a counselor to help you work through your feelings of anger. At some point, in order to be honest with your partner, you may need to talk with him, but in a rational way. Screaming, threatening, or acting in a violent manner will not help either of you. If initially you have dealt with your feelings apart from him, you will be better able to be honest without being either physically or verbally brutal.

The time may come when you do indeed wish to send your partner packing. However, you will have had a chance to make the decision after a calmer assessment of your feelings and wishes. Because of this you will be better able to live with your decision without undue regret, because it was not dictated either by impulsive anger or the knee-jerk reaction of blaming.

In any case, blaming is unproductive. It does not enable you to deal constructively with your life as it now is. By putting responsibility for your happiness and well-being on someone else, you are giving away your inner power.

"Shortly after being diagnosed, I examined what my life had been—the kind of choices I had made, how I'd lived my life," "A. J." Roosevelt Williams told Michael Callen. "I did this out of the belief that some part of my having this disease was my responsibility." He mentions the years he had hung out in gay bars, the money he had spent on alcohol, cigarettes, and marijuana. He does not see such an assessment as blaming himself. Instead, he believes that the degree of responsibility he takes for his disease means he can have the same degree of control and influence over his chances of living. Callen calls Williams' words the most "succinct statement of the empowerment that can come from taking responsibility for one's choices."[3]

Taking responsibility for dealing with your disease and your health often sets in motion the process of true healing—a word not to be confused with cure. Such responsibility means "acknowledging and participating in the *now*, in the well-being of the now, wherever that is to be found." It means stepping out of the victim-rescuer-persecutor triangle.[4] Victims are powerless people who need someone else to rescue them from their persecutor. As you become your own rescuer, you assume power to make decisions and choices, to find the beauty and power of living in the moment with dignity and purpose.

Instead of anger or blaming, your first reaction may be

one of extreme self-pity. "Why did this happen to *me*?" You may compare your actions to those of someone else who is not HIV positive but took far more risks than you.

"Roberto" tells of going through an initial "why me?" period that led him to a painful emotional housecleaning. "When I was diagnosed in '82 I went into shock," he said. "I had daily crying bouts, wondering what I had done— 'Why me?' I was a *total* victim." When Roberto finally stopped crying, he began to take stock of his life. He realized that the first thing he should do was give up drugs. But that would cut him off from many of his friends, and he was afraid he wouldn't have any friends left. "And then I started analyzing all of my friends and how many of them did drugs, and I realized very clearly that none of my real friends did drugs. . . . I went cold turkey off drugs and I started out one day at a time."[5]

Self-pity, which bears an unhealthy relationship to blaming, may be a necessary phase for you to go through, but let it be only a phase. It encourages the unfortunate-victim attitude that implicitly says, "Someone must rescue poor me," thus cutting you off from taking any initiative to help yourself.

Guilt—feeling bad about what you did or failed to do— is another primary component of grief. It may be hard not to heap guilt on yourself at this point. Such feelings may be well deserved, or they may be largely false. In either case, the best antidote is to assess honestly your share of responsibility, if any, for acquiring the virus, acknowledge your part in it, and then set about doing all you can to strengthen your body and your spirit.

Blaming somebody else for what has happened may seem to absolve you from guilt, at least for a while. But you are wasting valuable time and physical and emotional energy you could better use in facing your situation and taking whatever positive steps are possible.

One destructive way of attempting to deal with guilt is through revenge. You may not know who passed the virus on to you, but you are going to get even by passing it on to others. Randy Shilts tells of Gaetan Dugas, "who [to avenge himself for having been infected with the virus] was having sex with people at various sex parlors and then calmly telling them he had gay cancer."[6]

Revenge is one of those very human reactions that promises much more than it delivers. It does nothing to strengthen your immune system or improve your health. All it does is deplete your precious store of vitality while you pursue a negative goal. Michael Callen puts the idea of revenge in the proper perspective when he writes, "Living is the best revenge."[7]

Depression and Possible Thoughts of Suicide

Another facet of grief into which you may plunge is depression. No one hears the diagnosis of a terminal illness, no matter how far in the future the end may be, and goes out and celebrates. Of course you are depressed!

At first, it may seem to you that with the diagnosis of HIV or AIDS, you are losing everything. You are not. What you are losing, among other things, is your idea of how life ought to proceed for you. Every loss must be grieved, and one of the ways of grieving is to feel depressed. Some depression in such a situation is normal. You feel sad, tired, uninterested in or discouraged by life's events. If within a few days or weeks you move out of these feelings, you can begin to take positive steps to deal with your situation.

Particularly with men, self-esteem may be wrapped up with job performance. Your ideas about yourself may depend in large measure on your working life. As your health declines, even to a small degree, you may be unable to work the long hours needed to perform to your former standard of excellence. Your self-image suffers a blow, and depression sets in. As the disease progresses, you may suffer a whole series of blows as you find your life growing bit by bit more limited.

Or you may have defined yourself as a man by the number of sexual partners you had. (This can be true whether a person is heterosexual or homosexual.) Now, if you have any sense of responsibility, you know that this kind of behavior must stop. Again, you are losing a way in which you have defined yourself. The prognosis for persons with AIDS is often depressing enough without the loss of your self-estimation as a person of sexual prowess.

If you have been wrapped up in your work and must cut back, or have had to quit work entirely, ask yourself what you would like to do now that you have time. If sexual expression has been the most important facet of your existence, how are you going to fill this void? As you try to discover new goals for your life, ask yourself why your life matters to you. What had you planned to do with it, besides concentrating on work and/or sex? What else can bring you satisfaction? Frequently, people find that getting involved in a cause where their help can make a difference brings a measure of joy.

There can also be immediate, small pleasures. When you wake up in the morning and think about the day ahead, ask yourself, "What might bring me joy today?" One man who entrusted me with excerpts from his journal wrote of getting up early one day and watching the sun rise. He had seen sunrises before, he wrote, and most sunrises are basically the same. "Yet this morning it was exciting and beautiful to me. I was seeing it for the first time from a different perspective." He was involved in experiencing living in the moment, rather than ignoring a present beauty as he focused on some future task or satisfaction.

This same man put the question point-blank to God about what he should do with his life after finding out he had AIDS. (He could just as well have addressed his question to the Universe or the Great Being, and received the same answer.) He repeated the question day after day, and the answer came to him: "Teach my children about AIDS." And he does. He speaks to individuals, to groups, anywhere and anytime the opportunity presents itself and he is healthy enough to respond. He suggests that people should not dismiss the ideas that occur in answer to such a question, even though they may at first seem impossible or crazy. The follow-up question can be, "How shall I do this?"

Depression often bears a relation to blaming, but in this case the person you are blaming is yourself. It stems from anger unexpressed and turned against yourself. If, as Edmund White observes, "psychologically anger replaces despondency,"[8] then conversely despondency can be a cover for unexamined anger.

You may be violently angry with yourself, but you may be too frightened to allow yourself to understand this. Hidden in your unconscious mind may be the idea that to exorcise your anger and guilt, you should commit suicide. This would be an extreme reaction, but our unconscious inner self registers *feelings* without consciously imposed limits on both feelings and actions. Consciously you are unaware of any impulse to suicide. Instead, your hidden feelings present themselves in a more nonthreatening way, as depression. Whatever may be the underlying "script" of your depression, the antidote consists of finding the true feelings within yourself, acknowledging them, and expressing them in ways that do no harm to yourself or to others. A further antidote is to discover meaning and purpose in your life under its present circumstances.

You may, however, remain mired in depression. The sad, hopeless feelings may fluctuate, getting better sometimes and worse at others, but they don't go away. You may be so tired you can hardly get out of bed. You may have trouble sleeping, may lose your appetite. Your sexual interest and activity may diminish or even disappear, or you may become hyperactive sexually in an unsuccessful attempt to alleviate your low mood. You may be plagued by feelings of worthlessness or excessive guilt that are not relieved by talking your feelings through with another person. All these symptoms are characteristic of clinical depression rather than the transient depression you might expect in your situation. You are in need of professional help. While clinical depression is the number one mental health problem in the United States, it is also one of the most treatable. Psychotherapy, mood-leveling—not mood-altering—nonaddictive drugs, or both can help you through this emotional slough.

Acknowledging your real feelings, assuming responsibility for dealing with them constructively rather than destructively, assuming realistic responsibility for your actions, and *deciding to take constructive steps in dealing with your HIV positive status* are energizing and empowering ways of handling your situation.

What matters with all the phases of grief reactions is the duration and severity of each particular phase. If you find yourself continuing month after month in one or more of these stages of grief, you need help in dealing with your reactions. Just talking with an understanding friend may help. Perhaps a spiritual counselor can help you out of the depths into which you have fallen. Reading one or more books may help you understand your situation so that you can deal realistically with it. Finding a support group may help. If you need a skilled counselor, search one out. Whatever is necessary to help you take charge of your life, *do it*.

Other Reactions

Shame

A feeling of shame may accompany your discovery of your positive HIV status. Why, you may ask angrily, should you be ashamed of having AIDS? After all, it is an illness, not a matter of morality. Yet our popular culture frequently attaches a stigma to AIDS. Often PWAs (persons with AIDS) are seen as present-day lepers. In addition, feelings about AIDS may gather power from societal attitudes about homosexuality that you internalized long ago. No matter how much you seem to have overcome those societal attitudes, now they may come back to haunt you. If you hadn't been one of "those people," possibly you would not now have AIDS. The very fear you feel about AIDS can also trigger shame. Popular cultural attitudes tell us that only the weak and cowardly feel fear; real men don't—and haven't you often heard that gay men aren't *real* men?

Guilt, we said earlier, is feeling bad about what we did or failed to do. It relates to outward actions. With shame we feel bad about who we are. Because it is connected to our foundational understanding of ourself, it is likely to be far more detrimental to our emotional health than guilt. Because shame is so much a part of our inner climate, we often fail to recognize it in ourselves. Without knowing it, we labor under blanket self-condemnation. Others, either in person or through articles and books, can assure and reassure us that we need not feel ashamed. Ultimately we are the only ones who can break the power of shame over ourselves.

What inside of you is causing your feelings of shame? Do they stem from thoughts or behavior that you can change? If so, the obvious answer is to change your shame-laden ideas and actions. This may not be easy. Often our actions and mental processes are rooted in habit, which provides a deceptive feeling of comfort because those habit patterns are familiar. For this reason we tend to cling to habits even when they are detrimental to our well-being. If you believe you are really a worthless human being, you may, for example, feel it necessary to inflate your tattered image with indiscriminate sex, counterfeit love. Or because you see yourself as "bad," you may unconsciously feel a need to flagellate yourself by internalizing right-wing condemnation of homosexuality.

You may have to engage in some deep soul-searching to find out why you prefer injurious thoughts and actions to those that will promote your welfare. If you are able to name the original source of your shame—ideas absorbed in childhood, societal censure of homosexuality—you begin to realize that you no longer need to carry this old burden. Instead you can respond to life out of a new understanding of yourself. Even though changing your thought habits may be difficult and painful, when you know the true cause of your shame you can respond to yourself with compassion and self-love.

Wholesome self-loving should not be confused with narcissism or an inflated sense of your own importance. The Bible instructs us to love our neighbor as ourselves. We may get a fresh insight if we turn that idea around: We should love ourselves as much as we are called upon to love our neighbor.

Louise L. Hay is an author, speaker, and workshop leader who has worked tirelessly to help PWAs fight their disease. One of her helpful suggestions consists of ten ways in which to love yourself. Some people would disparage positive thinking as merely a bandage or gimmick. Unless you face your underlying shame issues, positive thinking may not help much. However, when it comes to a choice between constantly criticizing yourself or constantly feeding your spirit with forgiveness and lovingkindness for yourself, it is not hard to guess which will be more helpful to you.

---

10 Ways to Love Yourself

Louise L. Hay

1. *Stop All Criticism.* Criticism never changes a thing. Refuse to criticize yourself. Accept yourself exactly as you are. Everybody changes. When you criticize yourself, your changes are negative. When you approve of yourself, your changes are positive.

2. *Don't Scare Yourself.* Stop terrorizing yourself with your thoughts. It's a dreadful way to live. Find a mental image that gives you pleasure (mine is yellow roses) and immediately switch your scary thought to a pleasure thought.

3. *Be Gentle and Kind and Patient.* Be gentle with yourself. Be kind to yourself. Be patient with yourself as you learn new ways of thinking. Treat yourself as you would some-one you really loved.

4. *Be Kind to Your Mind.* Self-hatred is only hating your own thoughts. Don't hate yourself for having the thoughts. Gently change the thoughts.

5. *Praise Yourself.* Criticism breaks down the inner spirit. Praise builds it up. Praise yourself as much as you can. Tell yourself how well you are doing with every little thing.

6. *Support Yourself.* Find ways to support yourself. Reach out to friends and allow them to help you. It is being strong to ask for help when you need it.

7. *Be Loving to Your Negatives.* Acknowledge that you created them to fulfill a need. Now you are finding new, positive ways to fulfill those needs. So lovingly release the old negative patterns.

8. *Take Care of Your Body.* Learn about nutrition. What kind of fuel does your body need to have optimum energy

and vitality? Learn about exercise. What kind of exercise can you enjoy? Cherish and revere the temple you live in.

9. *Mirror Work.* Look into your eyes often. Express this growing sense of love you have for yourself. Forgive yourself looking into the mirror. Talk to your parents looking into the mirror. Forgive them too. At least once a day say: "I love you, I really love you!"

10. *Love Yourself* . . . Do It Now. Don't wait until you get well, or lose the weight, or get the new job, or the new relationship. Begin now—and do the best you can.[9]

Fear

One of the almost inevitable feelings that accompany the realization that you are HIV positive is fear. When gay men see twenty or fifty or seventy of their friends and acquaintances die, it is only natural to fear the agent of so much death.

How do you deal with the fear that assails you at times like an immense, overwhelming wave, and at other times like a furtive ghost lurking in the background of even your happiest moments, corroding everything with a subtle poison?

When you are assailed by fear, your muscles become tense; your emotions tighten up. Such tenseness throws you off balance, both physically and psychologically. Physically, you are more apt to get sick. Psychologically, you are robbed of enjoyment of life. What can you do? Ignoring the fear does not help. Neither does bravado. Only as you look your fear in the face can you find relief. In the case of AIDS, you have reason for trepidation. However, you can decide that you will not be immobilized by your fear, that you will take action. But how?

One way of dealing with fear is to channel it into constructive effort. When the *New York Post* persisted in what Arnie Kantrowitz called "blatant fag-baiting," the Gay and Lesbian Alliance Against Defamation (GLAAD) organized demonstrations against the paper. "Fear turned to rage," Kantrowitz says, "and rage soon became determination."[10]

Undoubtedly ACT UP (AIDS Coalition to Unleash Power) draws at least some of its constituency and a good deal of its energy from rage that has found a purpose and an outlet: demanding more government action and research for AIDS, as well as a shortened time between development of a potentially effective drug and its release to the public. Members of ACT UP have found a way of doing something about the immense fear and resulting sense of powerlessness that AIDS has brought to gay people. While some of the ACT UP demonstrations may seem to be unnecessarily graceless, the basis for them is sound: moving people out of fear into action aimed at producing helpful results.

Norman Cousins, who has done a great deal to show us how emotions and illness interact, speaks of the "biology of hope." Such emotions as hope, faith, love, will to live, festivity, playfulness, purpose, and determination are "powerful biochemical prescriptions."[11] Cousins says practically everything influences the immune system, which he describes as "a mirror to life, responding to its joy and anguish, its exuberance and boredom, its laughter and tears, its excitement and depression, its problems and prospects. *Scarcely anything that enters the mind doesn't find its way into the workings of the body.'*"[12] You would not knowingly feed your body poison day after day. Therefore don't feed your mind the poison of negativity. It is only a more circuitous way of poisoning your body.

In practical terms, how can you implement such things as will to live, festivity, playfulness? Often when people learn that they are HIV positive they see only that their life has suddenly been put in a very small box. "I will never be able to do . . . " becomes a despairing refrain. This may or may not be true. What they are experiencing is the loss of a dream, the loss of a sense that there are no limits to what they can do in life, the loss of a sense of endless time. In this case, grieving such losses may not be the best way of dealing with them.

Photographer Carolyn Jones has put together a portfolio she calls "Living Proof," more than three dozen photographs of smiling PWAs or HIV positive people. The pictures present a model of what living with AIDS can be. Each of the people, she says, decided that even though they had only a limited amount of time to live, they would do at least some of the things they had always meant to do but never did. They had taken a positive approach.[13]

An experienced counselor tells me she talks with her clients about their hopes and dreams, helping them explore the possibilities of making at least a few of these desires and ambitions come true. "Are you sure you can't do that?" she will ask. "Why do you think you can't?" If her clients find that even one or two of the things they have wanted to do are still possible, their sense of limitation lifts. Their desires may be relatively small—play touch football at family get-togethers, go camping with their children or nephews and nieces, take a particular trip or vacation. "Consult your doctor to learn what you realistically can or can't do," the counselor advises. "Talk it over with your relatives. If you want that trip and your doctor OKs it, scrounge up the money and go.

If your dreams are so great that even if you had remained in excellent health you might not have achieved them, or achieved them at a detrimental cost to yourself (become a millionaire, have a record number of sexual partners), it is time to reassess them. Would your dreams really bring you the happiness you thought they would? If so, why? If not, what can you put in their place that is achievable and can bring you deeper joy and satisfaction?

Part of the fear and grief you feel results from the knowledge that almost surely you will not have sixty or seventy years in which to do your living. Your friends have been cut down perhaps even before they reached their prime years. You grieve the waste of their talents and potential, the loss of their hopes and dreams. You don't know how much time you yourself may have.

How can you deal with your own HIV status and the emotional numbness that comes from seeing friend after friend die of AIDS? "One day at a time" has long been a staple of twelve-step programs for dealing with dysfunctional living. If you begin to live one day—*only* one day—at a time, you find you need deal only with a manageable fraction of reality. What had seemed impossible becomes, bit by bit, possible. Focus on the day you are living. You probably have commitments you must fulfill in this particular twenty-four-hour period. You probably also have some discretionary time. What use of that time will bring you some joy or satisfaction? If you find you usually have no discretionary time, perhaps you have overcommitted yourself. In that case, reexamine your priorities and see where you can make changes.

It is important to your well-being that you have some time to fill with an activity you enjoy. Try to do something each day that will feed your emotions or your spirit. Such small satisfactions can add up to feelings of contentment with life. You are still alive. Therefore live! Depression and the loss of your will to live cannot bring your friends back from the dead. Honor the memory of a friend by dedicating your discretionary activity on a particular day to that friend, and take joy in so honoring him. If remembering the friend brings tears, weep. Choked-back emotions fester. Expressed emotions, even if expressed to no one but yourself, help to cleanse the wound that loss inflicts.

Spend Time with Your Nightmare

One of the most powerful ways of dealing with fear is to spend time with what causes that fear. Dan Turner, a

PWA, had apparently dealt with other AIDS deaths by not letting himself "feel" them. He began to spend time with his nightmare in August 1984 when Bobbi Campbell died. Campbell, a registered nurse, was the first Kaposi's sarcoma patient to go public as a person with "gay cancer" and begin awakening the gay community to the threat of immune-deficiency diseases.[14] His was "the first death that really got to me," Turner has said. "I realized that I had never cried about my cancer, about AIDS, about any of it. But I cried for fifteen minutes solid when I heard Bobbi had died."[15]

Avoiding your intense feelings and fears will not help you subdue them. In a classic children's book, *There's a Nightmare in My Closet* by Mercer Mayer, a little boy shoots a Nightmare. Instead of getting angry or running away, the Nightmare begins to cry. The little boy finds that the only way he can get the Nightmare to stop crying is to tuck him into bed and sleep next to him. Anna Quindlen, commenting on this story, says that much useful therapy is based on this principle of adopting one's nightmares, rather than denying or ignoring them.[16]

Rev. Christine Oscar tells how she learned about spending time with her nightmare. Following the death of Paul, a gay friend, from AIDS, she was feeling extraordinarily depressed one day. When she got to her office, Paul's friends David, Curtis, and Edward were waiting for her. Shutting herself in her office, she refused first David's and then Curtis' attempts at drawing her into their company. When Edward, Paul's closest friend and roommate, put his head in the door, he looked so forlorn she let him come in. He began telling story after story about Paul.

When she and Edward joined David and Curtis, the three men began talking about who would die next. Her first impulse was to view the conversation as insane. And then she realized, "*This was sanity for them, the realest of realities*. Just because I feared their deaths and was uncomfortable discussing [them], didn't mean that they didn't need to talk about [them]." Slowly it dawned on her what a moment of miracle and grace she was witnessing. "They were including me, trusting me and involving me in the most intimate experience they would ever face—death. We could talk, joke, laugh and cry about everything else, why not this? So we talked about the untalkable, that day and many days afterward."[17]

Another way to spend time with your nightmare is to read about facing death. Stephen Levine's book *Who Dies? An Investigation of Conscious Living and Conscious Dying* can open your heart, mind, and spirit to the richness and beauty of this last and greatest adventure each of us will ever have.

"Most people begin to open to their life not because there is joy, but because there is pain," Levine writes. "Pain often denotes the limit of . . . the 'safe ground' of the self-image, beyond which a kind of queasiness arises at being in the midst of the uncontrollable. This is our edge, . . . the place the heart closes in self-protection. . . . Playing the edge means being willing to go into the unknown. *It means approaching that place where real growth occurs.*"[18]

How can you go about "playing the edge"? Levine suggests that if you "sit down with yourself each morning and allow the mind to quiet, you will begin to see that edge."[19] It is the place from which your mind draws back in fear, not wanting to look. You may have a hundred edges, sore spots in your relationships and in your soul that need examining. Only as you begin dealing with these sore spots can you grow both in your living and, if necessary, in your dying.

When your mind becomes quiet you begin to meet yourself. Not the self you would like to be, but the self you really are. As you meet your real self, you experience a kind of salvation not generally spoken about in religious circles. May Sarton understood this when she wrote of a young woman: "I am myself, she thought, walking down the stairs like a princess. And it meant, I am saved."[20] When we begin truly to know our inner self, we begin to know God, the creative energy at the center of the universe. It is as if this creative energy takes up residence inside us, so that it makes no difference whether we address our prayers or our meditations to a being out there or to our inmost soul. The results are the same.

A Positive Side to HIV Positive

If you are serious about getting in touch with your inmost soul, you will find time—make time—to be alone and quiet so that your soul can communicate with you. In doing this, you may discover to your utter surprise that being HIV positive can bring a positive aspect—an unsuspected new, healing dimension—to your life.

A number of gay men have discovered and experienced this positive dimension. Jim Batson, a young man with AIDS, has testified out of his personal experience that he has seen people with AIDS realign their priorities in life. The process, he has written, is relentless and uncompromising: "As health and prosperity falter, you have to make decisions about what is important in life. Then you have to direct all of your energies to securing and nurturing those things." In his life he has experienced abundance, "and AIDS has been part of my path leading to it."[21]

Michael Callen says that AIDS has been a challenge to him "to *finally* begin living fully" rather than a sign to begin dying. While he would never have chosen to have AIDS, "the plain truth is that I'm happier now than I've ever been. . . . AIDS has taught me the preciousness of life and the healing power of love."[22]

Probably not many people would think of AIDS as a gift from God, as Brian Coyle wrote in his journal on April 26, 1991. Coyle, a Minneapolis city council member for eight years before his death from AIDS in August 1991, saw his disease as "an occasion to change and learn more about myself and the human spirit."[23]

What has happened to you need not be an unrelieved calamity. Stephen Levine, who has worked with many people with terminal illnesses, writes:

> I see the incredible grace of what so many consider tragedy. I see how much connectedness with something deeper has ensued from the investigation of such suffering. . . . The greatest loss is never touching the essence of fulfillment, our original nature, the source of peace in one's life. What brings pain to my heart is seeing beings who have lost the most important loved ones: themselves. . . . We might even say that satisfaction cannot be found in the world of desires, but is only to be found in the uncovering of our true nature.[24]

Such uncovering comes because we spend time in silent expectation. Whether we say we spend time with God, Creative Energy, the Infinite, or ourselves does not matter. The results are likely to be the same.

Finding Spiritual Dimensions

In the midst of a busy and successful life, Barbara Bartocci, businesswoman, wife, and mother, felt an emptiness inside. At a friend's urging she decided to set aside an hour a day for prayer. The first day she set her alarm for 5 A.M., a cold, dark time in February in the Midwest. She found it strange to be alone with God. "No church rituals. Just me. And God. For an hour. . . . 'Well, God, here I am,'" she said. "'Now what?'"

What she discovered as she sat, with nothing happening, not even able to frame a prayer, was that her mind eventually quieted, as did her breathing, "until I sensed a stillness within me. . . . Then I felt the warm presence of love. . . . All my life I'd been *told* God loves me. On that cold February morning I *felt* his love."[25]

"I just sit still and clear my mind—get in tune with the Infinite," Marilyn Morgan Helleberg's father told her in answer to her question about what he did in the half hour before his noon meal at home when he went into the den and closed the door. Even though he was "an old-fashioned, 24-hour-a-day doctor who made house calls to farm homes in snowstorms in the middle of the night," getting in tune with the Infinite was important enough that he set aside time to do this every day.[26]

The key to discovering spiritual dimensions is perseverance. If you continue steadfastly day after day with a half hour or an hour of quiet time, you will find rewards for your commitment. They probably won't come quickly, and they probably won't be spectacular. Many times they may be uncomfortable. But because you are listening to your spiritual self you *will* experience salvation in one way or another.

If you are in tune with the theology that teaches salvation through Jesus Christ, very likely you will experience such salvation within the orthodox Christian framework. Those who follow other avenues of belief will experience salvation differently, as new insights, new horizons, a need to deal with painful issues, as preparation for more life, or preparation for death. The spiritual dimension of the world is limitless, inexhaustible, rich beyond our wildest imagination. When you faithfully set aside time every day, sooner or later you will experience results. Listening to your soul is a process that cannot be hurried.

Besides waiting in silence, you may want to spend some of your time in prayer or meditation; perhaps in some reading with a spiritual emphasis; perhaps using deep breathing exercises or some yoga-type activity; sometimes using guided meditations or visualizations. All of these help you to allow the spiritual dimension more and more scope in your life.

Affirmations can be a great help in these spiritual sessions. As the universe contains celestial bodies in such staggering abundance that we cannot even imagine their numbers, in the same way it has an unimaginably great spiritual abundance waiting for us to claim it. We cannot, however, simply put a quarter in a slot, turn a handle, and expect spiritual abundance to pour forth. We must reach out for it, spend time making some part of that inexhaustible abundance our own.

What do you feel you need? Write out a sentence that states—affirms—that you are receiving what you need, and say it over and over to yourself.

"I receive the love of God (or, the love of the Creator)."

"I receive all that is necessary to live my life."

"I surround every cell in my body with love (or, the love of God)."

"I surround the AIDS virus in my body with love (or, the love of God)."

"I hold my parents in the Light."

"I hold myself in the Light."

"The Light (or, the Light of God) shines through my whole body."

As you can see, the variations are limited only by what you want to accomplish. They are valid for the believer in God or for the believer in nothing, because the Infinite lives within us, whether we know it or not, whether we want it to or not, by whatever name we may call it. The Spirit is there and is waiting to cooperate with us in bringing healing and wholeness to our souls, which in turn may contribute to the healing and wholeness of our bodies, here or in the dimension across the threshold.

Discovering and nurturing your spiritual dimensions have one ultimate focus: to move yourself into the flow of unconditional love in the universe, however you may name that energy. As you touch this flow, even in a small way, you can pass it on to others. In so doing, you are helping in your own survival. Victor Frankl has spoken about those persons—rabbis, nurses, doctors, laypeople, priests—who escaped the gas chambers and survived the typhus, dysentery, pneumonia, and despair of the Nazi death camps, mostly because they wished to help others. Year after year they survived while most others simply disintegrated. "Reflecting on those times [Frankl] said, 'It did not really matter what we expected of life but rather we had to ask ourselves what life expected of us.'"[27]

Finding Meaning

Ultimately, if you are honest and at least a bit introspective, you will confront the question of the meaning of your life. Why are you here? What do you want from life? What does life expect from you, particularly in your present circumstances?

Before you learned you had AIDS, your ideas of such meaning may have been bound up with making a lot of money, achieving success in your field, finding a handsome partner, living for pleasure, having abundant sex. Your whole focus was on gratifying your material and physical desires. Now your focus may change radically as you discover a dimension to life far deeper than anything you had experienced before. As this change comes about, you may realize that life is not only a taking; it is also a giving, and in the giving lies the reason for existence.

Perhaps, however, your idea of life's meaning did indeed lie in what contribution you could make to humanity, what service you could perform in your particular areas of talent and interest. Now more than ever you want to continue to make a contribution to life while you still have time.

Frequently people who are HIV positive want to serve in some capacity related to AIDS. You may or may not want to do this. You may feel you can make your best contribution in some other area. What life expects from you may be the job you presently hold, a different job, or service performed in your free time. How can you discover the place most suitable for you? Ask—your inner self, the Spirit, the Creative Love at the center of the universe, God.

At some point, because of physical limitations brought on by HIV/AIDS, your goals may have to change. How do you find a new focus in these circumstances? What can life expect from you when your physical stamina is greatly curtailed? Again, the answer can be summed up in one word: ask. If you find you are tired much of the time and don't have the energy to take on anything extra, you can serve in less physically strenuous ways.

The time you spend in nurturing your spirit is not selfish time. Every spiritually aware person makes a contribution to the totality of the world's spiritual dimension, helping bit by bit to heal the world of its spiritual emptiness. That may be too nebulous a concept for you. How do you know that this is happening? You want to do something that requires a less enormous leap of faith.

The fact that you are often tired and need to rest need not limit you as you search for meaning in your life. Caring for your bodily needs is a first priority and can provide an unsuspected avenue of service. Don't be ashamed, therefore, to take naps as you are able to and as you need them. Often we are almost embarrassed about indulging in longer hours of sleep at night as well as periods of rest during the day. We think only young children and old people should do this. Forget such ideas. Do whatever is necessary to maintain your physical well-being.

As you allow yourself rest periods, you will discover that these can be prime times for doing affirmations. Instead of letting your mind dart here and there, perhaps getting into repetitive cycles of worry, relax and begin saying an affirmation over and over. If it puts you to sleep, no matter. As you awake, let yourself feel the flow of love in the universe. If you don't feel that flow, don't think you have been shut out. Lay your hands palms up by your sides and say to yourself, over and over, "I receive the flow of love in the universe"—or, if you prefer, "the flow of God's love." In time, as you keep doing this, you will begin to be conscious of an interior climate different from the old negative thoughts. As you find yourself filling with love, in your thoughts you can begin to surround one other person with that love. Not your love, but the flow of love that is the gift of the universe to each one who will accept it.

If you want to see results, to know that your meditation matters, choose one or two affirmations and concentrate on using them day after day. One affirmation might be for yourself. The other affirmation might be for someone else—a friend who is ill, a person who is in some way your enemy, your parents. It is not necessary to tell the universe/God specifically what to do for this person or these persons. Simply hold them up into the Light. Continue to hold them up, day after day, week after week. The time will probably come when, for one reason or another, you begin concentrating on someone else. This is no doubt the guidance of your spirit, leading you to a new endeavor. You may also change the affirmation for yourself.

The writer of the letter of James in the Bible says, "You do not have, because you do not ask" (James 4:2). Or, the writer goes on, you don't receive because you ask for unworthy ends. Jesus phrased the idea positively: "Ask, and it will be given you; seek, and you will find; knock, and it will be opened to you. For every one who asks receives, and he who seeks finds, and to him who knocks it will be opened" (Matthew 7:7, 8). Although these statements have been made in the Christian Bible, they express universal spiritual truth. They are not limited in their application exclusively to Christians.

Similarly, Jesus' words in John 7:38 can be understood in

a specifically Christian or in a more universal context. "If any one thirst," Jesus said, "let him come to me and drink. He who believes in me, as the scripture has said, 'Out of his heart shall flow rivers of living water.'" Affirmations are a way of filling the thirsty soul. "Coming to me" and "believing in me" can mean either the actual person of Jesus or the spiritual forces of the universe. Many will argue, even heatedly, against this more generalized interpretation. No matter what the skeptics say, when we fill our souls from the abundance of the universe, we will find "rivers of living water"—love, light, forgiveness, even joy, flowing from our hearts to those of others. Such spiritual adventures and healing of yourself and others are available to you, even in a weakened condition. They prepare the way, if this is the course of your life, for a death that will become a spiritual blessing and adventure for you and those around you.

Ultimately, finding the meaning of life is an intangible spiritual achievement, a gift that comes from a meeting of your spirit with the Spirit. In religious terms, it is the meeting between you and God, earth and heaven, the temporal and the eternal. It may be expressed through either outward or inner spiritual service. Life's meaning comes in many ways, but seldom without being sought.

Long-term Survival

Why do some PWAs become long-term survivors and others don't? There are any number of possible reasons: your genetic and hereditary makeup combined with previous health habits, drug use, positive or negative attitudes, fear, hatred, love and acceptance by your family or lack of love from your family, church, and society because you are gay, luck, fate—the list could go on.

Dr. George F. Solomon, who pioneered in the field of psychoneuroimmunology at UCLA, has found these characteristics among long-term survivors of AIDS:

- They are realistic and accept the AIDS diagnosis but do not take it as a death sentence.
- They have a fighting spirit and refuse to be "helpless-hopeless."
- They have changed life-styles.
- They are assertive and have the ability to get out of stressful and unproductive situations.
- They are tuned in to their psychological and physical needs, and they take care of them.
- They are able to talk openly about their illness.
- They have a sense of personal responsibility for their health, and they look at the treating physician as a collaborator.
- They are altruistically involved with other persons with AIDS.[28]

Michael Callen, writing about surviving AIDS, has made his own list of "What I Would Do If I Were You" (the title of a chapter in his book). It includes deciding if you really want to live; setting reasonable, achievable goals for yourself; preparing for the worst, then hoping for the best; and making peace with uncertainty and contradiction.[29]

*"Prepare
for the world to come as thou shouldst
die tomorrow"* says
the Book of Delight,
and: *"Prepare for this world as thou
shouldst live forever,"*[30]

Callen strongly urges joining a support group. "Sharing survival strategies with other people with AIDS can be invaluable." Plugging into the PWA network will give you access to the latest treatment news, often before you will find out about it anywhere else, Callen says. Those who are experiencing the same problems as you often have a wealth of practical information that can make your jour-

ney easier. Callen urges that you attend at least three sessions of a support group before deciding whether it is the
group for you. If not, he recommends shopping around
for one that meets your needs.[31] Those who do not have a
support group available may be able to plug into a computer network that can provide a somewhat similar function.

Particularly if your family is not available to help you,
whether because they are at a distance or because they
choose not to be available to you, find a PWA group, a
circle of friends, a religious constituency, or a social services organization to stand by you in your efforts to combat the disease, to stay with you when the going gets
rough.

How are you going to manage when you can no longer
work to provide for yourself? What will you do for shelter?
What about medical care and medication? In many cases
this is where the family steps in and provides at least
shelter and care. If your family is not willing or able to do
this, what are you to do?

Make plans well ahead of time. This cannot be stressed
strongly enough. Even if at present you are living successfully with HIV, make plans now. Even before you tell
your family of your HIV/AIDS status, make sure you develop your networks of help and support, emotional and
financial. If at all possible, you do not want to make your
family responsible for the thousands of dollars your medications and hospitalizations will cost. Making financial arrangements may involve the painful discipline of acknowledging your future need. You know, as a man, that men
have egos that frequently are bound up with their careers,
their achievements. To say, "I will not be able to do this
alone. I will need help" may be exceedingly difficult. It
represents loss in many forms: loss of control of your life,
loss of your health, your self-esteem, loss of all the mone-
tary rewards for which you have worked, because finan-

cial help comes only after you have spent yourself into poverty. You may have to quit your job in order to qualify for services because it is almost impossible to earn enough to cover them. Accepting government aid—Supplemental Security Income, food stamps, disability payments, Medicaid—may be a bitter experience. Even to think about it may be very hard for you. Being dependent on others, whether your family or service institutions, may seem at this point to be unthinkable. In the future, however, self-sufficiency may be a luxury you will no longer be able to afford.

A PWA has told me there is no reason to be out on the street. Whether this is an entirely accurate assessment or not, certainly you need to overcome your reluctance to accept help from any quarter, government or otherwise. You need to investigate all avenues of aid as you look to the future. If you are in an area without adequate support services, you may have to consider moving to one where such services will be available. Even if you have a family or a support group who can provide care, you need to consider all possible sources of financial help.

It is also important to consider making a will. If you have possessions to leave to others, *be very sure that you make a will*. Particularly if you want to make certain your partner receives what you want him to have, put this into the most ironclad form possible. Parents and siblings may try to seize everything that is left, even those things in your house or apartment that actually belong to your partner. Put your wishes in writing, very plainly, and make sure your family and your partner know of these wishes ahead of time.

As you consider your financial situation and the fact that you could end up in technical or actual poverty, you may discover that there is an important spiritual principle to be apprehended in all this. It is a time to learn the dignity and grace of receiving, and to discover what you may supply in return. In the past you may have thought of giving in terms of money and things. There are other intangible, nonmonetary gifts you can give. To learn what these may be and to value them can become deeply meaningful and satisfying experiences in your pilgrimage through AIDS. If you cannot imagine what such gifts might be, begin asking yourself, God, and/or the universe to show you. As you live each day, you will be given the lessons to learn. At first you probably won't recognize them as lessons until after you have failed to grasp them. You cannot go back, but you can be sure you will be given another chance!

Depending on your particular circumstances, the gifts you give may include such things as patience, lending a listening ear, giving voice to your love, expressing appreciation, sharing faith, exhibiting courage. You will discover other ways of sharing as you attune your spiritual ear to yourself and to others. There may be times when you are hurting so much you feel you can give nothing. Know then that you do not have always to give. Simply receive with gratitude whatever help is given you at that moment. Gratitude also is a spiritual discipline.

Letting Go

The time may come when your body is utterly weary, in pain, and the prospect of the death you have fought against so hard becomes the promise of release. Attitudes in our society do not favor giving up, seeking death in one way or another. The medical profession is geared to saving life, often at almost any cost, not to letting it go. There is a stigma attached to quitting and a deeper stigma attached to conscious suicide.

The brutal ugliness of some of the late stages of AIDS may cause us to rethink such cultural assumptions. Before his death, Jim Strout explained his choice to discontinue treatment: "This disease turns people bitter and angry and scared. That is the last thing I want to be. If I did, I would have lost. . . . Look, this is a terminal disease. There's no shame in giving up. In fact, I'm not giving up. I feel I've won the battle."

He won by taking charge of his death, stopping medical treatment for the pneumocystis pneumonia that had put him in the hospital. He was tired of the nausea from the medication, tired of feeling IVs flowing cold into his veins. He wanted no more of the seizures, the spinal taps, the brain scans. He was tired of the racking cough left from his first bout with pneumocystis. He was, as he said, "sick of being sick."

The day after he made his decision to stop treatment he said, "I feel wonderful about it. It just means I'm not going to live as long."[32]

When prolonging life means prolonging misery, pain, and suffering with no hope of ultimate cure, it becomes a punishment rather than a boon.

Until we are face to face with cessation of life, however, we do not always know how we will react. Dr. Richard Selzer tells of receiving a phone call from an acquaintance asking if Selzer would intervene on behalf of a friend who was dying of AIDS. Selzer agreed, though with misgivings, and a plan was set up. He would visit the dying man's apartment after the man had taken a lethal dose of pills. If he was not already dead, Selzer would administer an injection of morphine. Then the conspirators discovered a flaw in the plan. According to law, because of the manner of death there would have to be an autopsy, and any injected substance would be discovered. The doorman at the apartment building could identify Selzer as a visitor at the time of the suicide. The man's partner advised Selzer not to go to the apartment to make the injection. He would not tell his dying friend Selzer was not coming.

On visiting the apartment, the partner discovered that his friend had not died from the overdose. Not knowing what else to do, he called an ambulance. Five days later, when Selzer visited the man in the hospital, he asked him, "Do you still want to die?" The man shook his head no. Twelve days later he succumbed to pneumonia naturally.[33]

This man, in the end stages of AIDS, with all its attendant wasting, diarrhea, and decay, still took charge of his life and acted on what he chose. When inadvertently he was given a second chance, again he made a choice. He was powerless against the course of his disease, but he was not without power in a different way.

The borderline between wanting to live and wanting to die can be very thin. It can vary with the acuteness of suffering. The PWA who thinks he wants to die may have spiritual and emotional reserves he did not know he had and that his family or loved ones were not aware of.

When Bert Henningson was ill with cryptococcal meningitis, his doctor, Michael Sampson, gathered Henningson's family in the hospital waiting room to explain the situation. The meningitis was an infection of the brain that kept Bert near-comatose and paralyzed. There was no way of telling if he could hear or understand.

Dr. Sampson explained that he could treat the meningitis with antibiotics, but the side effects could be harsh: muscle cramping, nausea, fevers. In Henningson's weakened condition he had a 10 percent chance of making it through the night. Almost certainly he would be dead by the week's end. At the moment Henningson was comfortable, Sampson told the family, adding, "It's not a bad way to die."

The members of the family, as they had always done, each expressed his or her thoughts on the matter, then voted. Unanimously they voted to let Henningson die. Sampson concurred: "He never wanted to prolong his life.

He saw what Dick [Henningson's partner, who had died of AIDS] went through and he said, 'That's not for me.' "

That night Sampson had a dream in which Henningson stood by the edge of his hospital bed. Sampson asked him, "Do you want to fight this or do you want to die?" Henningson didn't answer.

The next morning, when Sampson went to the hospital, nurses told him that they had found the sick man teetering at his bedside, asking for food.

"He didn't answer me in my dream," Sampson told the family when he met with them. "But I sure think he's answering me now." The family voted again, this time to treat the meningitis.

Henningson survived and returned to his parents' home, though not to real health. Long before, he had decided not to prolong his life artificially. "I tried to work everything out with the doctors about critical care and not taking heroic measures," Henningson said. "But things don't stay black and white. They turn to shades of gray. . . . When it comes right down to it, there's only one question. What do you want to do—live or die?"[34]

Many times the unconscious will to live overrules the conscious, rational decision to let go. At other times it can be just the reverse—the unconscious death wish takes charge and the person dies, even though the prognosis is positive.

Particularly because of our societal conditioning, we often wonder how a person can muster the courage to commit suicide. Even when we understand that it represents a way out of insoluble difficulties or pain for the hurting person, we also see it as a leap into an unfathomed realm. "It seems there are only two kinds of beings who enter death willingly," Stephen Levine comments. "One whose heart is wide open, not holding to the body, melting into the next moment, openness to the unknown. The other, whose mind is weary and whose heart is frightened, jumps into death to escape life. The first moves toward the light. The second backs away. They are due equal respect and compassion, the prayers and acceptance of those left behind."[35]

Our conditioning, Levine says, tells us that suicide is a heinous act, a sin. It arises out of a complex web of cultural values that include our fear of the unknown, of death, our sorrow for ourselves at being deprived of the other's presence, our perception that we have not done enough for our loved one, our idea that if only we had done something more, or not done something, the person would still be alive. Choice of death, whether as a single once-for-all event or as a slow deterioration without heroic measures, can activate all of these feelings. In the end, we have to acknowledge that each person must act within the context of his or her own life. We need to forgive the one who chooses death, forgive ourselves for what we may perceive as our failure to keep that person alive, forgive our anger at his or her choice to leave us.

"The being who commits suicide as a means of escaping life is a manifestation of the pain of us all," Levine says. "Suicide is not the answer. But neither is a life of coping and holding to a hope that things will be different or that survival must be maintained at any cost." He counsels those whose friend or loved one has committed suicide to investigate the pain in their hearts "and let it be met by a commitment to serve others, for the cessation of the suffering of all."[36]

Judgment needs to yield to compassion, both for the one who has departed from this life, and for those who are left. Only compassion can heal.

Because there is so much more that could be said about dealing with HIV/AIDS both before and after you tell your family, you may wish to read several books that can help you. Some of these are listed in "For Further Reading" at the end of this book. The library may have others, and often you can get helpful lists from support groups and other services for persons with HIV/AIDS.

Telling Your Family

Once you have begun to come to terms with your HIV positive state, you may think about telling your family.

If your parents don't yet know that you are gay, your first task is to tell them this. Chapter 4 can help you in this venture. Even if you have been reluctant, for whatever reasons, to tell them of your same-sex orientation, you must now give serious consideration to letting them know. If you don't tell them that you are gay, in the event of your death you will present them with an agonizing triple blow: their child has died; they discover that their child was gay; and they discover that he died of AIDS. The death of a child, whether juvenile or adult, presents parents with one of the greatest traumas they can experience. To learn at the same time that that child was gay and died of AIDS would compound the trauma enormously. Not only do the parents lose their child to death; they also lose the child they thought they had, so that even the memory of him as they thought he was eludes them.

Although you may not expect to tell your parents that you have HIV at this time, be prepared with your answer if they ask about it. If you are HIV positive but do not yet have AIDS, you can explain the difference to them. Because this is likely to be an extremely emotional time for them, don't expect them to grasp the fine points of difference between HIV and AIDS or remember the distinction later. You may have to repeat your information on a future occasion.

If they do not ask about HIV, be content to let them deal with the fact that you are gay and get used to this first. Quite possibly they will experience enough grief over your announcement without having to deal with a further cause of grief. You can tell them of your positive status later.

In chapter 4 we discussed possible mixed motives for wanting to come out to your parents. Again, in wanting to tell them you are HIV positive, you may have mixed reasons. Is your main goal to secure their love and acceptance at this difficult time in your life? Do you want to share this most profound event of your life with them because they are among the people who are most important to you? Do you want to tell them because they were such rotten parents and this is a way to strike back at them? Do you, like a tired child, simply want to come home? The fact that you are aware of possible mixed motives can be helpful to you in deciding whether or not to tell your family. As with the coming out process, work through any possible negative motives before you try to deal with your family.

You can do some of this by yourself, but your understanding will be expanded if you talk the matter over with wise friends or counselors.

Telling your family may seem overwhelmingly difficult, but deciding not to tell them has its own pitfalls. For instance, you may experience considerable stress from trying to keep your health problems secret. Such stress can hinder you as you work through your own grief reactions and progress toward acceptance of your HIV/AIDS status. If you do not tell your parents and they find out, they may be angry with you for not confiding in them. In other words, if you decide not to tell your family, you should have some compelling reasons for your decision.

Sometimes, as people become sicker, their original reasons for not telling their family may shrink or disappear. If, after deciding not to tell your family, you find you need the relationship with them, tell them. There is no reason you should not change your mind.

All that was said in chapter 4 about ways of telling your parents you are gay or lesbian holds true as you tell them you are HIV positive. What is the best time for your disclosure, the best place? One counselor suggests that you begin by telling the family member with whom you have the safest relationship. Go gently, she says. Test the waters. This person's reactions can give you support as you consider your next step. In some cases, you may feel the need of telling your family in a more structured setting, with a counselor present.

Again, as chapter 4 suggests, act out in your mind, or with another person, how you visualize yourself telling your parents and how you imagine they will react. Rehearsing the whole situation, not once but a number of times, can prepare you for a variety of reactions and can give you a greater degree of calmness than if you step unprepared into the actual situation with your parents.

All of the grief reactions dealt with in the earlier part of this chapter as well as earlier in this book will undoubtedly come into play when you tell your parents of your HIV/AIDS status. There may be anger, guilt, denial, bargaining, depression, as well as, perhaps, recriminations, futile questioning such as "Who gave it to you?" and a whole range of hurtful comments. Try to understand that these reactions arise out of deep pain within your parents, rather than out of lack of love, ignorance, intolerance, or malice. If you are able to control your responses, *do not retaliate in kind*. This may be exceedingly difficult for you, but it is worth the most strenuous effort to guard what you say at this point.

If your family patterns have always been dysfunctional, it would be unrealistic to expect your parents to react in a helpful, loving, caring way unless you take specific steps to remedy the situation. No matter what kind of relationship you have with your parents or what kind of family patterns exist, you will be wise to prepare for your disclosure about HIV/AIDS with prayer, affirmations, meditation, and visualization, blessing your family day after day for an extended period. Visualize holding them in the Light. Make affirmations of love for them, and in general surround the situation with as many positive thoughts and prayers as possible. The actual encounter may not produce the results you want, but the procedure might have been much worse without spiritual preparation. Remember to include yourself in this process of making ready. Even though the waves of loving prayer and thought you send your parents ahead of time may not seem to do much for them, these affirmations can do wonders for your attitude as you face the task of telling them about yourself.

If negative thoughts arise as you prepare yourself, look at them honestly and deal with them. Perhaps, for example, the anger within you says, "They always have been lousy parents. Why should I expect them to be anything but lousy in this situation?" Maybe they have been lousy parents, but if you expect nothing else from them, it is practically certain you will get the reaction you anticipate. Instead, make a conscious effort to replace negative thoughts with positive ones such as, "I surround my parents and myself with love and understanding." It is not a matter of what you *feel* at this point. It is a matter of moving your will in the direction of love and understanding between you and your parents.

Let your parents know in whatever ways you can that you care about them and have told them about yourself because you want to remain in relationship to them. In telling them, you are giving them an opportunity to learn and grow in circumstances that present them with rare— albeit difficult—opportunities for their growth. Some of the interactions that have taken place between parents and children in the last weeks of life are nothing short of amazing. Bought at the cost of much suffering, they are miracles of grace that reveal the depth of the spiritual dimensions and rewards of life. At least give your parents the opportunity to receive this last gift that you can give them.

If you have no relationship with your parents, if they

wrote you off long ago or if you wrote them off, you may think none of what has been said concerns you. Don't be too sure. Should you die of AIDS, one way or another your parents will find out. Try to visualize their reactions to such information. Your first thought may be glibly cynical: "They'll say, 'Good riddance.'" Go beyond the flip retort, and picture them as they get up the next morning, and the next, and the next, knowing that they will never see you again. In order to get a different perspective, reverse the situation and imagine yourself receiving word that your parents have died in a plane or car crash. Begin to explore the conflicting feelings you would undoubtedly have. As long as they were alive, in the back of your mind there was always the possibility of making contact again. Now that possibility no longer exists. You are left with, "What if . . . ," "If only . . . ," "Why didn't I . . . " If it seems possible these would be your feelings, very likely your parents' feelings would be similar, but more intense. After all, they were responsible for bringing you into the world. No matter how angry they may have been with you, how much they or you may have wanted separation, death puts a different light on the matter. In such circumstances, for your sake and for theirs, make whatever spiritual preparations may be necessary so you can reach out to them, and then do it.

But suppose you tell your family that you are HIV positive, and your worst nightmare comes true. They tell you you are no longer their child. What can you do?

Weep. Rage. Express your feelings. Doing this in your parents' presence is not likely to help, but your instinctive reaction need not necessarily be held back. On the other hand, you may do your weeping and raging privately. Expressing your intense emotions can in itself be healing. Voicing your feelings means that you acknowledge them; you no longer need to use energy pretending to yourself that you can tough it out. Instead, you can use the energy to work out arrangements for your care and companionship. None of this means you should not talk about your feelings of bitter disappointment, abandonment, and pain to your friends.

All that was said earlier about finding a support group and making financial and care arrangements is doubly important now. If you do not already have a nonrelated family, now is the time to build one. Because circumstances differ so greatly, it is difficult to make specific recommendations about how you should do this. Perhaps the best that can be said is follow every lead, every clue, every possibility that seems to give promise of adding a member to your family circle.

You can also use prayer and/or affirmations as a way to help locate those who will stand by you when the going gets rough. "I receive those who will be friends with me as time goes on, knowing that as they contribute to my life, I too can contribute to theirs" might be a way to draw to yourself those who will walk with you. The time may come when you are ready to send thoughts of forgiveness—perhaps even of love—to your family. Whether or not this changes your parents' attitude, it can be helpful to your spiritual growth. It means you have, in large measure, transmuted your bitterness into an attitude that can heal your soul rather than filling it with poison.

Sometimes, without your being conscious of it, abandonment by your parents may seem to mirror abandonment by God. When we were very young, our parents were the gods of our lives and their words carried almost supernatural weight. Something of that feeling still clings like cobwebs in the back corridors of our minds. If you can become aware of this shadowy identification, you can separate the faulty human beings who are your parents from the Spirit at the center of the universe.

The Meaning of AIDS

Over and over, at odd moments of the day, in the dark hours of the night, our hearts ask: Why AIDS? What is the meaning of this disease that so readily fits the psalmist's description (91:6) of "the pestilence that stalks in darkness . . . the destruction that wastes at noonday"—the noonday, and often even the morning, of life?

Part of the trouble is that we do not understand the nature of life. We have been led to believe that life is a linear affair, running from the cradle into the distant future (we prefer not to dwell on the end of that line), and because our technology has performed so many miracles for us, we have come to believe that we can order life to our specifications. When we find we can't always do this, we think life has betrayed our trust.

The ancient Chinese symbol of yin and yang gives us a much truer image of life as a circle divided by a wavy line into light and dark halves, but with a seed of dark in the light and a seed of light in the dark. Life is made up of polarities. The problem is not to choose one or the other, but somehow to give space to both. Our trust in our own power has in it the seed of our betrayal. Yet if we embrace betrayal totally, we lose the seed of trust that moves us into a wider circle of power, intangible but nonetheless real. Our soul will lose the transcendent experience of forgiving life its treachery, allowing the salt of bitterness to be transformed into the salt of wisdom, "that union of love with necessity where feeling finally flows freely into one's fate, reconciling us with an event."[37]

AIDS does not give us a choice between life and ultimate death. Nor does life give us a choice. If we are born, it is certain that we will die. The choice we have is what we do with the time we are given. When love can flow through the time we have here, we will find peace of heart. Just to have had our feet set on a different path, to have glimpsed a less materialistic, more spiritual aspect of life, is a triumph dearly bought but never wasted. We have enlisted our soul in the service of Light.

From the Parents' Side

Several years ago Lucinda and Jim received word from their son's wife in Texas that their son was dangerously ill with pneumonia. When they flew to see him they found him in isolation, beneath an oxygen tent, close to death. As they walked down the hospital corridor after leaving their son's room, his wife asked if he had told them anything. No, the parents replied. Their son was dying of AIDS, she said, and he had asked her to tell his parents this in case he could not summon courage to tell them himself.

A number of years earlier, Lucinda and Jim's son had told them he was gay, but somehow this information had failed to lodge in their minds. Denial had taken over and kept them in a comfortable blindness. Now, suddenly, they were catapulted into an anguished reality.

Amazingly, they rose to meet the situation with grace, wisdom, and faith. Their son's widow is a person of great courage and integrity, which undoubtedly helped Jim and Lucinda through the ordeal. Although their denomination is not particularly tolerant of a same-sex orientation, they held a memorial service at their church for their son, not hiding the fact that he had died of AIDS.

Since their son's death, Lucinda in particular has dealt with her loss first by learning all she can about homosexuality and then by helping to educate her fellow church members. An outgoing person, she has undertaken her self-assignment with strength, courage, and at times, humor. Of course it has not been easy. There have been many tears, much pain. In Lucinda's case it is apparent that her strong Christian faith has been the rock beneath her feet as she has dealt with the waves of grief, anger, guilt, and bitterness that could have overwhelmed her.

Confronting Your Child's Illness

How many parents rally to their son's side when they discover he is HIV positive or has AIDS? How many simply turn their back on their child? There are no reliable statistics to show whether more parents respond helpfully or by abandoning their ill family member. What is apparent is that often families forget their smaller foibles and complaints in the immensity of the crisis they face. They draw together against the greater enemy.

Initially your impulse may be simply to remove your child from your family circle. Already you have a foretaste of the emotional pain, which will worsen in time. You may be overwhelmed by the myriad of problems you envision: the expense of time, physical energy, and money that may be demanded, and the relational problems both with your child and with his partner, if there is one. Geographic distance may be a complicating factor, as well as the reactions of your own parents and siblings, your other children, your friends, neighbors, co-workers, church or synagogue members, and so on. Life would be infinitely simpler in the days ahead, you think, if you disowned your child. Some parents do this.

My word to you at this point is "Don't." You may think that cutting off relationship with your child will spare you unbearable pain. Instead, you are simply issuing life a promissory note that you will have to pay later on. We cannot escape the painful elements of grief by closing a door on them. One way or another, through stress-induced physical illness or emotional turmoil, we pay for locking away our feelings. It is no light matter to abandon your child at the most crucial point in his life.

Whether you stand by your child or abandon him, whether you acknowledge your feelings to a greater or lesser degree, you still will have to deal with denial, anger, guilt, blaming, depression, self-pity, fear, shame—all the emotions we looked at earlier in this book and again in this

chapter. If we don't deal with these emotions straightforwardly, we deal with them in more devious and less helpful ways.

You may be terribly angry at your child: "Why did he
behave that way?" Or you may be angry at his partner:
"He gave it to my son." You may think, "He got himself
into this by living in ways we have never approved of;
now he's on his own."

It is not surprising that you feel anger, though not for
the reasons just mentioned. After all, your life's pattern is
being disrupted. Children should care for their parents
when they get old; the parents should not have to care for
their adult children. Furthermore, children shouldn't die
before their parents. Through his illness your child is implicitly or explicitly demanding far more of you than you
ever thought you would be asked to give.

Sometimes, perhaps because it is too frightening to
name the object of our wrath, our anger remains free-
floating and unfocused. One mother I talked with after her
son's death said, "I am angry." No, she was not angry at
her son, or herself, or God. She was, she said, just angry.
But because she could not attach her anger to something or
someone, she could not deal with it. "I'm running," she
said.

If she could name the objects of her anger, she might be
able to stop running. She would know at least a measure
of the truth about herself, and out of that knowledge
would come strength to deal with other aspects of her life.
Was her anger related to guilt? "I messed up my life. I was
a bad mother. I should have done . . . " Or could she dare
to be angry at this son who had died? Yes, she could be
angry at him for behaving in a way that brought about his
death. After acknowledging her anger to herself, she
could begin to see that being angry at her son need not
keep her from also loving him.

Expressing anger at God, as we saw earlier in this chapter, can be cathartic. Anger expressed in ways that do not physically harm or heap verbal abuse on yourself or others can clear a lot of garbage out of your soul. You can yell at AIDS, write out your rage at this disease, draw or paint the way you visualize the disease and your feelings about it, and clear away more garbage so that you can see clearly to plot constructive steps for your life.

Your anger may be genuine and uncomplicated. It may also be a camouflage for other emotions—guilt, shame, fear. Only as you separate your feelings and call them by their specific names can you begin effective grief work.

As you maintain the relationship to your child, know that you are stepping out into what will surely be a difficult, draining, trying experience, but one that also has potential for emotional and spiritual growth and rewards. Remember also that what you do for your child may have a value to him impossible to measure. "Family, friendship, stillness, balance—these may sound sappy, but they are sometimes the only tonic for this disease," Jim Batson has written. "They do not necessarily cure the body, but they can heal the soul."[38]

One woman described her experience with her gay son as always having to learn one more thing: First she had to learn that he was gay, then she had to learn what it meant to be gay. She had to meet his friends. Then there was her first gay parade, her first gay dance, the first support group she attended, her first P-FLAG meeting, the first gay blessing of union—and then learning that her son had AIDS. She saw her journey as one of continually needing to take the next step of growth.

When her son called to tell her how sick he was, he did not use the word AIDS. Instead he told her he had no immune system. But of course she knew—had known for a long time—that he had all the indications of the disease. He is not the only PWA who has avoided calling it by name. Parents have told me, "He never said he had AIDS" or "He called it 'this thing I have,'" as if by refusing to name the disease the ill person retained a certain distance from it or power over it.

Issues to Be Faced

As you confront your child's illness and its implications for your own life, you undoubtedly find a daunting array of questions facing you. The problems of single parents will be different from those who have spouses. If you live in a different part of the country from your child, that will present other difficulties. Is it feasible for you to make an extended stay with him to care for him? What is his financial situation? At some point he will have to stop working, and his money and insurance may run out. Will you have to assume his financial burdens? What is your financial situation? Must you save for retirement, thereby cutting down on any financial assistance you can give? Is there room in the family home for this adult child to move back in? Are there younger children in the family who must be considered?

"I can't do that . . . "; "He shouldn't expect me to . . . "; "If he thinks I'll . . . he's mistaken," and so on. These may be some of the thoughts that fill your mind. Simply to tell yourself that you must stand by your child no matter what may seem to be a heroic decision. Undertaking a course of action without sufficiently exploring what it will mean in the long term, however, can be a prescription for all sorts of disastrous situations.

Don't ignore your feelings. Jot them down on a piece of paper so that you can consider them rationally. Some of your thoughts may express anger, some guilt, and so on. Recognize these feelings. You need not be ashamed of them; they are natural and real. In the end, however, they may not be the basis on which you want to make your decisions. Instead, gather information about how you can deal in the future with potential problems. What is the role your child wants you to play in his life and care? Until you have some idea of his plans, you won't be able to make yours. He may expect you to do more than you feel able to do, or he may want you to provide love and acceptance but not physical care. Gather all the information you can, from him and from all other available sources. This will give you a realistic look at what you may be facing later on and will help you decide what part you are willing or able to play in your child's future care. In addition, gathering information is a constructive way of *doing* something. Useful action can reduce your feelings of helplessness.

Even while you are striving to make a plan, you can begin your grief work. If the need for care for your child is not yet acute, you have time to pay attention to your feelings before you are plunged into the harder choices you may have to make later.

It may be that, for many different reasons, you cannot bring your child home. You may live in an area without the medical expertise necessary to deal with the disease. Your child may need to stay in the state where he has established residence so he can receive state aid. He may want to stay where he has friends and support groups. You may live in a small community where people quite possibly would turn their backs on you and him. Your health may be such that you cannot take physical care of your child. No matter how strong you are, there will almost certainly be times when you need help from others—hospital care, hospice guidance, friends to give you a rest from unremitting day and night care. Can your community provide such help for you?

Even if you can't provide actual care your attitude can make a great difference. There are many ways of showing love besides taking actual bodily care of your failing child. Letting him know you love him is important. "Be a family," one couple said. "Do things together." What you do depends on your child's state of health and your geographical nearness. One mother quit her job, took all her savings, and for four months traveled all over the world with her son. (It should be noted that he worked for an airline, which made air fare minimal, and she had traveled extensively and was not afraid of dealing with health problems her son might experience in foreign countries.) If all your child can manage is to watch a sunset, watch it with him and enjoy the beauty together.

One mother was so devastated by her son's approaching death that she could not bear to sit with him for an evening and simply be there, even though she knew he wanted her to do just that. (Her son was receiving excellent care so she knew she was not neglecting his physical well-being.) A father came to see his son daily in the hospital, but he sat in a chair in the corner, far removed from his son's bed. A friend and counselor of this young man also visited him daily, sitting by the bed, taking his hand, embracing him when he left. Somehow the father could not bring himself to this degree of intimacy with his son, perhaps because such intimacy had never been part of the family pattern.[39]

Typically, mothers are more likely to be able to deal with the fact of a son's illness. Many fathers find it extremely difficult. Others, although they may not "understand" their son's gayness, nevertheless are supportive in their own ways. One father in a semirural area told me, "I don't get this men loving men business, but he's family, and families stick together. I told him to come home whenever he needed to." (At the time his son was in an experimental drug-testing program in a big city hospital.)

Allen Hanson, a widower and retired farmer in rural Minnesota, visited his son Dick, who lived nearby, on a fairly regular basis. Usually the conversation centered on the family, the failing farm economy, their common political dreams. One night Allen uncharacteristically spoke at some length about two experiences he had had in his life with faith healers. "I just know if I could find someone like that, they could help the doctors and take away this illness of yours," Allen said. At that Dick, overcoming the great weakness he had felt for days, stood up and took his father's hand in both of his. They stayed that way for a long, awkward moment—"two proud Norwegian farmers who seldom shared a handshake in all the years they shared a life." Still holding his father's hand, Dick told his father how good it was to see him and how much he appreciated his father's concern.[40]

If you are at a distance, frequent phone calls may have to substitute for your actual presence with your child. Make those phone calls. Time spent with your child, and honest expressions of love and concern, can mean more than you know.

Pitfalls

There are many pitfalls in dealing with your child. "How can I take back my anger when I told [my son] I'd as soon have him dead as gay?" one parent asked. The answer is simple, if not easy. Tell him you remember saying those words, but now you are sorry. Tell him that, though you cannot take back those words, you want him to know you would give a great deal to have him remain gay and live to old age. Tell him you love him and want to stand by him as he lives his life with HIV/AIDS.

How can you help your child while still allowing him as much autonomy as possible in making his decisions? He has been an independent adult, managing his own life. Now he may be increasingly dependent—and such loss of control over his life is very hard for him. Talk things over with him. If he gets angry, try to keep your own anger under control. If you explain your position to him calmly, it may help to defuse the situation.

You may find that you are in continual conflict with his partner. You want to care for your ill child, and you don't want this stranger getting in your way. Although you may only recently have met your child's partner, he is not really a stranger, either to you or to your child. If society and the church gave to committed gay relationships the same legal, emotional, cultural, and religious support that they do to marriage, your son's partner would be your son-in-law. This might make it easier for you because he would have a seemingly more legitimate claim on helping to make decisions. On the other hand, not every parent likes or trusts heterosexual in-laws. Remember that your child cares greatly about this person (although you may not understand why) and that this person cares greatly about your child.

One man, in the final stages of AIDS, wanted to be sure that his partner would be welcome to sit with the family at the funeral.[41] This may be a difficult hump for the parents to get over. It challenges their "possession" of their child and is an acknowledgment to the community of a fact the parents may want to hide, that their son was gay. You may have far more serious differences with the partner, such as whether or not to take heroic measures of treatment. You feel that because this is your child, you should make the final decision. If your son were legally married to a woman, however, she would have the final say. In this case, from a strictly legal standpoint you are the next of kin. You could lose far more than you gain, however, by insisting on your "rights." If you can understand even a bit of your child's feelings—he loved this man—as well as the partner's feelings, you and he may be able to work out your difficulties. Of course if your child is at all able to express his wishes, neither you nor his partner may have to make the decision.

Be aware that you can easily suffer from stress and burnout, particularly as your son's disease continues. Some of the symptoms that can alert you to your condition are changes in blood pressure, stomach pains, anxiety attacks, depression, irritability, difficulty in relations with people at work or in other settings, increased drinking, overeating, escape through an unusual amount of sleeping, reading, or television watching. Changes in your daily emotional life patterns can alert you to begin taking steps to help yourself cope.[42]

As you care for your child, you may find yourself isolated. This may come about because you fear rejection, ridicule, or persecution at work, from friends, from those in the community, from the groups to which you belong. It is important to find whatever support you can for yourself. There may be established support groups in your community. Call the national Parents FLAG Federation to learn about groups operating in your area. Even if you cannot attend group meetings because of distance or other considerations, perhaps they can put you in touch with someone with whom you can talk by phone. Call an AIDS hotline. Talking with even one nonjudgmental friend, one caring doctor or pastor can help greatly. Several books can help you realize that the problems and feelings you are experiencing are common to people in your situation. (See "For Further Reading.")

If you feel that you are sacrificing everything in your life to your child, it may be time to set limits. You need time off, away from the constant care, away from the visible deterioration of your child. This doesn't mean that you don't love your child. It means you care enough to acknowledge and make provision for human physical and emotional limitations.

Although in your inmost soul what you want to do is save your child, this is not your real role in his life. You are there to walk with him, perhaps to provide physical care for him, certainly to provide emotional support. You are there as a human being, reaching out to another human being. The time will come when you can no longer do anything to make him get better, when you will be called on to let him go. You may need to tell him it is all right for him not to fight anymore, that it is all right with you for him to step over the threshold into his next life. Many times people hold off their dying until some member of the family has arrived from a great distance, until they have made peace with someone, until someone tells them it is all right to go. This may be one of the last loving things you can do for your child, to open your hand and help him let his soul float free.

Rewards

As you read the preceding pages it may have seemed to you that, as the parent of a child with AIDS, you will give, and give, and give some more, without recompense or reward. You may feel that life is cheating you—and you are angry. Even to think such thoughts may be shocking to you. Your situation, however, need not be a one-way street. Recognizing your limitations of time, strength, and money can keep you from overspending your physical, material, and emotional resources and falling into bitterness and self-pity.

As you go along, you may also find intangible rewards that you could not have been aware of as you looked ahead. Jim Batson voiced one possible satisfaction you may discover: helping to heal your child's soul at this difficult time in his life. One caregiver assigned to help a PWA spoke of the "'gifts' from the dying person: trust and love of a kind rarely experienced, and the dying experience itself." Later the caregiver spoke of having been "a part of something . . . holy."[43] The parents of a forty-year-old man who died of AIDS acknowledged the incongruity of receiving recompense in such a situation when they said, "Blessings come in odd packages."

Your son's death and the period immediately following can be times of real blessing. Chris Glaser tells of going with his partner to the hospital to see his friend Lyle

Loder's body an hour or two after Lyle had died. The orderly who was cleaning the room left, leaving the two men alone with Lyle. His face was uncovered, and someone had placed rose petals in the form of a cross on the bedding covering Lyle's slight frame. "Seeing him and taking his hand in mine (cool, but not cold) comforted me enormously," Chris writes. "I hoped his spirit might have hung around long enough to see us there."

Later Chris marveled that, even in death, Lyle should have provided comfort: "Lyle Loder had led us beside the still waters of death and somehow restored our soul. The one who seemed in need of healing had healed us."[44]

Such a reaction is not unusual, according to Stephen Levine, if family and friends are allowed to remain a number of hours with the body of the person who has just died. If the person dies at home or in a hospital that allows time with the body after death, Levine suggests tidying up the room, removing medications and any life-support paraphernalia, dressing the body in the person's favorite clothes, playing favorite music, bringing in flowers, lighting candles or incense, and simply spending time with the person who has departed. Society has encouraged us to turn the body over as soon as possible to the professionals who will ready it for cremation or burial. The idea of being with a dead body has been presented to us as ghoulish. Instead, it can be a time of rare comfort and peace.

Levine says that often, if one places the tips of one's fingers gently on the crown of the head, for some hours after death one can feel the vibrancy of the life force as it leaves the body. If one observes the face carefully in the hours after death, one often perceives a greater and greater lightness. The face softens and falls into a smile not due to stiffening of the muscles. Those sitting close to the body, touching it, feel a sense of completion.[45] Quite possibly, as Chris Glaser hoped, Lyle Loder's spirit had indeed hung around to be with Chris and his partner.

The departure of the spirit can be very real. Chris' friend, John, whose partner had died of AIDS, told Chris, "He died in my arms. I felt him leave his body. That's why I'm sure I'll see him again."[46]

Stories of the last hours with PWAs often indicate that a number of friends and caregivers were "watching" with the family, awaiting the moment of death. When death takes place with family and friends at hand, both the one who is dying and those who are present are blessed.

"His final gift was to those of us who were at his bedside when he died," a minister-neighbor wrote in a sermon. Although one of the outstanding characteristics of this young man had been his intense will to live, a few hours after he entered the hospital in an emergency situation he said to his grandmother, who had cared for him, "Grandma, I want to die." "It was as if he were saying, 'the time has come.' Twenty minutes later he died quietly without struggle. His eyes squinted as they do when one sees an extremely bright light. Then there was a faint smile on his face and a look of serenity and peace in which he was telling us, 'Don't worry, I'm fine. All is well.'"[47]

This minister, who had spent many hours with his young neighbor, told me—groping for words to express something inexpressible—"Because of him, I know now—I *know*—that life is stronger than death." What too often is a cliché in Easter or funeral services had become for him a real and overwhelming experience. Somehow to know, powerfully, deep within, that death does not hold the winning hand was an unexpected and immeasurable return for the time, energy, and love given in the preceding months.

Dick Hanson, who had been a farmer and a politician, died at 5:30 A.M.—"farmer's time." The morning before, he had suffered a seizure that doctors said had probably left him unaware of his surroundings, "beyond pain and—finally—beyond struggling. Yet those closest to him swore he could hear them, knew what was happening, and knew it was time. 'Three times during the course of the night he brought his hands together and his lips would move, and you knew he was praying. I can't help but think he was shutting himself down,' said Roy Schmidt, a Minnesota AIDS Project official and longtime friend who stayed with Hanson that last night. Hanson died holding the hands of the two people most dear to him— his sister, Mary Hanson-Jenniges, and his partner of five years, Bert Henningson. 'Amazing Grace' was playing softly on a tape machine in the corner of the room."[48]

Gus and Charlotte Sindt said that when their son David died in Chicago, the apartment was filled with "family"— relatives, local caregivers and friends, and many who had come from around the country to be with David in his last days and hours. David had been the moving spirit in forming Presbyterians for Lesbian and Gay Concerns, which had developed into a nationwide network.

As David breathed his last, everyone gathered in the living room in a spontaneous prayer circle, hands joined, as they said farewell to David and committed him to God's care. For those participating it was an unforgettable moment, a benediction at the end of their vigil, a recognition of an ending here but a beginning there, a moment no one had planned or could have planned. For a brief period eternity and time were joined.

Miracles of the Heart

A Good Friday/Easter story comes from an unknown chaplain through a gay computer bulletin board. Steven was of Puerto Rican birth, the shining star, the pride and joy of his loving Catholic family. They did not know he was gay, certainly not that he had AIDS, only that he had a rare and difficult type of pneumonia. Steven's girlfriend knew, however, and as his condition worsened she urged him to tell his family. "You're not being fair to them or to yourself," she told him. Because of papers the parents would have to sign after his death that would name the disease, they would eventually find out, and they would be left "with only a grave to talk to. Don't let them go through this alone. Don't hold back from them such a vital part of you. Do this for them and trust the love that exists between you." Steven, unable to talk because of a tube in his throat, printed on a large yellow pad, "I'll think about it." That was early Thursday morning.

Friday morning Steven's pad contained the stark words: "I have A.I.D.S. I am Gay." His mother stood by him, her love unwavering. His brother, expressing nothing, stayed also. But his father was angry: "You brought this disease upon yourself. It is God's judgment for your sin. I have no sons who are fags. . . . I disown you . . . You can rot in Hell!" And he left before he could see the words Steven was printing in large shaky letters, "I love you."

All day Saturday the father stayed away. On Sunday he returned and sat alone in the intensive care cubicle with his son. Later he recounted some of the conversation: "Steven, you have turned my world upside down. . . . [Yesterday] I was angry that you had not told me sooner. I was angry that you told me at all. . . . I have been taught that the Church speaks for God and says that being a homosexual is wrong and AIDS is a consequence of Sin. But I love you and so now nothing is clear anymore. . . . I wanted you to tell me you were sorry. I do not say that I will ever understand about this Gay business, but you are my son and I know of your goodness. . . . I must wrestle with all that you are and love all that you are, not just the pieces that fit in with my Church's rules. So now I tell you that it is I who am sorry, and I ask your forgiveness."

"There were tears," said the unknown author. "There was joy. The rest was all private, the kind of communing that occurs between people who have resolved their differences and are reconciled. . . . Three hours later, Steven slipped into a coma and died. We were all with him, and he died in peace. The father tore off the page from Steven's pad which said, 'I have A.I.D.S. I am Gay' and which also said, down at the bottom in large five-year-old letters, 'I love you.' He folded it carefully and put it in his pocket."

Later Steven's doctor, who knew nothing of what had taken place, said to the chaplain, "Too bad that Steven succumbed to panic last week and asked for that breathing tube. He and his family could have been spared this extra week of suffering."[49]

Panic? Spared extra suffering? Sometimes the soul chooses more wisely than it knows.

Many a mother in particular has prayed for a miracle—that her child's life would be spared. But miracles come in many forms, though we may need inner eyes to see and hearts that understand about things of the spirit. Bill Falk writes about a miracle that took place as his brother Byron died slowly with AIDS.

> I knew when I first saw my brother's gaunt face last year I was beginning the most agonizing year of my life. I didn't foresee that it would also be the most wondrous and most miraculous. All that had gone unsaid between my brother and his family, that formidable blockage of words and emotions, dissolved. All that mattered was that he was under attack and that he was ours—our flesh and blood.

The family came to know Byron's partner, John, and together they cared for Byron. Bill himself was

> surprised to discover, once the wraps were off, how strong were my brother's feelings for me. I think he was surprised at the strength of mine. I tucked him under a blanket I'd bought one day, and said, "I love you." His smile was full of happiness, everything else forgotten.

I was surprised, too, to see my father throw off the prejudices of his generation like an outworn coat. Many times at the hospital I marveled as this 63-year-old retired banker and Army vet blended seamlessly into a room full of gay men, joking with my brother's friends, touching them with affection, sharing their pain.

My mother, too, traveled light years. At the end, in St. Vincent's Hospital in Manhattan, my mother and John were as one person, spooning food to Byron's mouth, putting a straw to his lips. We cried together. We laughed together when Byron flashed his humor and his independence, prizes which he held high above the flood until it overtook him.

"Your arms are still very muscular," I remarked one day, as Byron lay in his bed.

He cast a glance at John and my mother, fussing with a meal he knew he couldn't escape. "It comes from pushing them away," he said.

At the wake, we were overwhelmed by more than 100 of my brother's friends, gay and straight, men and women. They told us about the life my brother created, giving texture and shape and color to years that we had seen only in silhouette. We saw that his life was full, that he contributed a great spark of joy.

Afterwards, his friends threw a party—a celebration of my brother's life. My father and mother, who once might have been so ill-at-ease in this setting, embraced his friends and were embraced. My father stopped the music, raised a glass and thanked everyone "for being so wonderful and making it so . . . easy." My mother had prayed so hard for a miracle. I thought then, as I saw my dad reflected in a hundred grateful and shining eyes, that we'd had our miracle, after all.

261

We shouldn't have waited, of course. We shouldn't have waited until it was so obviously right, so obviously necessary. But regrets would be a foolish indulgence now.

His illness presented a final chance to give Byron the love and acceptance that he needed so badly and that we needed so badly to give. We gave it. He got it. He gave it back. We were all, in a very real sense, healed.

The day he died, I sat in his hospital room clenching his hand, telling him we were all there and not to be afraid. . . . He was beyond speaking then but he squeezed back, hard. The love that poured through me was pure and brilliant and without condition or boundary and I will never forget that feeling. . . .

And I know this: Though Byron, my little brother, is gone, he will be part of me all of my days.[50]

The Journey of Grief

These are beautiful and comforting thoughts. Yet the reality is that days lengthen into months, months into years, and it is impossible for us not to move on. How we move on is the important question. William E. Wallace speaks of grief as a journey during which we accept the loss, experience the pain of the loss, learn to live in an environment from which the loved one is missing, and remove our emotional energy from the loved one in order to invest that energy in other significant relationships. This does not mean that we get over the loss of a loved one. Rather, completing the journey of grief deals with function, not with forgetting: one has completed the journey of grief when one is functioning as well as before the loss.[51]

The length of time involved in this journey differs from person to person. Our society would like recovery to be quick, the quicker the better, because on the whole we do not want to be reminded of death. Others' grief makes us uncomfortable, because it makes us think about death, and we want to avoid such thinking in every way possible. Even to mention a time span for working through grief can be a trap, because if your experience differs from this, you may think you haven't grieved enough or you are grieving too much. People often give indications that the griever ought to be over it in a couple of months instead of the more realistic figure of a year or two or three. Your timetable is your own. If grief goes on year after year, however, you need some outside help.

"Grief is a wound that needs attention in order to heal," Judy Tatelbaum says. "To work through and complete grief means to face our feelings openly and honestly, to express or release our feelings fully, and to tolerate and accept our feelings for however long it takes for the wound to heal." Because this is a big order, she says, *it takes courage to grieve*. "It takes courage to feel our pain and to face the unfamiliar. It also takes courage to grieve in a society that mistakenly values restraint, where we risk the rejection of others by being open or different . . . willing to journey into pain and sorrow and anger in order to heal and recover."[52]

Your grieving may be more complicated because in many cases you are grieving in isolation. One of the ways people cope with their grief is to tell their story over and over, to friends and relatives who will listen, or else in support groups. Simply to find a nonjudgmental, listening ear is helpful. If you have not been open with people about the disease your child died from, you can experience no release in talking with people about his death. Certainly the church or synagogue ought to provide such an outlet. Depending on the stance of your congregation, however, this avenue may not be open to you. People at times have had difficulty finding a place to hold a funeral or memorial service because of the congregation's attitude toward homosexuality and AIDS.

The Realities of Grieving

"I should have been in that bed instead of him," parents and grandparents have said. "I'm old anyway. He still had so much of his life before him." Such statements reflect a number of ideas. One is that the normal progression of life, with the older dying before the younger, has been upset. These words also reflect the guilt of the survivor: "Why him? Why not me?" They may reflect the shame, the anger, the hopelessness you are feeling. These are complicated feelings. Deep down you may be ashamed that *your* child behaved in such a way as to get AIDS. You may be angry with him for getting AIDS—but it does not seem acceptable to be angry with a person who has died. Society tells us we should feel pity and sorrow, so dutifully we feel pity and sorrow, and the anger gets buried where we can't see it. Because these feelings are not acknowledged, much less expressed, they seethe far below the surface of our minds and send up such feelings as depression and hopelessness. Feelings of failure may also be present, acknowledged or unacknowledged. After all, an interior voice tells us, *if we had not failed somewhere along the line our child would not have died of AIDS.*

How can you cope with such thoughts and feelings? If you live in or near a town or city that has a group for parents of children who have died of AIDS, or even a group for parents of same-sex-oriented children, make every effort to participate in the group. It is a safe place to grieve, to express yourself. If you do not find a group, perhaps you can find an individual counselor—a minister, priest, rabbi, doctor, therapist—to whom you can pour out your heart and who can accompany you on your journey of grief. You may be blessed with one or more wise friends in whom you can confide. If you do not have access to such help, consider calling a hotline to talk. You do not need to limit yourself to one call. You can make contact a number of times.

Whether you can find outside help or not, read one or more books about grief. Judy Tatelbaum gives various exercises and activities to help the bereaved person work through grief. Many other books can assist you in threading your way through the maze of feelings that make up grief.

Rituals help us to break up our overall grief into smaller, more manageable pieces. Making a square for the AIDS quilt is one ritual that has been meaningful to many thousands of people. Simply reading the book *The Quilt: Stories from The NAMES Project*[53] can be a private ritual of grieving. When you sit down to read, light a special candle and tell your child you are doing this in memory of him.

You may want to select a poster that displays a picture or words that convey a particular feeling or message to you and put it somewhere in your house for six months or a year.

You may want to construct an altar. One woman, Kaia Svien, constructs altars not as worship centers, but as a way of meditating on a particular theme while she is making the altar.[54] She keeps each altar in her home for a period of time to remind her of her feelings, her thoughts, her prayers around this issue. You might want to make such a center as a memorial to your child. You may construct it on a table, a wide windowsill, the top of a bookcase, on the floor in the corner of a room, on a piece of fabric hung on the wall. The whole family could contribute articles that hold meaning for them.

It should be understood from the outset that the altar will remain in place for a limited time only, that it is not a permanent adjunct to your home. In the beginning you may set a limit of perhaps a month, with the understanding that at the end of that time you and your family will review whether you want to keep the altar in place for another month, and so on. Any posters and altars should be gone by the end of the first year.

Other small rituals can help you express your grief: a special candle lighted at the table (better than placing an empty chair—light conveys a different message than vacantness); a fresh flower for special days of remembrance; a weekly verse from the Bible or a brief quotation, repeated each day that week before the evening meal. Part of the process of healing is simply being conscious of your grief and giving it a space in your life in various ways. This is not morbid. Instead, by giving defined places and ways of expression to your grief, you prevent its spreading out like an amorphous mass that could absorb your whole life.

Completing Your Journey

And then . . . you complete your journey of grief. You are functioning as well as you did before the loss. What does this mean in your particular case? Something is gone from your life that can never be replaced. "Grief, like manure, is meaningless until we learn how to use it," Judy Tatelbaum says. "Making our grief meaningful can be the antidote to despair and suffering as well as the steppingstone to personal growth and achievement. We each must find our own meanings in order to transform our suffering into something of value."[55]

Even while you are in the midst of your grief, you can be searching for the meaning of this tremendous event in your life. You cannot go back to business as usual, because you can never be the same again. What direction do you want your life to take? Through this whole experience you may have encountered your inner self in ways you never did before. You may realize that you need to spend time finding out anew who you are, what direction you want your life to take now. "Each of us can be a creative survivor. We can choose to turn great personal tragedy into life-affirming action or personal change. The more we reach toward life, instead of withdrawing into our tragedy, and the more we aim for achievement or accomplishment, the more we expand our own possibilities."[56]

One father wanted to help people understand about homosexuality and AIDS. He began the process in the memorial service for his son when he asked the minister to include the information, unmentioned before in the wider family circle, that the deceased man had been gay and had died of AIDS. Months later the father was willing to talk with me at length about his experiences and his feelings, because he wanted to further people's understanding. A mother with whom I corresponded is an artist, and she is using her art to bring people to an awareness of AIDS. A counselor told me that many parents come back to the support groups that helped them in order to help support other parents who are dealing with an HIV/AIDS child.

You may not be ready immediately to undertake any new activity. Refilling your physical and psychic energy reservoirs takes time. You may not know where to direct your impulse to service. It may or may not be AIDS or gay related. Whatever you choose, whether in a new area where you can learn and grow or in one that already fits your skills and talents, let it be compatible with your available strength. If you don't know where you might serve but want to do something, let the field of service find you. Simply tell yourself or God that you want to do something to help and to bring the need to you. Repeat the offer daily until a door opens before you.

If you could talk now with your deceased child, what would he say? Sit down with pen and paper and write the letter you think your child would send you if he could.

My guess is that his letter would read something like this:

Dear Dad/Dear Mom,

If I could tell you what I learned in my life with HIV/AIDS, it would be this: Don't spend your life grieving for me. Always remember me, and know that I loved you then and I love you now. But don't waste a minute of the precious time you have for enjoying life. Enjoy the sunrises and sunsets. Enjoy the food you eat, and a good night's sleep. Enjoy your family and friends. Enjoy your work. Don't waste the suffering you have been through with me. Use it to help others in a way that will enrich both you and them.

I'm fine. I'm healed. I'm whole. I am growing in love and service. Because you are still in space and time, there will undoubtedly be other circumstances that cause you pain and suffering. Don't whitewash the pain, but know that in time you can use that pain too as an opportunity for growth.

I love you.

"In the midst of life we are in death," says a line in the service for the Burial of the Dead.[57] It could just as well read: "In the midst of death we are in life." Life and death are the ultimate yin and yang of existence, the two sides of the same coin. Go back and reread the section of this chapter titled "The Meaning of AIDS." We cannot choose never to die. The choice lies instead in what we do with the time we are given.

As you bid farewell to your child, let the words of a thirteenth century Persian poet and mystic be a benediction:

> Having seen the going-down, look upon the coming-up; how should setting impair the sun and the moon?
>
> To you it appears as setting, but it is a rising; the tomb appears as a prison, but it is release for the soul.
>
> What seed ever went down into the earth which did not grow? Why do you doubt so regarding the human seed?[58]

Chapter 11

The Goal and the Reward

The lounge was crowded with gay and lesbian persons and their parents after the Mass that begins the monthly meeting of Dignity, the national gay/lesbian Catholic organization. Every available chair was taken in the rows that had been set up. Many people were standing, and many more were sitting packed together on the floor.

This night Ellen—like me, the mother of a gay son—and I were speaking to the members of the Twin Cities chapter of Dignity and to their mothers and fathers about the interaction between parents and same-sex-oriented children when the children come out to their parents. We made our presentations, and then the meeting was opened for discussion and questions. A brisk exchange went on for some time.

Then a mother stood up and began to tell what had happened to her on Mother's Day, a week or two before. Her account went something like this:

For a long time Thomas has been wanting me to meet some of his friends. I told him, "I accept you. I love you just as much as I did before, but I want no part of your gay life, I don't want to meet your gay friends, and if you have a lover don't tell me about it."

This past Mother's Day I had one of the most beautiful Mother's Days anyone could have. My son had wanted to take me to the Sheraton-Ritz, but the workers there were on strike, and he told me instead that one of his friends had invited me to his home for brunch.

I'm happy that I went. I loved each and every one of them. They're beautiful people! I was ashamed of the feelings that I'd had. And I'm sorry to say this to the heterosexual world, but I saw more love in this church tonight than I've seen in a long time.

You should have heard the applause as she finished! A lot of eyes were damp too.

I do not remember what Ellen and I said that evening; I do not remember any of the discussion or questions. But several years later I remember clearly what that mother said. Her spontaneous account of an important turning point in her relationship with her son summed up the purpose of the meeting. She was a living demonstration that even parents who are in their sixties and seventies *can* readjust their thinking. The satisfaction and joy she radiated because of the change in her thinking made a powerful impact on the whole gathering.

Ellen, who shared the program with me that night, is another parent who has discovered a new dimension to life because of her gay son. I had not known her before she learned about her son's sexual orientation. When I met her I met a vital, concerned, outgoing woman. She has since told me she used to be quiet and retiring. Sometimes the hard experiences of life do cause the opening and flowering of unsuspected characteristics and talents.

I think of another mother who, two years ago, was devastated to learn that her son is gay. Today she, her son, and his partner share a home. This *can* happen. This *does* happen. Why should this not happen?

If death comes—and today, with AIDS, early death comes more frequently than it used to—we have to accept it. We can do nothing else. But to shut the door on a child because she or he does not fit our expectations is a double cruelty—to us and to the child. We cannot afford to lose even one of our children simply because of our discomfort with his or her sexual orientation.

"I feel terrible sadness and pathos over the beautiful 'children' many parents are missing because sexuality gets in the way," writes Peggy Way, a United Church of Christ minister who has counseled many lesbian and gay persons. "All the rich humanness, spirituality, commitment, kindness I get to enjoy and share is lost to parents who cannot deal with the homosexuality of their own children, regardless of their other fine qualities."[1]

The ever-present shadow of AIDS lends a note of poignancy and urgency to the words on the next several pages, most of them written on the eve of our recognition that a new, serious menace had entered our world. In view of this menace, your effort to cope with the information that your child is lesbian or gay takes on greatly increased importance. Even if coming to terms with your child's sexual orientation requires the investment of a considerable amount of time and perhaps even a good deal of money, the effort will be worthwhile. It may take courage; it may be painful; it may require hard work and determination on your part as you learn about a same-sex orientation, meet your child's partner, meet some of his or her other friends.

Is it worth all this? A thousand times yes! This is, as Robert Browning said in a different context, "the last of life for which the first was made."[2] Do not cheat yourself of the years when you can enjoy your grown children. Do not cheat yourself of what Joan Mills has called "the best part of parenting; the final, firmest bonding; the goal and the reward."[3] There is no reason why, simply because one of your children happens to be same-sex-oriented rather than other-sex-oriented, you should miss out on this reward. Don't let the fact that your child is different from what you had thought rob you of a relationship that can, perhaps against your expectations, enrich your life.

Any experience that wounds has the potential for cracking open the tight, constricting husk that often imprisons a part or all of one's soul. Confronting your child's same-sex orientation is one of these experiences. You will not escape the confrontation without pain. Your only choice is whether the pain is going to be destructive to you, to your enjoyment of life, and to your relationship with your child, or whether you are going to allow the pain to be a constructive influence in your life. Are you going to allow it to open you up? Are you going to allow yourself to grow? Are you going to come to grips with this unwelcome circumstance and make it into something that broadens and deepens your life?

Use all the resources that are available to you—those mentioned at intervals throughout this book and those you may discover for yourself.

None of us wants to experience the destruction of his or her hopes, dreams, goals. It seems to us that a dark cloud has descended on us, obliterating the familiar landscape about us. Before us stands a bleak, forbidding door that promises us nothing but separation from everything we had hoped for. We can choose to remain outside this door for the rest of our lives, but we cannot go back to life as it was before. We can also, by our own volition, step through the doorway. Probably the majority of parents of same-sex-oriented children are dragged, protesting, through the doorway into what may seem to us to be the utter void on the other side.

"There was no strain of music from within, no smell of eternal orchards at the threshold," C. S. Lewis wrote about his experience of being "dragged through the doorway" as his atheism yielded reluctantly to faith.[4] Each of us at some time in life is dragged through a doorway we would not have chosen. We see only what we believe is the everlasting extinction of our dreams. We cannot imagine that there will ever again be music or fruitful orchards in our lives.

There can be joy on the other side of bleakness, of darkness. How could I have known that out of divorce and then out of learning of my son's gayness would come some of the most fulfilling experiences of my life?

Even if your child has AIDS and, sooner or later, dies—even in such a loss deep experiences of something akin to joy may be hidden. You may touch a spiritual realm of which, until now, you were ignorant. The loss of your child cannot be anything but bitter. Yet there can be a kind of radiance that defies description or explanation if you can surrender the bitterness and ask to find the meaning in your loss. Against all reason, you may discover that blessing can come out of calamitous circumstances, in strange ways.

One final recommendation is important: Start now to move toward acceptance of your child. For a time denial may be necessary for you to survive. Do not make it a way of life.

Begin to take hold of the circumstance that has befallen you. Act now. None of us knows what time allotment we may still have in which to accomplish this reconciliation of our feelings. Judy Tatelbaum, a much younger woman than I, writes: "Time is passing quickly. . . . At twenty I disliked the sense that life felt endless, and I liked the idea that I had plenty of time. Now I no longer feel that I have plenty of time. I want to act now, before it is too late."[5]

Further on she writes: "Frequently after a loss I have heard people say something like, 'Never again will I hide my love from my family and friends.'" We bring great sorrow on ourselves when we have to live with unexpressed feelings of love after the death of a loved one. It is, Tatelbaum says, a painful lesson that many people have to learn.[6]

You do not have to learn this lesson. You can decide not to withhold your love from your child. Approval is not the same as love. You do not need to approve of *everything* your child does in order to love him or her. Surely you do not approve of *everything* your heterosexual children do.

If AIDS does not add urgency to your particular situation, be grateful. If it is an ingredient in your case, you have a compelling reason to express your love and care *now*.

Do not withdraw from your emotions: your anger at your child, at yourself—yes, even perhaps at God; your feelings of guilt; your fear of pain and of the unknown; your anger at your vulnerability and your fear of this vulnerability. Most important, do not withdraw from your love. The person you hurt most by withholding love is yourself. Yes, you *do* hurt your child, but of even more significance is the fact that you shrink and wither yourself. The floodgates that shut off or release pain are the same floodgates that shut off or release all emotions, including love. You cannot shut off pain or anger without also shutting off love.

Let yourself hurt; let yourself weep; let yourself be angry; let yourself love; let yourself live. Life is too short to waste in the chill, gray winter of blighted hopes and chosen separation from a loved one. No one else can end this winter for you. You have to make the effort yourself.

A new chapter of your life awaits you. It may even contain music and fruitful orchards. It can still bring you the rewards of parenting—the final, firmest bonding of adult parent to adult child, the goal and reward for which you gave up many of your own desires, worked, walked the floor nights, hauled carfuls of squealing youngsters, attended PTA meetings and Little League games, and sat through such milestone ceremonies as graduation.

And if the reward for your years of love and service must, because of AIDS, be different from what you might have hoped or imagined, know that it need not be an unworthy substitute. It is impossible to say what the reward in your particular case may be. Whatever it is, it will fit your situation and no one else's.

For one father, it was a folded note in his shirt pocket that told him at last that his son loved him, that as a father he mattered tremendously—and that his feet had been set on a journey that, a few days before, he could not have imagined. Another father and mother gained a miracle. Not the sparing of the life of their son, but an entrance into a whole new life for themselves that in their wildest flights of fancy they would never have envisioned.

Your daughter, your son, is reaching out to you, wanting to maintain a real, loving, caring relationship with you. Your child has shared with you a significant part of her or his life. For this you can rejoice. Your child is reaching out to you in love. Accept this love and give back yours.

All life is a process, a pilgrimage. You are being asked to set out on a new part of your journey, one you never expected to be called upon to make. Yet almost by definition pilgrimages run through difficult terrain. Do not lose heart. Against all expectations, against all odds, there can be joy. Open your heart to that joy. Open your heart to your child.

Appendix 1

Coming-out Letter from Rick
to His Family

New York City
December 20, 1978

Dear Family,
 Merry Christmas. I hope this note finds you all in good health and humor.

 You have not heard much of me, and unless you've been reading between the lines, you know even less of the story of my last year. I hope to give all of you autographed hardcover editions when I can settle down to write it; but at this point I have only the energy to give a summary of what it feels like to be me as I stand at the summit of 1978 and look out over the prospect of 1979.

 As for my '78: My list of acquisitions does not include a bank account of any great weight; but I do own a beautiful oriental rug, a desk, several tables and chairs, many books, and a considerable (though used) wardrobe. I also have a decent job and a habitable one-bedroom apartment at reasonable rent in a fair neighborhood. But my most prized possession at this moment is one purchased only in small part by money; that is, my survival. As I survey my wealth, I am not displeased.

 My calculation of my image is more difficult. In the eyes of those who truly know me, I feel it has been enhanced in 1978; they have told me as much. However, among many who would, or feel they should, know me—but do not—my image is unclear. This is due, in part, to a conscious decision on my part a year ago to restrict information based on which family, friends, and acquaintances could alter their impressions. I went through some wrenching changes and didn't want to have to explain or justify myself as I was doing it.

A year ago I left Arizona, where I was involved in, among other things, a very intense loving relationship with Karla.* She is an open, honest, intelligent, and sensitive human being, and I loved her as a lover and an ally, and I loved her son in a way as close to parental as our relative proximity in ages and our newness to each other would allow. I was, in a way and to an extent previously inconceivable, happy.

Her love did everything I'd always hoped a love would do . . . almost. The only disappointment was that her love did not overwhelm or subsume my sexual and emotional attraction to men.

There. I said it.

For some reason, I'd always assumed that the love of the Right Woman would "mature" me out of my "aberrant" feelings and so had never experienced relating to men other than in rather narrowly defined ways—ways acceptable to our homophobic society. When, after a year of various degrees of intimacy with Karla—most of it wonderful, all of it satisfactory—I still found my eye wandering and my heart wondering, I could lie to her no longer. Nor would I lie to myself. So I told her then what I am telling you now. And I left her and pursued the only thing I really know: that is, how I feel.

It's been a long year, easier in many ways than most years because of the relative lack of dissimulation I've felt I had to put out; but difficult in the intensity of the overhaul (emotional, spiritual, interpersonal, etc.) I've subjected myself to. It's been worth it: I feel much closer on the track toward a view of life and love and my role with others than I did a year ago. I have honest relationships based on affection and respect with both men and women. I hope to find a life/love partner with whom to share the years, and at this point I feel I would prefer a man. This may not always be so, but my attraction to men goes back at least seventeen years, and I have never been particularly attracted to women, at least not physically. (Although I must say that emotionally I find more women more compatible than most men.) It's possible that I may not find a partner in any traditional sense, and so I am striving for the strength to face life autonomously or in nontraditional relationships. Since I have few expectations, I have less than most to fear from loneliness.

*Name changed

Appendix 1: Coming-out Letter

My image? Whether it be enhanced or diminished in the eyes of any particular person is of less concern to me than this: I have never felt clearer, more honest, more self-directed, and more confident . . . in my life.

So, my memories of 1978? They are too many, too complex, too extreme, and too personal to recount here. But I'll tell anybody anything they're willing to hear with an open mind. I love you all and would like to know you. I welcome you to know and love me.

1979? There is much work for me to do, and a changed, freer person goes about the tasks. I have sifted through a couple hundred pounds of seven years of writings, correspondences, and memorabilia over the past week or two, and I think some of the writings are in near-publishable form. My intention is to polish and try to sell some lyrics and short stories. The specific time and space plans haven't jelled yet.

So. That's the main of what's new in my life, and I want to end this before I decide not to send it. The time for these things never seems right; but today I feel strong and have faith in your love.

All my love, and a hope that 1979 brings to you the peace and hope I have found this past year.

Rick

Note: For the sake of brevity several parts of the letter have been deleted. All that pertains to Rick's coming out to his family has been retained in his own words.

Appendix 2

How Successful Are "Ex-Gay" Ministries?

A number of persons who founded or led ex-gay ministries have since disappeared from public view or returned to their same-sex orientation.

Colin Cook, the Seventh Day Adventist from Reading, Pennsylvania, who started Quest and Homosexuals Anonymous, resigned in November 1987 from Quest and closed the ministry. Fourteen young men told of "a series of episodes of sexual misconduct [with Cook] over the last six years."[1] Six men eventually sued Cook and the General Conference of the Seventh Day Adventist Church for $20,000 each as well as restitution of the fees and expenses incurred in the program, citing Quest's failure to rid them of their homosexual urges as promised.[2]

An early ex-gay ministry, Eagle Ministries, and its leader, Greg Reid, have long since vanished from the scene, as has Guy Charles's Liberation in Jesus Christ. Charles was discovered having homosexual encounters with those to whom he was ministering.[3] As early as 1978, Roger Grindstaff's Disciples Only, Saugerties, New York, had gone out of existence and Grindstaff himself disappeared. Dave Wilkerson's Teen Challenge had referred people to Disciples Only for deliverance from homosexuality.[4]

The co-founders of Exodus, Michael Bussee and Gary Cooper, left the organization some years ago and have since spent several years in a loving relationship with each other.[5] John Evans, who at one time believed himself to be ex-gay and founded Love in Action, has since reverted to his real orientation.[6] In the book *The Third Sex* Evans, under the name Ted, was one of the six cases described.[7] Of the other five, at least two believe "they can be gay and Christian" and a third is out of contact with Love in Action.[8]

Rick Notch of St. Paul has long since left The Open Door, the ex-gay ministry he started in St. Cloud, Minnesota, in 1978 with support from Outpost, the Minneapolis/St. Paul ministry. Very early in his work, in October 1978, he represented Exodus on "Donahue." By 1980 he realized that he never had been ex-gay, that because of his belief at the time that homosexuality was a sin, he simply had suppressed all knowledge of his homosexual desires. In June 1991 he appeared on "Geraldo" as an opposition member of the panel dealing with the ex-gay movement.

Ed Hurst, who in 1980 worked with Outpost and published a thirty-seven-page pamphlet about ridding oneself of homosexuality, eventually left Outpost and went to Texas. In late 1984 he returned to Outpost, and he again resigned in April 1988, saying that his major sexual problems (apparently his continuing same-sex orientation) still had a great impact on his sexual struggles.[9] In summer of 1990 he appeared in public wearing a Gay Pride button, and he has since been seen as a part of the gay community in Minneapolis/St. Paul.

Dr. Jeff Ford, another former director of Outpost and now a counselor in private practice, eventually realized he was still gay and subsequently took part in a public demonstration in St. Paul against the Berean League's "strong anti-Gay and anti-Lesbian agenda."[10] Doug Houck, who founded Metanoia Ministries in Seattle, resigned in 1989 because of "continued homosexual acting out."[11]

Tim Stafford's conclusions concerning ex-gay ministries make several points. Frank Worthen ("Brother Frank") readily admitted to him that many leaders of the early ministries had dropped out. Anyone who had just left a homosexual life and attempted to function in an ex-gay ministry faced temptation as he (or she) tried "to meet enormous needs without adequate resources." Most of these ministries had no church ties or board oversight. Exodus now has strict standards for ministries that want to affiliate with it, thus reducing the need to discipline these organizations or provide intensive counseling to erring heads of the ministries.

Further, Stafford cautions that "the ex-gay movement is young, small, and operates in unknown territory." All ministry, he says, operates at risk, and this kind of ministry is riskier than most. In addition, the church has given very little support to such ministries, waiting to see if they fail. Such an attitude could become for the ministries a self-fulfilling prophecy. "Most congregations know nothing about the needs of homosexuals, and many don't want to know." If the church were to embrace such ministries, Stafford says, it would better understand their work and the results would perhaps be greater and more positive.[12]

The need for ex-gay ministries is predicated on the belief that the Bible condemns homosexuality. Those who hold this belief refuse to acknowledge any validity to interpretations of biblical passages such as Victor Furnish, Robin Scroggs, and John Boswell give.

Luke Timothy Johnson has some wise words for churches as they deal with the issue of a same-sex orientation:

It would be wrong-headed to deny the complexity or difficulty of this issue. It is certainly one about which I know too little. But I have listened to enough stories to make me question my presuppositions about where God *cannot* be at work. That homosexual activity can be sinful, I have no doubt, any more than I doubt that heterosexual activity can be sinful. That a style of life built upon sexual promiscuity and pleasure, while claiming to be Christian, is self-contradictory, I am certain— whether it is gay or straight in orientation. . . .

I have been forced to wonder, for example, at the way committed, sincere, and intelligent believers have discovered that their lifelong struggle against a homosexual orientation has been in effect a rejection of the way God has created them. For some of these men and women, the acceptance of this "fact" about themselves has been the *beginning* of a genuine search for God's will in their lives. In the disciplined, by no means self-indulgent spiritual journals of some of my students, I have read how the acknowledgment of their sexual identity has been tantamount to a conversion experience. I report this, though I have not digested it myself.

How can we begin to exercise discernment in the church on this question, without the narratives of both gay and straight believers? . . . Is faith in God and the obedience of faith not available to gay people? I do not like to think about these things, for they call my presuppositions into question. That is why we need the narratives of those involved. And if we discover, when we hear these narratives, that "they have received the same gift as us," what will our response be? Will the church, like Peter, say, "Who are we to withstand God?" Or, will it deserve his rebuke, "Why are you testing God?"[13]

Appendix 3

Resources

Parents and Friends of Lesbians and Gays
One of the most helpful organizations that you, as a parent, could become involved with at this time in your life is a Parents and Friends of Lesbians and Gays group. To find out if there is such a group near you, write to:

P-FLAG
PO Box 27605
Washington, DC 20038
(202) 638–4200

Enclose a long (#10) stamped, self-addressed envelope.

Lesbian and Gay Religious Groups
For a listing of the national headquarters of various same-sex-oriented religious groups, such as Integrity (Episcopal), Dignity (Catholic), Lutherans Concerned, Presbyterians for Lesbian and Gay Concerns, and Universal Fellowship of Metropolitan Community Churches, write to me:

Mary V. Borhek
c/o The Pilgrim Press
700 Prospect Avenue East
Cleveland, OH 44115–1100

Enclose a long (#10) stamped, self-addressed envelope and an extra first-class stamp to cover printing and handling costs.

Computer Bulletin Boards

Computer Shopper, a listing of available bulletin boards, is available at many magazine stands. Libraries may also have this publication or others that may supply some of the same information. Two bulletin boards, CompuServe and America Online, carry forums and discussion groups on a great variety of subjects. Both are generally supportive of gay and lesbian issues.

AIDS Hotlines

There are many national organizations and a number of hotlines dealing with AIDS, too numerous to list here. Many of the books mentioned in "For Further Reading" contain the names, addresses, and telephone numbers of such organizations. The books more recently published are more likely to have current information. Two organizations to start with are:

P-FLAG family support and HIV/AIDS helpline:
1–800–4-FAMILY
(1–800–432–6459)

National AIDS Information Clearinghouse
PO Box 6003
Rockville, MD 20850
1–800–458–5231

Have paper and pencil with you before you call to jot down information.

Notes

Introduction: A Two-way Mirror

1. Alan P. Bell et al., *Sexual Preference* (Bloomington, IN: Indiana University Press, 1981), p. 222.

Chapter 1: So You Want to Come Out to Your Parents

1. M. Scott Peck, *The Road Less Traveled* (New York: Simon & Schuster, 1979), pp. 131, 16.

Chapter 2: The Big Decision

1. Mary V. Borhek, *My Son Eric* (New York: The Pilgrim Press, 1979).
2. Augustus Y. Napier, with Carl A. Whitaker, *The Family Crucible* (New York: Bantam Books, 1980), p. 208.
3. Don Clark, *Loving Someone Gay* (Millbrae, CA: Celestial Arts, 1977), p. 68.
4. Napier, *The Family Crucible.*

Chapter 3: Grief Often Does Not Look Like Grief

1. Peter Marris, *Loss and Change* (Garden City, NY: Anchor Press/Doubleday, 1975), p. 9.
2. Ira J. Tanner, *Healing the Pain of Everyday Loss* (Minneapolis: Winston Press, 1976), pp. 54–55.
3. After the Federation of Parents and Friends of Lesbians and Gays—P-FLAG or Parents FLAG—was formed, the Minneapolis/St. Paul group, Families of Gays and Lesbians, affiliated with the national organization and became P-FLAG Minnesota. I have continued to use the former name throughout the book.

4. Judith Guest, *Ordinary People* (New York: Ballantine Books, 1977).

Chapter 4: Getting Ready to Make the Big Announcement

1. Ira J. Tanner, *Healing the Pain of Everyday Loss* (Minneapolis: Winston Press, 1976), p. 24.

2. Judith Guest, *Ordinary People* (New York: Ballantine Books, 1977).

3. Theodore Isaac Rubin, *The Angry Book* (New York: Collier Books/Macmillan, 1969).

Chapter 5: Working Through Grief—Together

1. Letha Scanzoni and Virginia Ramey Mollenkott, *Is the Homosexual My Neighbor?* (New York: Harper & Row, 1978), pp. 32–34.

2. Lawrence J. Hatterer, *Changing Homosexuality in the Male* (New York: McGraw-Hill, 1970), and Donahue Transcript #10141, with Phil Donahue, Alan Bell, and Lawrence Hatterer, p. 32; available from Multimedia Program Productions, P.O. Box 2111, Cincinnati, OH 45201.

3. Aesthetic realism is a philosophy founded by Eli Siegel and taught by him and others since the early 1940s. It explains the cause of homosexuality thus: "(1) All homosexuality arises from contempt of the world, not liking it sufficiently. (2) This changes into a contempt for women." A fuller explanation is contained in the book *The H Persuasion* (New York: Definition Press).

4. See Betty Fairchild and Nancy Hayward, *Now That You Know* (New York: Harcourt Brace Jovanovich, 1979), pp. 77–81, for an explanation of the Kinsey scale.

5. William H. Masters and Virginia E. Johnson, *Homosexuality in Perspective* (Boston: Little, Brown & Co., 1979). The Lutheran Campus Ministry study group referred to earlier had this to say concerning the book: "(a) Masters and Johnson report a treatment failure rate (note carefully the term!) of 28.4 per cent in

their treatment of 54 males and 13 females who expressed *dissatisfaction* with their homosexuality. (b) Masters and Johnson do not treat homosexuality, which they consider a natural sexual expression. They treat only the sexual dysfunction or dissatisfaction of those who want to *convert* (Kinsey's 5s and 6s) or *revert* (Kinsey's 2s, 3s, and 4s) to heterosexual expressions. The key component in their therapy is a rigorous neutrality on the part of the therapists. (c) The results of the Masters and Johnson study are not easily generalized beyond their mode of treatment. They are highly selective of their subjects and refuse those who come to them under opprobrium of the court or threat of job loss. Those selected must be highly motivated and willing to spend two weeks in St. Louis in a sophisticated program with a very competent staff. (d) The Masters and Johnson treatment is an *in vivo* modification of the erotic response system of an individual with a supportive partner. Thus they present a new approach to the treatment of sexual dysfunction and dissatisfaction."

6. In *Homosexuality and the Miracle Makers* Jim Peron writes: "To the vast majority of people 'ex-gay' would seem to mean someone who no longer has homosexual desires and is reoriented towards heterosexuality. But to Exodus [an ex-gay organization] the word has a different meaning. . . . On tape produced by Love in Action, an affiliate of Exodus, in San Rafael, CA, specifically states that an 'ex-gay' is only a homosexual who has turned his life over to Jesus Christ and been 'born-again,' it does not mean someone who has been reoriented sexually" (Glen Ellyn, IL: privately published booklet, 1978)

7. Alan P. Bell et al., *Sexual Preference* (Bloomington, IN: Indiana University Press, 1981). New research is introducing information about possible biological and genetic causes of male homosexuality. Similar studies of lesbians will add a further dimension.

8. Ibid., p. 222.

9. Victor Paul Furnish, *The Moral Teaching of Paul* (Nashville: Abingdon Press, 1979), pp. 62–63.

10. Erving Goffman's book *Stigma* (Englewood Cliffs, NJ: Prentice-Hall, 1963), examines in detail the reaction of all stigmatized persons and the strategies they employ in dealing with

the refusal of others to accept them on the same basis as everyone else.

Chapter 6: The Other Side

1. *Minneapolis Tribune,* April 9, 1978.

2. *Minneapolis Star, Saturday,* November 12, 1977.

3. No inference should be taken from this that any child who is not getting along well with his or her peers is same-sex-oriented. There are many reasons for a child's difficulties in relationships with others. Similarly, it is normal for children to hang around with other children of the same sex. Either of these behaviors can be indicative of other difficulties—or of nothing more than usual developmental patterns.

4. Del Martin and Phyllis Lyon, *Lesbian/Woman* (New York: Bantam Books, 1972).

5. *Minneapolis Tribune,* April 20, 1978.

6. *The PFLAGpole,* Fall 1992.

7. Ibid.

8. Morton Kelsey and Barbara Kelsey, *Sacrament of Sexuality* (Warwick, NY: Amity House, 1986), p. 182.

9. This is not the place to go deeply into this matter. The beliefs of Saint Augustine in the fourth century and Saint Thomas Aquinas in the thirteenth exerted great influence on the principles of morality that the Catholic church incorporated and promulgated. Because the Catholic church was so influential for many centuries, these ideas entered mainstram thinking. Reay Tannahill points out that "the very personal attitudes of some leading Christian thinkers" such as Tertullian, Jerome, and Augustine left a lasting impression on all subsequent Christian sexual ideas. These men had led full sex lives "before being converted to celibacy, and they had reacted with sometimes morbid revulsion against the sins they now abjured. . . . Just as Augustine had given a rationale to the Church Fathers' distaste for the heterosexual act and rendered it acceptable only in terms of procreation, so Thomas Aquinas consolidated traditional fears of homosexuality. . . . It was not difficult to prove, especially as he started from Augustine's proposition that the sexual organs had been designed by the Creator specifically for reproduction, and could only be legitimately used in ways that did

not exclude the possibility of it. Homosexuality was thus, by definition, a deviation from the natural order laid down by God . . . a deviation that was not only unnatural but, by the same Augustinian token, lustful and heretical" (*Sex in History* [New York: Stein and Day, 1980]), pp. 141, 161.

10. Arno Karlen, *Sexuality and Homosexuality* (New York: W. W. Norton & Co., 1971), p. 618.

Chapter 7: Letting Go

1. *St. Paul Dispatch*, December 5, 1979.

2. Florida Scott-Maxwell, *The Measure of My Days* (New York: Knopf, 1968), pp. 16–17.

3. Erich Fromm, *The Art of Loving* (New York: Harper & Row, 1956), pp. 42–43 (italics added).

4. Ibid., pp. 36–37.

5. Thomas A. Harris, *I'm OK—You're OK* (New York: Harper & Row, 1969), clarifies the concepts of parent, child, and adult and gives an insight into the ways in which we all relate to other people out of these three modes.

6. Scott-Maxwell, *The Measure of My Days*, p. 16.

7. Fromm, *The Art of Loving*, p. 17.

8. Judy Tatelbaum, *The Courage to Grieve* (New York: Lippincott and Crowell, 1980).

Chapter 8: Parents Also Come Out

1. Carl Whitaker, in Augustus Y. Napier, *The Family Crucible*. (New York: Bantam Books, 1980), p. 253.

Chapter 9: Religious Issues and a Same-sex Orientation

1. *Where We Stand: Social Action Resolutions Adopted by the Union of American Hebrew Congregations*, rev. ed., prepared for The Commission on Social Action of Reform Judaism, 838 Fifth Avenue, New York, NY 10021, 1992, pp. 126–27, 205–6, 211–12.

2. *Homosexuality and Judaism: The Reconstructionist Position* (report of the Reconstructionist Commission on Homosexuality) (Wyncote, PA: Federation of Reconstructionist Congregations and Havurot and the Reconstructionist Rabbinical Association, 1992).

3. Telephone conversation with Rabbi Robert Gluck, March 23, 1993.

4. *Homosexuality and Judaism*, p. 35.

5. Ibid.

6. Ibid., p. 29.

7. Ibid.

8. Ibid., pp. 29–30.

9. Ibid., p. 36.

10. Ibid., p. 37.

11. See "For Further Reading" for availability of these two publications.

12. *Homosexuality and Judaism*, p. 33, as well as actual resolution passed at the "last Biennial Convention," forwarded to me by Sarrae Crane, director of the Department of Social Action and Public Policy of the United Synagogue of Conservative Judaism.

13. Ibid., p. 34.

14. Press release, National Jewish Community Relations Advisory Council, New York, November 2, 1992.

15. Ibid. *Halacha* is the body of Jewish oral laws supplementing the written laws, or both oral and written law together, or any particular law or custom prescribed by the legal codices.

16. John Boswell, *Christianity, Social Tolerance, and Homosexuality* (Chicago: University of Chicago Press, 1980), p. 335.

17. Francis Schaeffer, *No Final Conflict* (Downers Grove, IL: InterVarsity Press, 1976), p. 16.

18. John Marsh, *The Gospel of St. John* (New York: Penguin Books, 1979), pp. 48ff.

19. Clyde S. Kilby, *The Christian World of C. S. Lewis* (Grand Rapids, MI: Eerdmans, 1964), pp. 153–54.

20. Richard Kroeger and Catherine Clark Kroeger, "Pandemonium and Silence at Corinth," *The Reformed Journal*, June 1978.

21. Virginia Ramey Mollenkott, *Speech, Silence, Action!* (Nashville: Abingdon Press, 1980), p. 135.

22. See James Strong, *The Exhaustive Concordance of the Bible* (Nashville: Abingdon Press, 1973 edition).

23. Victor Paul Furnish, *The Moral Teaching of Paul* (Nashville: Abingdon Press, 1979), pp. 57–58.

24. Boswell, *Christianity, Social Tolerance, and Homosexuality,* p. 100. Lev. 11:7 prohibits eating of pork; Lev. 15:24 prohibits intercourse during menstruation.

25. Ibid.

26. Strong, *The Exhaustive Concordance of the Bible.*

27. Furnish, *The Moral Teaching of Paul,* pp. 73–78.

28. "Sexuality," unpublished paper by the Right Reverend Arthur Freeman, Ph.D., Moravian Theological Seminary, Bethlehem, PA; February 26, 1992, p. 13.

29. The "due penalty" has been variously interpreted. Robin Scroggs mentions venereal disease as a possible penalty in *The New Testament and Homosexuality* (Philadelphia: Fortress Press, 1983), p. 115. Dr. Ralph Blair, in "The Bible Is an Empty Closet," a pamphlet available from Evangelicals Concerned, 311 East 72nd Street, Suite 1G, New York, NY 10021, suggests the penalty could have been the self-castration that male devotees of Cybele and other goddesses sometimes inflicted upon themselves. Perhaps the "debased mind" of Rom. 1:28 was the penalty, elaborated in Paul's list in Rom. 1:29: "They were filled with every kind of wickedness, evil, covetousness, malice. Full of envy, murder, strife, deceit, haters, insolent, haughty, boastful, inventors of evil, rebellious toward parents, foolish, faithless, heartless, ruthless."

30. Furnish, *The Moral Teaching of Paul,* p. 63.

31. Ibid., p. 65.

32. Boswell, *Christianity, Social Tolerance, and Homosexuality,* pp. 106–7.

33. Ibid., pp. 344–45.

34. Scroggs, *The New Testament and Homosexuality,* p. 125.

35. Ibid., p. 126.

36. John J. McNeill, S. J., *The Church and the Homosexual* (New York: Pocket Books, 1976); Letha Scanzoni and Virginia Ramey Mollenkott, *Is the Homosexual My Neighbor?* (New York: Harper & Row, 1978).

37. Tim LaHaye, *What Everyone Should Know About Homosexuality* (Wheaton, IL: Tyndale House Publishers, 1978), p. 62.

38. *RECORD,* Newsletter of Evangelicals Concerned, Inc., New York, Winter 1987. The report of the study was published in the *Archives of General Psychiatry.* Two researchers, Lee Ellis,

Ph.D., and M. Ashley Ames, Ph.D., have gathered the results of many such tests and synthesized them into "Neurohormonal Functioning and Sexual Orientation: A Theory of Homosexuality-Heterosexuality," originally published in *Psychological Bulletin* 101:233-58. A summary of Ellis and Ames' article has been published as "A Lay Person's Summary," prepared by Douglas and Molly Webster, and is available from Parents-FLAG, Box 15515, New Orleans, LA 70175, at $2.00 to defray the cost of printing and mailing. Robert Pool's article "Evidence for Homosexuality Gene" (*Science* 261 [July 16, 1993]) forms the basis for "Born Gay? Studies of family trees and DNA make the case that male homosexuality is in the genes" (*Time*, July 26, 1993) and "Does DNA Make Some Men Gay?" (*Newsweek*, July 26, 1993).

39. LaHaye, *What Everyone Should Know About Homosexuality*, pp. 37–38.

40. Ibid., pp. 52–53.

41. Ibid., pp. 42–43, 58.

42. Ibid., p. 49.

43. Ibid., p. 190.

44. Ibid., p. 202.

45. Arno Karlen, *Sexuality and Homosexuality* (New York: W. W. Norton & Co., 1971), pp. 256–57.

46. Greg L. Bahnsen, *Homosexuality: A Biblical View* (Grand Rapids, MI: Baker Book House, 1978), p. 23.

47. Ibid., p. 25.

48. Ibid., pp. 37–38.

49. Ibid., p. 127.

50. Joe Dallas, *Desires in Conflict* (Eugene, OR: Harvest House Publishers, 1991), pp. 267–82.

51. Leanne Payne, *The Broken Image* (Wheaton, IL: Crossways Books, 1981). The quotation is from the back cover of the 1991 book.

52. Kathryn Kuhlman, *I Believe in Miracles* (Englewood Cliffs, NY: Prentice-Hall, 1962), p. 212.

53. Agnes Sanford, *The Healing Gifts of the Spirit* (Philadelphia: J. B. Lippincott Co., 1966), p. 76.

54. C. S. Lewis, *The World's Last Night* (New York: Harcourt Brace Jovanovich, 1960), pp. 4–5.

55. Karlen, *Sexuality and Homosexuality*, p. 440.

56. *RECORD*, Winter 1989, quoting Alan Medinger of Regeneration ministry, from the *Washington Times*.

57. Radio program on KKLA, January 25, 1991, quoted in *RECORD*, Spring 1991.

58. *Mid-Atlantic Affirmation News* (United Methodist Gay/Lesbian Group), November 1989. Quoted in *RECORD*, Spring 1990.

59. Tim Stafford, "Coming Out," *Christianity Today*, August 18, 1989, p. 20.

60. Donald Goergen, *The Sexual Celibate* (San Francisco: Harper San Francisco, 1974), pp. 2–3.

61. James B. Nelson, *Embodiment* (Minneapolis: Augsburg, 1978), pp. 198–99.

62. *Homosexuality and Judaism*, p. 31.

63. L. William Countryman, *Dirt, Greed, and Sex* (Philadelphia: Fortress Press, 1988), p. 174. I am indebted to Countryman's whole book, as well as to Bruce J. Malina, for my quick summary of the societal and cultural structure of ancient Hebrew life.

64. Countryman, *Dirt, Greed, and Sex*, p. 175.

65. Ibid., pp. 141–42.

66. William E. Amos, Jr., *When AIDS Comes to Church* (Philadelphia: The Westminster Press, 1988), p. 70.

67. Ibid.

68. Ibid., p. 71.

69. Ibid., p. 74.

70. Ibid., pp. 74–76.

71. John 4:9. The New English Bible says: "Jews and Samaritans, it should be noted, do not use vessels in common," and the New International Version offers a footnote: "do not use dishes Samaritans have used."

72. Mollencott, *Speech, Silence, Action!*, p. 133.

73. Ibid., p. 134.

74. Ann G. Suzedell, *Accent*, April 1981, Vol. 10, No. 2, published by Moravian Theological Seminary, Bethlehem, PA. The Bible passage she refers to and quotes is Isa. 43:2, 4.

75. Henri Nouwen, *Out of Solitude* (Notre Dame, IN: Ave Maria Press, 1980), pp. 32, 36.

76. Ira J. Tanner, *Healing the Pain of Everyday Loss* (Minneapolis: Winston Press, 1976), p. 167.

77. Nouwen, *Out of Solitude*, p. 57.

Chapter 10: Living with HIV/AIDS

1. After AIDS succeeded GRID as the name of the disease, pre-AIDs status was referred to as ARC, AIDS-related complex. In some cases, this designation is still in use.

2. Michael Callen, *Surviving AIDS* (New York: HarperCollins Publishers, 1990), p. 1.

3. Ibid., p. 112.

4. Jack Hamilton and Vicki L. Morris, "The Psychosocial Aspects of AIDS," in *The AIDS Caregiver's Handbook*, ed. Ted Eidson (New York: St. Martin's Press, 1988), p. 83.

5. Callen, *Surviving AIDS*, p. 141.

6. Randy Shilts, *And the Band Played On* (New York: St. Martin's Press, 1987), p. 200.

7. Title of a chapter in Callen, *Surviving AIDS*, pp. 227–34.

8. Edmund White, "Esthetics and Loss," in *Personal Dispatches*, ed. John Preston (New York: St. Martin's Press, 1989), p. 152.

9. Louise L. Hay, "10 Ways to Love Yourself," Hay House, PO Box 6204, Carson, CA 90749-6204. © 1987, 1988 Louise L. Hay. Used by permission.

10. Arnie Kantrowitz, "Friends Gone with the Wind," in *Personal Dispatches*, p. 23.

11. Norman Cousins, *Head First: The Biology of Hope* (New York: E. P. Dutton, 1989), p. 73.

12. Ibid., pp. 35–37 (italics added).

13. Degen Pener, "Finding Something, Many Things, To Smile About," *New York Times*, August 9, 1992.

14. Shilts, *And the Band Played On*, p. 107.

15. Callen, *Surviving AIDS*, p. 121.

16. Anna Quindlen, "Things That Don't Go Bump," *New York Times*, October 30, 1991.

17. Rev. Christine Oscar, "Talking About the Untalkable," in *The Valley Star*, a publication of the Metropolitan Community Church of the Lehigh Valley, Fall 1991.

18. Stephen Levine, *Who Dies? An Investigation of Conscious Living and Conscious Dying* (Garden City, NY: Anchor Press/Doubleday, 1982), p. 34 (italics added).

19. Ibid.

20. May Sarton, *The Bridge of Years* (New York: W. W. Norton & Co., 1985), p. 160.

21. Jim Batson, "Tonics for the soul when you're living with AIDS," *Minneapolis Star Tribune*, August 4, 1991.

22. Callen, *Surviving AIDS*, pp. 2, 10.

23. "Brian Coyle: A chance to educate a city about AIDS," journal excerpts printed in the *Minneapolis Star Tribune*, May 12, 1991.

24. Levine, *Who Dies?*, p. 5.

25. Barbara Bartocci, "One Hour That Can Change Your Life," *Reader's Digest*, March 1984; reprinted from *Catholic Digest*, August 1983.

26. Marilyn Morgan Helleberg, "Finding the Kingdom of God Within You," *Guideposts*, April 1980.

27. Levine, *Who Dies?*, pp. 202–3.

28. Bernard Gavzer, "Why Do Some People Survive AIDS?" *Parade*, September 18, 1988. See also Cindy Mikluscak-Cooper and Emmett E. Miller, *Living in Hope* (Berkeley, CA: Celestial Arts, 1991), pp. 249–50.

29. Callen, *Surviving AIDS*, pp. 190–201.

30. Denise Levertov, "Sparks," in *Poems 1960–1967* (New York: New Directions Publishing Corp., 1983), p. 87.

31. Callen, *Surviving AIDS*, p. 192.

32. Kim Ode, "Living and Dying with AIDS," *Minneapolis Star and Tribune*, December 7, 1986.

33. Richard Selzer, "A Question of Mercy," *New York Times Magazine*, September 22, 1991, pp. 32–38. See also his book, *Down From Troy* (New York: William Morrow and Co., 1992), pp. 282–96.

34. Jacqui Banaszynski, "The Epilogue," *St. Paul Pioneer Press Dispatch*, April 3, 1988.

35. Levine, *Who Dies?*, p. 216.

36. Ibid., p. 219.

37. James Hillman, "Betrayal," in *Loose Ends* (Dallas, TX: Spring Publications, 1975), p. 79.

38. Batson, "Tonics for the soul."

39. Both of these incidents were told to me by a relative or a friend.

40. Jacqui Banaszynski, "AIDS in the Heartland: Chapter II," *St. Paul Pioneer Press Dispatch*, July 12, 1987.

41. Letter from Dr. Robert J. Perelli at AIDS Family Services, Buffalo, NY.

42. Hamilton and Morris, *The AIDS Caregiver's Handbook*, p. 141.

43. Ibid., pp. 171, 173.

44. Chris Glaser, "Minister in Death," *More Light Update*, February 1988, p. 5.

45. Levine, *Who Dies?*, pp. 221–23.

46. Chris Glaser, "Restoring Easter Hope," *More Light Update*, June–July 1989, p. 7.

47. "Patrick," sermon preached by Rev. Charles Staples at College Hill Presbyterian Church, Easton, PA, August 30, 1992.

48. Jacqui Banaszynski, "The Final Chapter," *St. Paul Pioneer Press Dispatch*, August 9, 1987.

49. From GayCom's SURVIVORS message base:Msg#:7811 *SURVIVORS* 07/31/89 18:53:00 Subj: SERMON #1. Good Friday, 4/1/88. Reprinted in *More Light Update*, October 1989.

50. "Brother's death leads to healing of a family," Parents FLAG Philadelphia Newsletter, July 1989. Reprinted from *Courier Journal*, Louisville, KY.

51. William E. Wallace, "Survivors of AIDS: Care for the Grieving," *Lutheran Partners*, July/August 1989.

52. Judy Tatelbaum, *The Courage to Grieve* (New York: Lippincott and Crowell, 1980), p. 9.

53. Cindy Ruskin, *The Quilt: Stories from The NAMES Project* (New York: Pocket Books, 1988).

54. Kaia herself has not made altars in connection with AIDS, but certainly constructing altars can be of great help in giving space to your grief.

55. Tatelbaum, *The Courage to Grieve*, p. 139.

56. Ibid., pp. 139–40.

57. *The Book of Common Prayer* of the Episcopal church, 1928, p. 332.

58. Jalal al-Din Rumi (1207–73), poem no. 118 from *The Mystical Poems of Rumi*, tr. A. J. Arberry, copyright 1968 by A. J. Arberry, in *The Oxford Book of Death*, ed. by D. J. Enright (New York:

Oxford University Press, 1987). p. 151. Reprinted by permission of the University of Chicago Press.

Chapter 11: The Goal and the Reward

1. Peggy Way, "Homosexual Counseling as a Learning Ministry," *Christianity and Crisis,* Vol. 37, Nos. 9 and 10 (May 30 and June 13, 1977), p. 128.

2. From Robert Browning, "Rabbi Ben Ezra."

3. Joan Mills, "Season of the Empty Nest," *Reader's Digest,* January 1981, p. 118.

4. C. S. Lewis, *Surprised by Joy* (New York: Harcourt Brace Jovanovich, 1955), pp. 230–31.

5. Tatelbaum, *The Courage to Grieve,* p. 4.

6. Ibid., p. 133.

Appendix 2

1. *RECORD,* Winter 1987.

2. *Parents FLAG Philadelphia Newsletter,* October 1988.

3. *RECORD,* Spring 1991.

4. Jim Peron, *Homosexuality and the Miracle Makers* (booklet) (Glen Ellyn, IL: privately published, 1978). Information given to Peron in a telephone interview with Mrs. Grindstaff, January 9, 1978.

5. *RECORD,* Summer 1990.

6. Ibid.

7. Kent Philpott, *The Third Sex? Six Homosexuals Tell Their Stories* (Plainfield, NJ: Logos International, 1975).

8. Ralph Blair, *Holier-Than-Thou Hocus-Pocus and Homosexuality,* booklet published by HCCC, Inc., New York, 1977, p. 29. Blair is quoting from a letter from "Brother Frank" to two parents, April 1, 1977, who enclosed the letter in their letter to Blair, April 25, 1977.

9. *RECORD,* Summer 1988. Also, information from a personal conversation with Rick Notch November 12, 1992. It should be noted that Hurst in his counseling never had or attempted to have any sexual relationships with his clients, as have some of the other leaders of ex-gay ministries.

10. *Twin Cities Gaze,* November 19, 1987.

11. *RECORD,* Fall 1990.

12. Tim Stafford, "Coming Out," *Christianity Today,* August 18, 1989, p. 21.

13. Luke Timothy Johnson, *Decision Making in the Church: A Biblical Model* (Philadelphia: Fortress Press, 1983), pp. 96–97.

For Further Reading

To list all the books available to help parents gain information and come to terms with a child's same-sex orientation would be impossible. The books included here have been helpful to me, but they are by no means the only ones. They represent at least a point of departure for a parent's pilgrimage. Some of these books also have listings for further reading. In addition, possibly the books, pamphlets, and articles cited in the Notes might catch the reader's interest.

Coming to an understanding of a child's same-sex orientation is not the only goal of this book. The deepening of understanding and relationships within the whole family is another important objective. For this reason I have listed books that, in many cases, do not mention a same-sex orientation but that might help to increase harmony within the family group.

For those who are having difficulties with a same-sex orientation because of religious views, I have included several books that take a positive view.

Books about Grief

Fortunato, John E. *Embracing the Exile: Healing Journeys of Gay Christians*. San Francisco: Harper & Row, 1985. This book contains several chapters organized around the subject of grief.

Grollman, Earl A. *Living When a Loved One Has Died*. Boston: Beacon Press, 1987. Heart talks to heart in the brief pages of this book. To keep beside your bed and read a few pages at a time.

For Further Reading

Miller, William A. *When Going to Pieces Holds You Together.* Minneapolis: Augsburg Fortress, 1976. Readable book with good insights into the grieving process.

Stearns, Ann Kaiser. *Living Through Personal Crisis.* Chicago: The Thomas More Press, 1984. Written in clear, jargon-free language for those who are now hurting or who have struggled with troublesome and hurtful feelings in the recent past.

Tatelbaum, Judy. *The Courage to Grieve.* New York: Harper Collins, 1984. This book deals mainly with grief resulting from death, but contains a wealth of material that can also be adapted to the process of grieving over a child's sexual orientation.

Westberg, Granger E. *Good Grief: A Constructive Approach to the Problem of Loss.* Minneapolis: Augsburg Fortress, 1962. Discusses stages of grief in ten brief chapters, from the initial state of shock to the last stage of struggling to affirm reality.

Information for Parents about a Same-sex Orientation

Barrett, Martha Barron. *Invisible Lives.* New York: Harper Collins, 1990. Subtitled "The Truth About Millions of Women-Loving Women." For parents this book offers a bridge to understanding, for lesbians a confirmation and validation of their lives.

Borhek, Mary V. *My Son Eric.* New York: The Pilgrim Press, 1979. How the author found out she has a gay son and the process she went through as her strongly anti-homosexual stand evolved into acceptance and positive action.

Fairchild, Betty. *Now That You Know.* New York: Harcourt Brace Jovanovich, 1989. A general, comprehensive book about same-sex orientation, written by parents for parents. Includes many parents' experiences.

Griffin, Carolyn Welch. *Beyond Acceptance.* New York: St. Martin's Press, 1990. A report of the experiences of twenty-three parents who worked together over a period of years in Parents and Friends of Lesbians and Gays. (P-FLAG).

For Further Reading

Muller, Ann. *Parents Matter*. Tallahassee, FL: The Naiad Press, 1987. Demonstrates the importance parents continue to have in the lives of their lesbian and gay children. Gives equal time to lesbian daughters and gay sons.

Rafkin, Louise, ed. *Different Daughters: A Book by Mothers of Lesbians*. Pittsburgh, PA: Cleis Press, 1987. Twenty-five mothers of lesbians tell of their struggles to accept and share their daughters' lives.

Scanzoni, Letha, and Virginia Ramey Mollenkott. *Is the Homosexual My Neighbor?* San Francisco: Harper & Row, 1980. Although written from a positive Christian perspective, this book contains such a wealth of information about the entire matter of a same-sex orientation—stigma, stereotyping, science, homophobia, etc.—that it is helpful to anyone.

Switzer, David K., and Shirley Switzer. *Parents of the Homosexual*. Louisville, KY: Westminster/John Knox, 1980. Deals not only with moral and religious aspects of a same-sex orientation from a positive standpoint, but also family—parent and child—relationships and the guilt parents so often feel.

Books Dealing with Understanding One's Self and Creating Better Family Relationships

Halpern, Howard M. *You and Your Grown-up Child*. New York: Simon & Schuster, 1992. Help for parents in adjusting to new roles when their children are old enough to lead independent lives. Could also help children understand the sources of conflict between themselves and their parents. Deals with human relationships as valid in homosexual and well as heterosexual situations.

Harris, Thomas A. *I'm OK—You're OK*. New York: Avon, 1976. Particularly good in explaining the specialized meanings of parent/adult/child as one way of understanding our interaction with others, especially our own parents or our own children.

Miller, Sherrod, et al. *Straight Talk*. New York: NAL-Dutton, 1982. Helpful in making one aware of why communication with other persons often misfires. Offers help in changing methods of communication to avoid unproductive, damaging exchanges and to substitute constructive dialogue.

Napier, Augustus Y., with Carl A. Whitaker. *The Family Crucible*. New York: Bantam Books, 1984. A readable, nontechnical book that can provide insights into why families behave as they do.

Peck, M. Scott. *The Road Less Traveled*. New York: Simon & Schuster, 1988. A book for both parents and children, with basic information about love, traditional values, and spiritual growth. Although written in a heterosexual context, Peck's analysis of love can also be illuminating to same-sex-oriented people.

Rubin, Theodore Isaac. *The Angry Book*. New York: Macmillan, 1970. Easily readable examination of the devious and unrecognized ways that anger shows up in our lives.

Sanford, John A. *Between People*. New York: Paulist Press, 1982. A book about communication one-to-one, from a psychological standpoint.

Books with a Positive Religious View for Parents, Gay Men, and Lesbians

In addition to *Is the Homosexual My Neighbor?* and *Parents of the Homosexual*, listed above, the following publications present further information and viewpoints.

Balka, Christie, and Andy Rose, eds. *Twice Blessed: On Being Lesbian or Gay and Jewish*. Boston: Beacon Press, 1991. Essays from many perspectives on the experience of being Jewish and lesbian or gay.

Boswell, John. *Christianity, Social Tolerance, and Homosexuality*. Chicago: University of Chicago Press, 1981. A minutely detailed analysis of scriptural references commonly supposed to deal with homosexual acts is found in chapter 4, "The Scriptures," and Appendix 1, "Lexicography and St. Paul."

Fortunato, John E. *Embracing the Exile: Healing Journeys of Gay Christians*. San Francisco: Harper & Row, 1985. The author's riveting personal story, three chapters dealing with grief (one of them "Grieving Gay"), and an invitation to heterosexual and homosexual persons alike to grow and deepen spiritually through the difficult experiences of life. Note: The "healing" referred to in the subtitle has nothing to do with cure or change.

Glaser, Chris. *Come Home*! San Francisco: Harper & Row, 1990. An invitation to gay men and lesbians to come home to their spirituality through Christian faith and community, written with courage, honesty, and insight.

―――. *Coming Out to God: Prayers for Lesbians and Gay Men, Their Families and Friends*. Louisville, KY: Westminster/John Knox Press, 1991. Sixty days of prayers; new vistas of prayer, discipleship, and the relationship between spirituality and sexuality.

―――. *Uncommon Calling*. San Francisco: Harper & Row, 1988. An account of Glaser's personal struggle to reconcile the gay man God created him to be with the minister God called him to be.

Gluck, Rabbi Robert, ed. *Homosexuality and Judaism: A Reconstructionist Workshop Series*. Wyncote, PA: Reconstructionist Press, 1992. Material for eight workshops to help congregations and Havurot learn about and prepare to implement the Reconstructionist policy on homosexuality. Accepting stance.

Gramick, Jeannine, ed. *Homosexuality and the Catholic Church*. Mount Rainier, MD: New Ways Ministry, 1985. Political awareness, theological reflection, sociological issues, and human personal and spiritual experiences combine in this many-faceted treatment.

Homosexuality and Judaism: The Reconstructionist Position. The Report of the Reconstructionist Commission on Homosexuality, January 1992. Published by the Federation of Reconstructionist Congregations and Havurot and the Reconstructionist Rabbinical Association, Church Road and Greenwood Avenue, Wycote, PA 19095. Excellent comprehensive consideration of being Jewish and lesbian or gay from the standpoint of Reconstructionist values, historical Jewish sources, discrimination and prejudice, and contemporary scientific understandings. Accepting stance.

McNeill, John J. *The Church and the Homosexual*. Boston: Beacon Press, 1988. While the whole book deals with material of a religious nature, parents may find chapter 2, "Scripture and Homosexuality," most pertinent to their interests. Especially good for Catholics.

———. *Taking a Chance on God*. Boston: Beacon Press, 1988. Explains how both tradition and scripture support love between people of the same sex and shows that a positive gay identity is compatible with Christian faith.

Nelson, James B. *Embodiment*. Minneapolis: Augsburg Fortress, 1979. Chapter 8, "Gayness and Homosexuality: Issues for the Church," deals with biblical interpretation, attitudes of the church toward homosexuality, a look at reasons why homosexuality is disturbing to many people, and implications for the church in ministering to same-sex-oriented persons.

Nugent, Robert, and Jeannine Gramick. *Building Bridges: Gay and Lesbian Reality and the Catholic Church*. Mystic, CT: Twenty-Third Publications, 1992. The authors deal with the subject of gay and lesbian reality from the viewpoints of educational and social concerns, counseling and pastoral issues, religious and clerical life, and evolving theological perspectives.

Scroggs, Robin. *The New Testament and Homosexuality*. Minneapolis: Augsburg Fortress, 1984. A careful look at homosexual acts in New Testament times and why we cannot use these passages to cover blanket condemnation of homosexuality today.

Where We Stand: Social Action Resolutions Adopted by the Union of American Hebrew Congregations. 1992. Only half a dozen pages deal with resolutions about homosexuality, but they supply definite confirmation of UAHC's positive approach. Order from UHAC, 838 Fifth Avenue, New York 10021.

Books Dealing with AIDS

Alyson, Sasha, ed. *You Can Do Something About AIDS*. Stop AIDS Project, Inc., 40 Plympton St., Boston, MA 02118, 1990.

(There are periodic updates.) A smorgasbord of short articles by many authors, usually well known, presenting a variety of opportunities to help deal with the AIDS phenomenon. Covers changing your own attitudes, volunteering, working with media, what a high school class can do, etc. Appendix of AIDS-related organizations, book list for further reading, telephone listings for local and state organizations.

Barbo, Beverly. *The Walking Wounded.* Carlsons', PO Box 364, Lindsborg, KS 67456, 1987. The story of Tim Barbo's life and how the Barbo family, in a small conservative town, dealt in a loving way with Tim's homosexuality and his eventual death from AIDS. Particularly good for evangelical and fundamentalist readers.

Dietz, Stephen D., and Jane Parker Hicks. *Take These Broken Wings and Learn to Fly: The Aids Support Book for Patients, Family and Friends.* Tucson, AZ: Harbinger House, 1989. Excellent help for those involved with a person with AIDS. Clear, understandable chapter about the AIDS virus, plus help in dealing with all aspects of living with AIDS. Extended glossary of AIDS-related medical terms, information, and advocacy resources, plus suggested reading list.

Eidson, Ted, ed. *The AIDS Caregiver's Handbook.* New York: St. Martin's Press, 1988. A manual for professional or volunteer caregivers covering all aspects of AIDS—scientific, medical, nutritional, psychological, interpersonal, and spiritual. Very practical, very helpful. Appendices about putting one's affairs in order, list of local and national hotlines and information groups, reading list. Index.

Hay, Louise L. *The AIDS Book: Creating a Positive Approach.* Hay House, PO Box 6204, Carson, CA 90749–6204, 1988. Many have found this book helpful in combating the fear and negativism that surround AIDS. The reader should understand that inner healing and outer cure are not the same and that one should not feel guilty for failure to effect complete bodily cure.

———. *You Can Heal Your Life.* Hay House, PO Box 6204, Carson, CA 90749-6204, 1987. A metaphysical aid to learning to love yourself, deal with relationships and stress, and work within your body toward healing. Not a final answer, but can be helpful to some people.

Jarvis, Debra. *The Journey Through AIDS: A Guide for Loved Ones and Caregivers*. Batavia, IL: Lion Publishing, 1992. A luminous yet very practical book to read and reread as one cares for a person with AIDS. Several guided meditations included, as well as appendix of resources and list for further reading.

Levine, Stephen. *Who Dies: An Investigation of Conscious Living and Conscious Dying*. Garden City, NY: Anchor Press/ Doubleday, 1982. Strictly speaking, this book does not deal with AIDS. Yet it shows how to open to the immensity of living with death. Includes a number of helpful guided meditations.

Martelli, Leonard J., with Fran D. Peltz and William Messina. *When Someone You Know Has AIDS: A Practical Guide*. New York: Crown Publishers, 1987. Comprehensive material on becoming a care partner, coping with the diagnosis, opportunistic infections, dealing with legal and financial matters, living with AIDS, getting the help you need, dealing with your relationship, conquering grief and loss. National directory of AIDS-related organizations. Bibliography, index.

Mikluscak-Cooper, Cindy, and Emmett E. Miller. *Living in Hope: A 12-Step Approach for Persons at Risk or Infected with HIV*. Berkeley, CA: Celestial Arts, 1991. Excellent material for those who test positive, their loved ones, and those who are health care providers. Resources appendix, reading list, imagery appendix, meeting appendix (how to start group meetings). Index.

Moffatt, Betty Clare. *When Someone You Love Has AIDS: A Book of Hope for Family and Friends*. New York: NAL Penguin, 1986. A mother's story of how she and her family dealt with her son's AIDS and the healing of family relationships in the midst of catastrophic illness. Good for those who use *A Course in Miracles* (Foundation for Inner Peace, PO Box 1104, Glen Ellen, CA 95442, 1992). Bibliography.

Peabody, Barbara. *The Screaming Room*. San Diego, CA: Oak Tree

Publications, 1986. Personal journey of a mother's odyssey in caring for her son with AIDS. Graphic description of what is involved in such care. A story of love, dedication, and courage.

Ruskin, Cindy. Photographs by Matt Herron. *The Quilt: Stories from The NAMES Project*. New York: Pocket Books, 1988. How the AIDS quilt project came into being, together with pictures of many of the quilt panels and the stories that go with them. Performs a function similar to the Vietnam Memorial: an important visual aid to dealing with individual and collective grief.

Tilleraas, Perry. *The Color of Light: Meditations for All of Us Living with AIDS*. New York: Harper/Hazelden, 1988. Brief, one-page meditations for each day of the year. Designed to lift the sights and spirits of those with AIDS, it could help loved ones and caregivers as well, both during their time of service and after the PWA's death.